NATURALIST
SUMMERS

NATURALIST SUMMERS

Pages from a Field Studies Journal

ANN TATE

Illustrations by Geoffrey Herickx

BLANDFORD

DEDICATED TO: Jan Dawson and all my other excursion-loving friends in the Leicester Literary and Philosophical Society: Natural History Section.

A BLANDFORD BOOK

First published in the UK by Blandford
A Cassell Imprint
Cassell Plc, Villiers House,
41/47 Strand, London WC2N 5JE

Copyright © 1994 Ann Tate

Distributed in the United States by Sterling Publishing Co., Inc.,
387 Park Avenue South, New York, NY 10016-8810

Distributed in Australia by Capricorn Link (Australia) Pty Ltd
2/13 Carrington Road, Castle Hill, NSW 2154

British Library Cataloguing-in-Publication Data
A catalogue entry for this title is available from the British Library

ISBN 0-7137-2484-6

Designed by Richard Carr
Typeset by Litho Link Ltd., Welshpool, Powys, Wales

Printed and bound in Great Britain by The Bath Press, Avon

Contents

Foreword

BY DAVID BELLAMY

As URBAN SPRAWL, motorways and factory farms have engulfed much of England's countryside, the bulk of its population has become cut off from its roots in natural history – from the delights of *Gasterosteus aculeatus* in a jam jar, *Lucanus cervus* on the wing and *Adoxa moschatelina* telling the summer hours.

Today, the seasons happen on the other side of double glazing, climate is the reason for high-tech gear and gamekeepers are nasty men with guns. What was once – and not that long ago – knowledge common to every child, has become the preserve of specialists. Magazines, newspapers, radio and television do their best to keep it all alive, but there is no substitute for personal contact with the countryside in the company of those who know the natural history of their local patch.

Naturalist Summers is living proof of the above, for the wisdom of rural ages bursts from its pages, a latter day Lammas tide to satiate the ravening hordes of townies.

All thanks to the Field Studies Council, now 50 years young, whose field centres have become oases of learning, hands on universities far from the madding crowd of urban life.

I, like the book's writer, Ann Tate, owe the FSC so much. Juniper Hall in Surrey, Flatford Mill in Constable country and Preston Montford in Salopia where John Sankey, Jim Bingley and Charles Sinker enthralled, entertained and educated me and thousands of others. There, they made Latin binomials and common names come alive, characters in a living, sustainable, well-managed landscape.

That is where I developed my biodiverse grass roots. That is why I will continue to fight for the rights of the people, plants and animals that make up the green and pleasant land that must be forever England – and Britain!

Read all about it in *Naturalist Summers*.

DAVID BELLAMY
Bedburn

PS *Bufo bufo* is mating in the garden pond right now.

Introduction

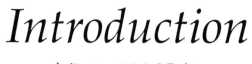

IN 1996 FLATFORD MILL FIELD CENTRE celebrates 50 years of 'naturalist summers'. Past students look back with affection and gratitude on time spent in the field with top naturalists of the day. The first centre of its kind in Britain, Flatford Mill opened wide its doors and offered 'environmental understanding for *all*'.

My own memories of Flatford date back to early spring, 1952. A week of dipping into ponds and streams with nets and jam jars was anticipated – but the weather decided otherwise. On 27 March, the day of arrival, the

Flatford Mill Field Centre, the first of its kind to open

temperature dropped, snow began to fall and the ponds froze over. Nevertheless – in the stalwart field centre tradition – we braced ourselves to face the bitter cold, shiveringly broke the ice, dibbled for freshwater invertebrates – and identified our catch.

We found net-spinning caddis fly (*Hydropsyche pellucidula*), water shrimp (*Gammarus pulex*), round-spired trumpet snail (*Planorbis spirorbis*), a freshwater leech (*Glossiphonia complanata*), stonefly larva (*Sialis lutaris*), square-tailed worm (*Eiseniella tetrahedra*), greater water boatman (*Notonecta glauca*) – a back-swimming bug, *Asselus* hog slaters, *Chironomus* midge larvae and *Cloëon* mayfly nymphs.

No, I'm not recalling the list from memory! I still have my old college file with its notes and sketches. On 29 March I wrote, 'Snow continues. Programme of Hydro-biology temporarily abandoned.'

A week of pond dipping in 1952. Author, fourth from the left

Instead we went for birdwatching walks in the snow-blanketed Suffolk countryside. Back at the Mill we dissected owl pellets and identified small mammal skulls: 12 field voles, 4 wood mice, 2 common shrews, 2 water shrews. In the evenings, we sat round a blazing log fire in Willy Lott's House and sang student songs to a strumming guitar. It all seemed incredibly exciting and romantic in those dreary post-war years.

Flatford Mill, once the family home of John Constable, was leased to the Field Studies Council (FSC) by the National Trust. The FSC had been founded three years before, in the middle of the Second World War. But you can read the whole story of the early beginnings and beyond in Catherine Broom-Lynne's excellent account, *A Vision Established*, published by the Field Studies Council (1994).

The National Trust continued its involvement with the field centre movement. Today the FSC owns 11 field centres, 10 of them residential. All are houses of character, set in some of Britain's most spectacular countryside. Malham Tarn in the Pennines is a National Trust property and so is Surrey's Juniper Hall.

As the decades passed, so visitors have enjoyed accommodation of increasing comfort. The atmosphere is relaxed and friendly, the range of courses is wide and the quality of teaching remains high.

But I have experienced breaks at centres run by other organizations too, for the idea soon began to spread. For example, Countrywide Holidays and HF Holidays – first in the field with walking holidays – include 'natural history weeks' in their guest-house brochures, the Youth Hostel Association offers field studies at certain purpose-built YHA hostels, universities ('continuing adult education') arrange residential 'field days' and Losehill Hall in the Peak District, the first of the National Park Study Centres, specializes in 'countryside courses'.

Private field centres are mushrooming and I have also sampled some of these.

No two field centres are alike. I've slept in a neat little bedroom in a converted cowshed; in the bunkbed dormitory of a stately home; and in a modern wing with *en suite* facilities. I've eaten packed lunches on a mountain side in pouring rain and dined by candlelight in a banqueting hall.

I've watched badgers at dusk and counted bats returning to their roosts at dawn. I've live-trapped small mammals; trekked across Exmoor after red deer; identified to species electric-blue damselflies and zooming hawker dragonflies; been buzzed by terns on Inner Farne; collected fossils from a ripple-marked wave-platform; dyed my own wool with natural dyes; infused delicious herbal teas; and met a sleepy dormouse in a hazel wood.

And I've met some fine naturalists.

Dr Robert Stebbings, who has an international reputation as a bat conservationist, runs his own Bat Consultancy. Dr Sara Churchfield is author of *The Natural History of Shrews* (Croom Helm, 1990). John Sankey's association with the Field Studies Council dates back to 1949; he retired as Warden of Juniper Hall in 1978, but his courses are as popular as ever. Adrian Bayley is an all-round naturalist and warden of Preston Montford Field Centre.

Dr Chris Mattison is author of *Frogs and Toads of the World* (Blandford, 1987) and several other books. Claire Dalby, a brilliant artist, is an elected member of both the Royal Water Colour Society and the Royal Society of Painters and Printmakers. Professor Robert Cameron co-authored *Collins Field Guide to the Land Snails of Britain and North-west Europe* (Collins, 1979, out of print) and *Land Molluscs of Britain and Northern Europe* (HarperCollins, 1994).

Penny Cresswell advises on badger 'problems' through her Bristol-based Badger Consultancy. Peter Skidmore wrote the FSC's *AIDGAP Key to Insects of the British Cow Dung Community* (1991). Doug Woods, area chairman of Somerset Trust for Nature Conservation, is a member, with Dr Pat Morris and Dr Paul Bright, of the Dormouse Project Team – and a winner of a Mammal Society Medal for his work with dormice.

Peter Hawkey was awarded the MBE on retirement after 20 years as National Trust warden on the Farne Islands. Dr June Chatfield, zoologist and past-curator of the Gilbert White Museum, co-authored Hamlyn's *A Guide to the Snails of Britain and Europe* (1983). Martin Catt, ex-Aerospace scientist, retrained as a field naturalist/tutor, perhaps a first for a Business Enterprise Scheme. John Whittle is proprietor of the award-winning Hull-based Fairfield Holidays.

Andrew Crawford works for the National Rivers Authority and is co-author, with Dr Elizabeth Andrews, of *The Otter Survey of Wales 1984–85* (Vincent Wildlife Trust, 1986). Grace and Paul Yoxon co-ordinate the International Otter Survival Fund from their Skye Environmental Centre. Dr Roland Randall is an authority on the history and natural history of the Orford Shingles in Suffolk.

Tony Wharton is an elected fellow of the Royal Photographic Society and a member of the Distinctions Panel in Nature. Dr Rasik Bhadresa leads safaris to his native Kenya for FSC Overseas. Dr Ted Benton wrote *The Dragonflies of Essex* (Essex Field Club, 1988). Malcolm Cullen is head warden of the Pembrokeshire Coast National Park.

I should like to express my gratitude to all these 'summer naturalists', and in particular for their kindness in reading through and commenting upon the final draft of relevant chapters.

I am indebted to Penny Kitchen, editor of *Home and Country* (National Federation of Women's Institutes) and Peter Frost, editor of *Camping and Caravanning*, for their invaluable help. Thank you to Christopher Hall for his permission to use material which first appeared in *The Countryman*; to the National Trust for the photograph of Peter Hawkey; and especially to Geoffrey Herickx for his delightful line drawings.

Most of all, I would like to say thank you to Larry Tate for his computer expertise (and much much more), and to Barbara, Helena and John for their support, encouragement and humour.

Ann Tate, Oadby, Leicester

CHAPTER ONE

Snuffle Holes and Totem Poles

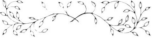

BADGERS
Adrian Bayley

•

Preston Montford Field Centre,
Shrewsbury, Shropshire

'WRAP UP WARMLY, wear drab-coloured, rustle-proof clothing – and don't forget to bring a torch,' advised Adrian Bayley, warden of Preston Montford.

It was May. Badger cubs born in February would be coming above ground on their very first outings. For a successful badger watch, Adrian warned, we'd have to stay still and quiet. Badgers have small eyes, so their eyesight is probably not all that good. But their hearing is sharp and they have a keen sense of smell.

'The badger's hearing,' said Adrian, 'is so sensitive that it can detect the tacky click of a slug's breathing tube.'

The wriggling of an earthworm 5 cm (2 in) below ground, the rustle of a leaf 30 m (100 ft) away or the ultrasonic squeak of a nylon anorak, all are enough to make a badger prick up its ears.

And its sense of smell is so acute that a badger has been seen to flinch and start away from a patch of damp earth where a whiff of human scent still lingers, though it may be several hours since the walker passed by.

Before emerging from the sett a badger will sniff the air. If the wind carries a smell that warns 'danger', it retreats into the tunnel and the watcher will see nothing that night.

Not in the least discouraged, we pulled on our woolly hats, laced up our walking boots and headed for the hills. Paths through bracken led us to a sett dug into a sandy slope. Adrian tested the air with his finger. If we stood with our backs to the stone wall opposite, the wind would be blowing away from the sett and towards us, and the badger would not catch our scent. It was a promising start.

It was not yet dusk. The first 15 minutes passed bearably enough as the orange ball of the

sun moved slowly towards the horizon. Honey bees visited bramble flowers on their last round of the day. Furry moths flew up out of the bracken, wings vibrating to generate heat. The evening chorus of birds was in full throttle: blackbird, robin, song thrush, great tit, willow warbler. And a pheasant clattered home to roost, making a tremendous crowing racket: 'GogOK, gogOK, gogOK'.

Another half-hour passed. I suffered an overwhelming urge to scratch the back of my neck. A twig snapped loudly beneath someone's foot and was followed by a quick intake of breath. Now my left leg had developed pins and needles. With infinite care I shifted my weight and a knee joint clicked: loud enough, it seemed in the silence, to frighten every brock in the parish.

The minutes ticked by. The air grew cooler. Tree tops swayed as the wind got up. It was past

9 o'clock. Yellow streaks in the west began to fade and merge into the greyness. A lone rabbit popped out of a hole to nibble grass. Two rooks flew over, cawing loudly. There was a bleating of sheep in the distance and a startled blackbird suddenly called 'chack' close by.

Staring at the dark entrance of the sett, my eyes played tricks, seeing shadowy shapes in the gloaming, movements in the bracken. When a badger's head finally did appear against the blackness of the hole, it was unexpected. The startling boldness of those black and white facial stripes...

The head ducked back. We waited, scarcely daring to breathe. We saw white-tufted ears and then the badger emerged into the open. Softly it padded along the badger path: bulky grey body, small sleek head. Half-way up the hill it paused to listen, sniffed the air, then padded on again into the trees. Two more adult badgers appeared and ambled after the first, disappearing into the treeline. There was a crashing through the undergrowth, some soft grunts, then silence.

Later, over pints in the village pub, the old hands began to reminisce.

'They'll sell their soul for a treacle sandwich...', 'honey buttie...', 'roasted peanut...'.

'You want to sit on a cushion in the fork of a tree, looking down on the sett.'

'I turned round and there were all these bullocks just behind me.'

'I've had a cub *that close.*'

'It's the midges I can't stand.'

'I get to the sett an hour before dusk...'

'I crash along at the last minute, they never seem to mind.'

All badgers are different, everyone agreed. Some are so shy that you daren't even blink your eyes. Others don't seem to notice your presence at all and almost trip over you.

I have had more exciting badger-watching since that first night and, yes, I have seen cubs romp and play, but no one ever forgets their very first sighting.

Next day we visited a number of setts to look for badger 'signs'. A few miles outside Ironbridge, Adrian led us up a steep, wooded escarpment.

'Snuffle hole,' he called back from half-way up.

'It had better be a good one, whatever a snuffle hole is,' I thought, as I clung to exposed roots of trees and laboriously hauled myself up.

A 'snuffle hole' turned out to be a shallow

scrape, rather like a rabbit scrape. But, imprinted in the damp soil was the clear tracing of a badger's lower jaw and snout. Even the short, stiff whiskers were visible. The badger, explained Adrian, had been rooting after earthworms with its flexible, rubbery nose.

A badger path followed the contours of the wood at this point, taking the easiest route. Perhaps centuries old, it was well flattened and bare of vegetation, a long-established 'brockway', leading to traditional feeding and watering places. On either side of the path grew dog's mercury, a green carpet, trampled where tributary paths radiated out. The fallen trunk of a silver birch tree blocked the way, its underside rubbed smooth and shiny, scoured of moss, where badgers had passed beneath.

'A fox would have jumped over the obstacle,' Adrian said 'or detoured round it.' Foxes, unlike badgers, wander where they please.

The brockway ended at a massive sett. A great spoilheap of excavated soil spilt down the hillside. Scattered hay showed that a fresh load had recently been dragged backwards into the tunnel to be used as bedding. In an underground chamber cubs are born between January and March. The sow suckles her young and at eight weeks they are ready to emerge. She will wean them gradually as food becomes more plentiful.

Adrian had brought his two children. Aged six years and eight years, they were sharp-eyed and quick at finding clues:

'Dung pit!'

Badgers dig conical pits to serve as latrines. Some are dug close to the sett. Other dung pits mark the outer boundaries of a home range. The dung was grey and sludgy with the remains of earthworms, their favourite food.

'A badger will chomp through 200 earthworms on a damp night,' said Adrian, 'working its way across the pastures.'

In areas where earthworms are not so plentiful, the animal will turn easily to other foods. Badgers are natural omnivores and will eat almost anything they happen upon.

'Clay ball,' sang out a young voice.

The sticky ball, 5 to 7.5 cm (2 to 3 in) in diameter, was lying on top of the spoil heap and, stuck to the clay, were badger hairs. Clay balls are part of badger mythology, mystifying their finders. But the explanation is prosaic. Lumps of clay stick to the badger's wiry coat and are rolled into balls as the animal journeys along the tunnel. (But why is it that regular badger watchers report from time to time finding golf balls at the entrance to a badger sett? This is another mystery, as yet unsolved.)

We investigated the spoilheap further. Badger palaeontologists sometimes kick out fossils with the loose soil. And there was the petrified shell

The brockway ended at a massive sett

of a bivalve mollusc and a stone bearing an impression of a crinoid sea lily.

The elder trees that were growing near the sett were creamy-white with blossom. Later the badgers would be eating the ripe purple-black berries. Seeds would pass undigested through the gut to germinate in the natural fertilizer of the dung pit.

'It's always worth looking for a badger sett where you see elder trees growing in profusion.'

The bark of one tree was frayed where it had been scored by claws. 'A badger totem pole,' said Adrian. 'Traditional scratching tree.'

On emerging from the sett, a badger will often head for the nearest scratching tree. Standing on its hind legs, it will bring its fore-claws down hard. Why does it do this? To scent the bark with the musk glands on its feet? To sharpen its claws? To get rid of the sticky mud between its toes? This is another mystery.

Close to the totem pole was the 'arena': a flattened area where adults squat to groom and scent each other, and where the young cubs play chasing games and king-of-the-castle.

We walked back through the wood, the children running on ahead.

'Bank vole's nest, look.'

Knowing it to be a good place to look for small mammals, they had lifted one corner of a discarded sheet of corrugated iron. A vole-sized runway led to a mossy nest – but it was empty. A litter of young mice or voles is a tasty snack for a hungry badger.

The children were soon finding more potential badger 'grub': a millipede with its legs in ripple-wave motion, the white eggs of a diadem spider, a torpid newt, which recovered quickly once we'd moved it into the warmth of the sun, a garlic snail ('Sniff it, Dad') on red campion and black slugs in a decaying log.

In wet mud, close to a little stream, they found a perfect print of a well-cushioned front paw, as broad as it was long, with five toe pads in an almost straight line and impressions of long, strong claws.

'Badger paw print,' they said.

Adrian fished in the stream with a stick, finding whirligig beetles, stonefly larvae with two-prong 'tails', pond skaters, and caddis fly larvae in tiny tubes of gritty soil particles cemented together with 'super-glue' saliva. ('Mum's not going to like your muddy boots, Dad.')

Away from the wood, on the outskirts of Ironbridge, birthplace of the Industrial Revolution, were more setts to visit: in an old quarry, in an abandoned brickworks and in loose coal waste along a geological faultline – for badgers have learnt to exploit man-made landscapes.

Preston Montford Field Centre

We took a quick look at the Ironbridge Museum and then we returned to Preston Montford.

That evening, in the laboratory – one of the smart new buildings added to the complex behind the elegant Queen Anne house – we began to analyse the samples of badger dung we'd collected.

The samples were first washed in a fine sieve to get rid of the 'gunge' (there must be a technical term for this). Microscopes were at hand to help us identify the food remains that were left behind.

What had the badgers been eating? We found hundreds of tiny bristles (chaetae), the remains of earthworms, beetle fragments, bits of snail shell, seeds, grass and bark.

'At other seasons of the year,' said Adrian, 'we'd find different items in the dung.'

In midsummer we could expect to find bones of mice, voles, hedgehogs, rabbits, frogs and birds. In late summer, droppings might be stiff and dry with cereal husks, or stained purple with the juice of blackberries or elderberries. In autumn there will be pips from windfall apples and pears, seeds of yew berries, rowan, hips, haws, and husks of acorns and other tree fruit.

A badger will dig up bulbs, rob a wasp nest, steal honeycombs from bees and swipe off the top of an anthill with its hefty paw to get at the pupae.

That night we went badger-watching again, taking cushions and sitting in comparative comfort at a woodland sett. But the moist wind blew first in our faces and then on our backs. Rain was forecast and the air was damp, trapping our scent and warning the badgers of our presence. Our vigil proved fruitless.

'But,' wrote Ernest Neal, the most famous badger-watcher of all, 'there is something about badger-watching that draws you on in spite of cold feet or a series of blank nights. There is only one question to be settled. When shall we go again?'

CHAPTER TWO

Neal Country

SURVEYING FOR BADGERS
Penny Cresswell

•

Leonard Wills Field Centre,
Nettlecombe Court, Williton,
Somerset

W E WERE WALKING back down the lane after an abortive badger-watch. It had looked a good spot: situated at the edge of a wood, wind blowing towards us, sett entrances in full view and plenty of cover on the slope opposite in which to hide. No one had fidgeted or coughed, or let the side down in any way. But it was all to no avail – in spite of the fact that this was Neal Country.

The lane was open to the fields on one side and a thick hedgerow bordered the other. Bats flickered along the tops of trees. Suddenly Penny, in front, stopped dead in her tracks, bringing the rest of us to a standstill.

A badger had slipped out of the hawthorn bushes and was trundling along the path, rear-end swinging, short legs padding softly. It swerved, ducked under the wire fence on the right and into the sheltered hollow where cattle grazed.

There was a snorting in the bushes – and out came two more badgers. They squatted on the track and gave themselves a good scratch. Then, slipping under the wire, they joined the first in the nightly search for earthworms. Snouts

down, all three went about their worming ways across the field. A fast pull, lick, snap – and another worm was gone. Dark clumps of nettles and the long shadows thrown by the rising moon made it difficult to keep track of the animals. A badger would materialize out of the gloom, its coat silvered by the moonlight and then, as mysteriously, melt away again.

We began to walk on quietly, but not quietly enough. Behind us came the thudding of badgers in a panic. Under the wire they scrambled and into the hedge.

'Practise walking without making a sound, like John Wayne did in the old Westerns,' said Penny Cresswell. And she showed us how. 'Watch out for pebbles, snapping sticks and dead leaves.' Sloping her legs, treading softly on the balls of the feet, she stepped with exaggerated care, but silently.

I bet Ernest Neal knew all about walking quietly. I don't suppose *he* ever caused his badgers to panic.

Although Neal's early work on badgers was in the Cotswolds, he spent many years of his life in Somerset. He taught and lived at Taunton

Nettlecombe Court in its secluded Somerset valley.

School from 1946-71, and then retired to Milverton in the foothills of the Brendons, where he lived until 1987. Now he lives in Bedford and is *still* engaged in writing about badgers.

His earliest book, *The Badger*, was published by Collins in 1948: the first of the monographs in the New Naturalist series. He took his own photographs and was proud of the fact that the book's frontispiece was 'probably the first colour picture obtained of a wild badger after dark'.

Amateur naturalists were starved for books during the war years and Neal offered the authoritative account, sorting out badger fact from badger folklore, that everyone had been waiting for. He had probably (said his editors) spent more hours studying badgers than anyone else before him.

'No naturalist who has once watched badgers is ever content with that one experience: he wants to go again and again,' he wrote.

The invention of radio-telemetry, infra-red cameras and light-intensifying binoculars in the 1970s added a new dimension to the study of nocturnal animals. Ernest Neal's second book *Badgers* (Blandford Press, 1977) brought the story up to date.

corresponding with other naturalists. Badgers, he concluded, seem to be very widely distributed. The largest colonies are to be found in the hilly country of the south and west, with the smallest in the flat landscapes of the east. He suspected that numbers were probably increasing from a 'low' at the beginning of the twentieth century.

'The more I get to know these grand animals the more fascinating I find them.'

It wasn't until 1963 that the Mammal Society organized its first National Badger Survey. Volunteer field workers were asked to record all badger setts. Conclusions agreed largely with Neal's findings. Some disturbing declines were noted and people began to campaign for better badger protection. In 1973 the Badgers Act was passed by parliament and in 1981 further protection was given under the Wildlife and Countryside Act 1981. It is now an offence wilfully to take, kill, injure or ill-treat a badger.

'In my own opinion, man is the most important limiting factor as far as numbers and distribution are concerned for most parts of England,' wrote Neal.

In 1990 the most scientific National Badger Survey thus far was undertaken. Entitled *The History, Distribution and Status of the Badger in Britain*, it was the initiative of the Joint Nature Conservancy Council. Penny Cresswell was appointed full-time organizer of the survey. Today Penny runs her own Badger Consultancy, advising developers and others when they encounter a 'problem' with badgers.

The Protection of Badgers Act 1992 extended legal protection to the sett. It is an offence to disturb the animal in its sett; to damage a sett in any way or obstruct access; or to send a dog into a sett. Illegal hunting is now punishable by fines up to £2,000 per badger, and may be coupled with the confiscation of dogs and vehicles.

We went to look for 'signs' on the edge of the Brendon Hills, where the soil is red and the woolly coats of sheep are stained as pink as pigs. The woods and sandy slopes are still home to a healthy population of badgers.

'It still gives me intense pleasure and a feeling of excited anticipation when I see that first glimpse of a striped face at the sett entrance,' wrote Neal.

The Natural History of Badgers (Croom Helm) followed in 1986. It was a synthesis of the latest observations, both his own and those of new researchers in the field: Hans Kruuk, Chris Cheeseman, Martin Hancox, Chris Ferris, Stephen Harris, Don Jefferies and Penny Cresswell.

In the 1940s Neal made his own subjective estimate of nationwide badger numbers by perusing the literature county by county and by

An upturned cowpat, and nose-prods and scratch marks in the exposed soil showed where a badger had grubbed for earthworms and beetle larvae. A strip of turf rolled back like a carpet was also the work of a hungry badger.

'A badger,' said Neal, 'eats practically anything that comes its way, but it does have its preferences with earthworms right at the top of the list.'

Badger paths radiated across the field to the sloping edge of the wood and the badger-sized entrance to a sett, with a spoilheap and wisps of bedding. Tunnels are normally 20 to 30 cm (8 to 12 in) in diameter and flattened oval in shape: wider than they are high. But entrances become eroded and worn, and foxes and rabbits also dig tunnels, so badger surveyors must make absolutely certain when identifying a sett.

Penny investigated. By lying flat on the spoilheap and stretching out an arm, it was possible to feel the shape and size of the tunnel.

The soft sandstone walls had been rubbed smooth, polished by the badger's shaggy coat. A faint, musky smell of ammonia lingered.

But how deep was it? How many chambers were there? The 'diggability' of the soil and the size of the spoilheap is some guide, but setts vary hugely. As Neal said, 'Each badger seems to be its own architect.'

The main sett may be extensive, with many tunnels and several sleeping chambers, or it may be quite small with just a single tunnel. Some of the largest setts are built on several different levels and there can be hundreds of metres of tunnel: a complex labyrinth.

Rabbits leave droppings (like currants) on the spoil outside the round entrances of their burrows. The smell of a fox is strong and rank; discarded bones and other debris may litter the entrance to a den. But rabbit droppings and fox litter do not rule out the possibility of badgers. Rabbits and foxes may be living amicably side

G.R.HERICKX

by side in different parts of an occupied sett, cohabiting with badgers.

'Like humans,' said Neal, 'the behaviour of badgers is greatly influenced by their need for homes and living space.'

We found more clues. A strong, wiry badger hair; black and silver, it had snagged on a bramble. Five deep scratches on a fallen branch suggested scent-marking to demarcate a home range, or perhaps it was made by the badger as it dragged bedding backwards down into the tunnel, hugging the stuff to its chest after shuffling backwards along the scent-saturated path.

Scent plays an important part in the lives of most mammals. Badgers are members of the *Mustelidae* family and all mustelids (pine marten, weasel, stoat, polecat, otter) rely on scent as a means of communication, but perhaps particularly so in the case of the sociable badger. Members in the same 'social group' scent-mark each other often and so come to share the same odour, which is chemically different from that of members of other social groups.

'Each badger has its own distinctive personality and temperament,' wrote Neal. 'Being social creatures, they too have their problems of learning how to live together.'

Close by the entrance, a dung pit was full to the brim with stiff corn husks and sludgy remains of earthworms. Dung pits are used, as well, to mark the boundaries of a home range (territory). Disputes can occur if a badger from another social group dares to trespass. Fighting is most common in spring when young males are looking for a mate, or old badgers want to gain dominance within a group. Horrible rump wounds are occasionally inflicted. But generally, at territorial borders, a badger will choose to avoid confrontation by turning back before things get too tense.

'A wary armed neutrality,' is how Neal describes it.

Social groups are complex with extended family-type relationships. Several different kinds of setts can occur within the same home

Badger hairs snag on brambles

range. Typically a main sett will have one or more satellite setts.

Penny worked out a sett classification for the 1985-8 National Badger Survey, based on categories suggested by Hans Kruuk. She asked her surveyors to look for: (1) a main sett; (2) annexe setts; (3) subsidiary setts; and (4) outlying setts.

The main sett is in continuous use and usually looks active; it has several holes, large spoilheaps and well-worn paths leading to and fro. Cubs are born in the main sett. Annexe setts are normally less than 150 m (500 ft) away and connected to the main sett by one or more paths. Subsidiary setts, not always occupied, are out on a limb with no obvious connecting paths. Outlying setts are only used sporadically, perhaps by a lone badger to lie up in by day or by an outcast; it can be temporarily exploited by other species, such as rabbits or foxes.

'But,' says Neal, 'any one group of badgers is as different from any other... as villages are different in the English countryside.'

By using this method of classification, the probable badger population in Britain, in 1985-8, was estimated to be 42,000 social groups: around 250,000 individuals.

Surveyors were shocked to find that 10 per cent of active main setts had recently been dug by badger diggers. An estimated 9,000 badgers a year are killed, often very cruelly: many more than was previously realized. The entrances to 14.5 per cent of main setts had been 'stopped', usually by hunts. Altogether 75 per cent of cubs are estimated to die in their first year. Around 30 per cent of adults die annually, one-third of these deaths being due to traffic; approximately 50,000 badgers are killed each year on our roads.

'Man is the badger's worst enemy,' said Neal.

But man can also be the badger's best friend. In the 1980s, people interested in the welfare of badgers began to form badger groups, often affiliated to their local Wildlife Trust.

The National Federation of Badger Groups was founded in 1986 and today there are over 50 groups countrywide, with around 30,000 members. Groups collect and record information on population and distribution of badgers in their locality. They work with English Nature, the RSPCA, the police, and others involved in badger welfare and protection. Badger groups advise property developers, liaise with landowners, offer evidence in badger-digging cases, relocate, if necessary, badgers from a threatened site and care for orphaned cubs.

Members swop badger-watching experiences. They contribute to newsletters, attend seminars and conferences, and keep a friendly eye on their local sett.

Walking back from the Brendon Hills down a narrow winding road to the car, we passed a regularly used crossing place. The banks of the hedge on either side had been worn smooth and denuded of vegetation by the passage of badgers: 'up-and-overs', Neal calls them.

That evening we sat once more in silence, with never a fidget, outside the sett at the end of the Nettlecombe lane.

'But,' wrote Ernest Neal, 'the appeal of badgers goes far beyond the magic circle of those who love to watch them in the wild. Badgers seem to typify the very essence of the countryside. They are part of our heritage.'

CHAPTER THREE

A Tarry Splodge of Spraint

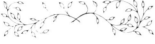

OTTERS

Andrew Crawford

•

Preston Montford Field Centre,
Montford Bridge, Shrewsbury,
Shropshire

'IT'S VERY UNLIKELY you'll actually *see* an otter,' Andrew Crawford warned us. 'Otters are secretive creatures. It's tracks and signs of otter presence we'll be looking for.'

Andrew confessed that, in spite of taking part in the Welsh National Otter Surveys of the late 1970s and early 1980s, he has seldom managed actually to catch a glimpse of the elusive creature.

The surveys had been designed to collect information on otter status: to serve as a baseline for the future. Andrew and his colleagues visited a total of 1,097 Welsh sites, and then revisited each several years later. He helped to write the *Otter Survey of Wales 1977–8*, published by the Nature Conservancy Council and the RSNC Wildlife Trusts Partnership. With Dr Elizabeth Andrews, the organizer, he co-authored the *Otter Survey of Wales 1984–5*, published by the Vincent Wildlife Trust.

'The data indicated a slight increase in numbers in some areas,' said Andrew, 'and we were cautiously optimistic. The increase has been accelerating since. Otters are making their way back down the Rivers Severn and Wye, reclaiming former haunts in Welsh border country, continuing on into the West Midlands.'

Andrew was enlisting our help this weekend to make spot-checks on several tributaries where he suspected *Lutra lutra* may have returned after many years of absence. So the first evening was spent preparing ourselves for the role of 'otter surveyor'.

The only other mammal to share a similar waterways lifestyle is the mink. We had to learn to differentiate between signs of otter and signs of mink.

Andrew produced plaster casts of the paw prints of both animals. An otter leaves a round print 5 to 9 cm (2 to 3.5 in) across. All five widely-spaced round toes may be visible with faint traces of webbing between. Mink prints are smaller, 2 to 4 cm (0.8 to 1.6 in) wide, and the five toes leave teardrop-shaped impressions. We compared mink and otter prints with prints of badger, fox, dog and cat.

'Droppings are the most important clues to an animal's presence,' said Andrew, 'but let's get the terminology straight. *Spraint* of otter and *scat* of mink.'

Glass petri dishes were passed round with samples. We sniffed obediently. Otter spraint smelt fishy, oily, spicy... sweetish. Not unpleasant. Mink scat? Yuk! Nasty. Then it was time for dinner, but none of us felt awfully hungry. Somehow we had lost our appetites. However, there is nothing quite like a spraint-sniffing session to break the ice...

Striding up river the next morning, clad in thigh-high waterproof waders, was another new experience. At first we had walked along the overgrown towpath, but it petered out, and the brambles and nettles forced us down into the water.

'Whoops! Take care,' warned the first one in.

There was a fast-flowing current and slippery stones on the river bed. An otter is equipped with horny, non-slip paw pads to grip with. Andrew had found himself a stout staff and we did the same. Criss-crossing from side to side, he inspected tree roots, fallen branches, gravel spits - any prominent feature that might serve as a spraining site. He approached a smooth boulder in mid-stream and on top was a tarry black splodge spiked with tiny white bones.

'Otter spraint,' said Andrew.

A boulder is a typical sprainting site, chosen by the otter to maximize the likelihood of it being found by other otters. Sprainting, to an

otter, is more than just a bodily function. It plays an important part in everyday social behaviour. An 'I have been here' calling card? A 'Keep off' warning? A means of staking out territory and avoiding conflict?

Otters seem to spraint often, impregnating the droppings with secretions from their scent glands. Work with tame otters suggests that an animal may have its own personal chemical 'fingerprint', but further experiments have proved disappointing. Can an otter discriminate between the spraints of other otters? Can it suss out male from female? Friend from foe?

Dominant bully boy from subordinate wimp?

'No one really knows,' said Andrew.

We waded on up river. 'Another spraint?' asked Pete hopefully, pausing by a tree root.

But the grey smudge was identified as a bird dropping, probably the dipper seen earlier, whirring fast below the bank: a plump little bird with a white 'shirt front'.

In a sandy bay at a bend in the river the roots of a sycamore tree had spread wide, forming a roof over the cavity underneath. Andrew beamed his torch into the hole. Inside was an otter paw print. All five toes were distinct and even the tiny pinprick marks of claws could be seen in the wet sand. This was proof that otters had returned to the tributary after 30 years of absence, as he'd suspected.

Solitary otters sometimes lie up in tree holes during daylight hours; or the hole could be the natal holt of a bitch otter with a family of cubs. Otters, like humans, have no special breeding season and cubs may be born at any time, staying with their mother for up to a year.

We climbed up the bank and stripped off our cumbersome waders. Then we lazed in the sun and watched house martins hawking after the midges that swarmed in the shade of riverbank trees.

Alder and willow, the commonest riparian species, have roots that shoot straight down vertically to reach the water table. Of much greater importance to the otter are the oak, ash and sycamore: trees with wide-spreading, cavity-creating roots.

As we ate our packed lunches, Andrew entertained us with stories of his life as an otter surveyor. He told us of encounters with bulls, of meetings with fishermen, canoeists, picnickers and courting couples, of the strange objects he came across: articles of clothing, odd shoes, old bikes, fishing tackle 'and *hundreds* of hard-boiled eggs'.

He always kept a change of clothing handy.

'I've lost count of the number of times I've fallen into the water and arrived back dripping wet.'

To find out more about otter diet, he collected spraints for analysis. Once, he said, he had returned, late in the evening, to his car, which he'd parked in a quiet spot. He found a policeman waiting for him.

'And what is this substance wrapped up in silver paper, sir?' the policeman asked suspiciously.

'Otter spraint, officer.'

'Otter spraint, sir? Oh, *yes*, sir?' queried the constable dubiously.

At parties, Andrew's job as an otter surveyor could be a great conversation stopper.

'What does an otter surveyor *do*?' people asked. And he told them and watched them recoil.

He steeps his spraints in fizzy Steradent overnight to free them of the slimy dark mucus and to whiten the tiny fishbones and scales. (Think about it next time you put your dentures in to soak!) Back at the laboratory that evening, he showed us how.

With the help of *A Guide to the Identification of Prey Remains in Otter Spraints*, by J. Conray et al., a Mammal Society Occasional Publication, we had a go at identifying bones. Most were from stickleback and eel. There was the jawbone of a trout and several vertebrae of a fish in the carp family. A tiny disc of calcium carbonate turned out to be an otolith from the inner ear of a chub. The wing case of a ground beetle and the gritty tube of a caddis fly larva had probably been in the stomach of a fish eaten by the otter. And a sliver of grey-speckled skin was identified - a great piece of detective work, this - as 'the nuptial pad on the thumb of a non-breeding male toad'.

The following day we crossed a suspension bridge that swayed alarmingly, to reach one of Andrew's favourite holts on a wide bend of a river where shallow water trickled across gravel beds. Dense stands of rosebay willowherb and Himalayan balsam provided good cover for otters.

Himalayan balsam is a recent invader of the riverbank. It is unpopular with conservationists for it spreads rapidly and smothers the more delicate native plants. The shape of the lush pink flowerhead is the reason for its popular name of 'policeman's helmet'. The ripe pods of the balsam are a temptation. Pinch a pod and it sets off the explosive trigger mechanism, and shoots a fusillade of balsam seeds in all directions. Pop! pop! pop! pop!

Scratch marks on the sandy bank showed where otter cubs had been at play. The bank was worn smooth and polished at one point. This was an otter slide, a short cut into the water. There were more signs: spraint on a discarded glove, on a chunk of metal, on the spit of gravel at a junction where a small stream flows into the river. A twisted tuft of grass was growing bright green where urine had acted as a fertilizer.

On a ledge beneath the bridge were two sets of paw prints. Otter print and mink print: the latter with impressions of the splayed, teardrop-shaped toes.

'Is the escaped fur-farm mink anything to do with the otter's decline?'

'You must be joking,' scoffed Andrew. 'Otters weigh seven to ten times more than the much-maligned mink and their bodies are about twice as long.'

The otter is a supreme fisherman. About 90 per cent of its diet is fish. The mink, more catholic in its feeding habits, is unlikely to

On a ledge beneath the bridge Andrew found two sets of paw prints

compete. Andrew's own experience tells him that where the two animals occur on the same stretch of river they appear to live amicably side by side.

'Mink are probably not the menace that the media like to make out,' he said.

The small dark mustelid, a native of North America, first escaped from British fur farms in the late 1950s and early 1960s. It was soon breeding on rivers left vacant by the otter. 'Filling a niche,' say the naturalists.

An adaptable and opportunistic carnivore, it kills efficiently with a bite to the neck, leaving small puncture marks. In summer, half its diet may be rabbit. Eels are a favourite food, and it will also eat fish, frogs, rats, mice, voles, ducks and other water birds. But the Waterway Surveys organized by the British Trust for Ornithology indicate that mink have had no overall effect on water bird populations. In fact numbers of moorhen and coot remain stable, and may even be increasing. (*Population Trends in British Breeding Birds*, BTO.)

Mink are undoubtedly guilty on certain counts. They do occasionally raid smallholdings and take hens, but several studies show that poultry and game birds make up less than 1 per cent of their diet. Mink predation appears to have played a considerable part in the decline of water voles on certain stretches of river (*The Water Vole in Britain 1989-1990: Its Distribution and Changing Status*, R. Strachan and D. Jefferies, Vincent Wildlife Trust/Joint Nature Conservation Committee, 1990). Ornithologists fear that terns and other ground-nesting birds could be decimated if mink ever manage to swim across to certain Scottish islands off the west coast.

'But to hear some people talk you begin to think that mink will get the blame for World War III if it breaks out,' said Andrew.

Mink are less nervous than otters, more likely to be seen peering curiously at us from the reeds. These cheeky newcomers can be recognized by their smaller size and fluffy tails.

'Larger than a cat, it's probably an otter. Smaller than a cat, it's a mink' is a useful rule-of-thumb.

It is the mink itself, say naturalists, that will ultimately limit its population size. The male is aggressive and will do battle rather than allow any other male to invade the stretch of river he considers to be 'his' territory.

The otter was equally controversial in times past. In the sixteenth century it was officially designated a pest in the 'Acte for the Preservation of Grayne'. Parish constables and church wardens were empowered to offer a bounty for each otter killed.

The earliest allusion to otter hunting was in the reign of King John (1199-1216). Hunting otters for sport became fashionable in Elizabethan England. The 1880s saw a revival of interest. By 1904, there were 21 packs of otter hounds in the UK, and otters were considered to be widespread and common.

'Otters are found on almost every river and stream in this country,' wrote Edmund Sanders in *A Book of Common Beasts* published in 1940.

But in the late 1950s and early 1960s the animal suffered a catastrophic decline. The major cause is believed to be the introduction of dieldrin in 1955: a pesticide used as a seed dressing and in sheep dipping. Numbers declined to such an extent that otter hunting was banned in 1970 and, under the Wildlife and Countryside Act 1981, the otter was given special protection.

We walked along more riverbanks where vegetation was sparse or absent, unlikely places for otters, unless special 'havens' could be created to entice them back.

Andrew was originally employed by the Vincent Wildlife Trust (VWT) as a regional coordinator on the Otters and Rivers Project. Later he worked for the RSNC, Wildlife Trusts Partnership when the RSNC took over the VWT project.

Andrew's brief was to encourage landowners and farmers to manage their land in a way that was beneficial to otters. Now Andrew has a post with the National Rivers

Authority, Severn-Trent Region. Today the National Rivers Authority implements otter-friendly policies and otters are slowly returning to our rivers. They have already reached Tewkesbury on the River Severn and Stratford-upon-Avon. Numbers of otters are reasonably healthy in Wales, in the north of England and in the south-west. There are also small, isolated populations in Hampshire, Kent, Sussex and East Anglia.

'Landowners are sympathetic, I find,' Andrew told us. 'Most are prepared to protect existing otter habitat and to permit the creation of otter havens on their land.'

To speed their return, the RSNC's Wildlife Trust volunteers plant trees and quick-growing shrubs. They encourage farmers not to cut back thickets of blackthorn, bramble and hawthorn. They put up fences to protect vulnerable areas of land against grazing cattle. They construct artificial holts with hollow logs, brushwood, heaped boulders and buried drainpipes (old tricks, 'borrowed' from yesterday's otter hunts).

Otters came top in a popularity poll organized by *BBC Wildlife Magazine* in 1991.

They are, apparently, Britain's favourite animal, followed closely by the badger.

That night we persuaded Andrew to take us on an 'otter watch' at a known holt.

'You won't see anything,' he warned. 'It's dark and it's raining... and I've more slides I can show you.'

But we insisted. Sitting on the damp grass we kept our gaze on the black hole in the bank opposite. Would a round, whiskery head appear? Would we see a sinuous, slender body with short legs, dense fur and long, tapering rudder-tail?

Quacks and loud plops: a family party of mallards had splashed down into the water. We heard the drip of rain falling off the leaves. Chain of bubbles, leap of fish, dark eddies and silver swirls. What was that? The high, piping 'contact whistle' of an otter? No, just the wind in the trees.

Otters, as Andrew had warned us, are scarce, nocturnal and secretive. On the waterways of England and Wales there is little chance of seeing one. To experience an otter I'd have to visit their strongholds, head west to Ireland or north to Scotland....

CHAPTER FOUR

Rainbows, Changing Skies - and Otters

OTTER-WATCHING
Grace and Paul Yoxon

•

Skye Environmental Centre,
Broadford Bay, Isle of Skye

T O CATCH A GLIMPSE of the elusive otter you need to travel to the wild western shores of Scotland, preferably in the company of a naturalist who knows the terrain.

In the lochs and inlets of the Scottish highlands and islands, otters can find the solitude and peace they require. And, unlike the elusive nocturnal otters of fragmented populations in England and Wales, Scottish otters are active by day as well as by night.

Grace and Paul Yoxon live on the Isle of Skye. They take a vigorous part in Skye Otter Surveys, mapping where otters are present, tracking down their holts and monitoring the most accessible of otter haunts. 'But,' warn the Yoxons, 'an otter sighting can never be *guaranteed.*'

I booked for an April 'Otter Weekend' and travelled north by overnight train to the Kyle of Lochalsh. From Inverness the scenic route traverses the Cairngorms. Mountain slopes were white with snow and dotted with brightly garbed skiers.

Grace was at Kyle to meet me at the station and together we boarded the midday ferry that crosses the Sound of Sleat to Kyleakin. From the open deck we kept watch in drizzling rain for seabirds, dolphins... otters?

Shags headed purposefully out to sea. Herring gulls swooped in the wake of the boat. And a small, tubby auk with a bold white wing patch bobbed on the waves; taking off, it whirred low over the water, displaying bright red legs.

'Black guillemot,' said Grace. 'Known locally as a tystie. It stays close to the island all winter and, in summer, nests among the boulders on the shore.'

My first tystie. But no otter.

From Kyleakin, Grace drove the 13 km (8 miles) to Broadford: a long, straggling crofters' township. Beul na Mara, the Yoxons' home and environmental centre, stands facing on to the beach and, from my bedroom window, I had a fine view of the length of the Broadford Bay.

'At low tide it is worth keeping watch through the telescope in the conservatory,' said Grace. 'The local dog otter can quite often be seen scrunching up crabs in the rock pools.'

The other guests included a newly-wed couple on honeymoon: a return to the house with romantic associations, for it was where they had first met, on an otter-watching holiday! We talked otters until bedtime and retired happily expectant for the morrow.

But on Saturday morning we woke to the sound of rain sheeting down. An early breakfast and then, well waterproofed and wrapped up against the appalling weather, we drove to a lonely peninsula and squelched our way across the soggy black peat. The narrow tracks we were following were otter paths: narrower than the tracks made by sheep. They were criss-crossing paths that led to a freshwater pool where bright green twists of grass marked otter sprainting sites.

There were different droppings too. 'Stoat,' said Grace, after getting down to sniff.

Greenish guano droppings betrayed where white-fronted geese had spent the winter. They would be gone by now, flying home to Greenland for the summer breeding season.

Prominent along the foreshore, slabs of rock tilted at a slant, forming natural caves with several exits: used by otters as holts to lie up in. The otter is a solitary animal. Each has its home range that may extend to 40 km (25 miles) with, perhaps, some 30 lying up places to use as it chooses.

We scrambled up the lee side of an outcrop of rock to get out of the wind, a blustering westerly. We were prepared for a long wait, but with a fine view of the beach, we settled ourselves as comfortably as we could.

'This is the spot,' said Grace, 'where an otter is regularly to be seen bounding across the sands to the sea.'

The shale rock was rich in fossils: small bivalves and other shelled creatures that had swum around in Jurassic seas.

The geology of Skye is extraordinarily diverse. Spectacular mountain ranges are the result of volcanic eruptions, liquid lava flows and gigantic earth movements that happened millions of years ago. Skye's rounded Red Hills are formed of pink granite. The jagged, sharply ridged Black Cuillins are of crystalline gabbro. And the basalt cliffs at Trotternish are a botanist's paradise, with a wealth of alpine plants. In more recent geological times, Ice Age glaciers scooped out great corries, shaped fantastic peaks and pinnacles, and left behind landslides of scree in their wake.

Skye is 96.5 km (60 miles) long from north to south. But, so indented with lochs and inlets are the hundreds of kilometres of magnificent coastline, that nowhere on the island is more than 8 km (5 miles) from the sea.

The rain stopped, shafts of light lit the gloom and a rainbow arched the sky – the first of several rainbows we were to see that fickle-weather weekend. We scanned the long empty beach once again. Our eyes stung with the cold and our fingers froze as they gripped binoculars.

A flypast of oystercatchers piped shrilly. Three seals hauled out on an islet. Boldly patterned shelducks pattered in pools. Lesser black-backed gulls stabbed at the sand. Eider ducks floated offshore, their crooning calls wafting across the water: 'Oo-OOO-oo'.

At the water's edge thick forests of ginger kelp heaved and swirled, exposing... a sleek, humped back? No, only a wet-black boulder. A floating piece of driftwood tossed by the waves raised hopes, but it was another false alarm. An otter can so easily be missed, swimming along the coast. With eyes and nose set high on a flat head, it needs hardly to break the surface to breathe.

Spring comes late to Skye, but from the windows of the minibus, we had seen yellow daffodils in the gardens of white croft cottages, primroses and lesser celandines in the hollows of mossy tree roots, and catkins swinging on the branches of hazel trees.

Now, perched on the craggy outcrop, hoping for an otter, we heard the 'Wheet, chack-chack' of a small spring migrant. A spruce, corn-coloured male wheatear had landed on a rock to whistle and chack. It flicked its white-patched tail and called again: 'Wheet chack-chack'.

'First wheatear of the year for me,' said Grace.

The sky darkened, storm clouds rolled and an icy squall of hail hit us. Abandoning all thoughts of otter watching, we belted back to the shelter of the minibus and reached for the Thermos flasks.

Next stop, Aird of Sleat. And a second rainbow. The sky began to clear and white clouds raced. A wooded path led down to the loch. Thousands of years ago, almost the whole of Skye was blanketed with trees: birch, hazel, elder, elm, oak. The ice retreated and humans arrived. Trees were felled for timber and for fuel, and spaces cleared for crop planting. The original 'wildwood' was whittled away. Today much of the island is bare and treeless, except where conifers have been planted. But the Sleat peninsula, sheltered from the worst of the Atlantic gales, remains wooded: rich in the lichens, mosses, liverworts and ferns that thrive in the damp pure air.

We were still some 30 m (100 ft) above sea level when Grace stopped beside a crevice in the rock. 'An otter holt,' she said. 'Used by a bitch otter to give birth to her kits.' Hidden by bracken, and on the south-facing hill slope, the chamber inside would be protected from rain and wind. After a few weeks, the mother would lead her young down the slope to a second holt close to the water's edge. There they would learn to swim and to fish.

'Scottish otters, unlike the all-the-year-round breeding otters elsewhere, appear to produce their litters most commonly in midsummer,' Grace told us.

A whisky-brown burn was trickling its way down the hillside. Fresh water is very important to a coastal otter, not only to drink, but also to bathe in. A sea-swimming otter must keep its coat free of salt. The long, outer guard hairs form a natural waterproof barrier that protects the dense, air-trapping thermal under-fur. But if salt is allowed to build up, the waterproofing properties are destroyed. Chilling can result in death. So an otter must bathe frequently in the fresh water of pools and burns if its coat is to be kept in good condition.

Heather, bog myrtle, tormentil, sedges, sphagnum moss and other acidic plants grew in the black peat at the loch's edge. A fallen tree trunk overlooking the loch served as a seat. In a little cove, a rowing boat had been hauled up on to the pristine sand, but there was no sign of its owner.

The light in the wide sky was constantly changing, transforming the scene. Hooded crows strutted yobbishly about on the rocks, scavenging whatever morsels they could find. Disgorged crow pellets littered the ground, shiny with the silver discs of periwinkle shells. A curlew took off from the far shore of the loch, its wild bubbling trill ringing out across the Sound. Higher and higher in pitch rose the trill, to culminate in the exhilarating 'cur-*lee*, cur-*lee*'.

But, after two hours of patient waiting and watching, the weather pattern changed once again and icy rain forced us to retreat. 'No otter': we had to report on our return to Beul na Mara. That night over dinner Paul told us about his very first otter sighting, which, he said, he would never forget.

He'd been watching a solitary grey seal 'bottling' offshore: whiskery head, limpid brown eyes. The seal sank slowly beneath the water without a hint of ripple. Then fronds of kelp began to heave and shake, moving in closer to the shore. Paul watched in puzzlement, until the 'kelp' turned into an otter shaking its coat into little spikes to dry.

Grace said that her most exciting otter sighting had been on the Isle of Canna; a wonderful experience. She had been walking along the boulder-strewn beach. On rounding one particularly large boulder, she'd almost stumbled over a bitch otter with two kits beside her.

'The mother and one kit were fast asleep but the other kit had its eyes open. It was quite unafraid and stared at me unblinkingly. A terrific moment. But then the adult stirred in her sleep and I crept away.'

Grace (a biologist) and Paul (a geologist) were students at the same university. They first met properly on a course at a field centre on Skye. They fell in love with the concept of field centres, with Skye and with each other. After graduation and marriage, they began to save hard. Paul worked on the oil rigs. Grace took a secretarial job. At last they had enough money to buy their house, Beul na Mara. Through the summer months, their Wild Explorer Holidays introduce people to the Scottish islands, not only Skye, but also Canna, Rhum, Muck, Raasay, Eigg and Lewis. And they are becoming more ambitious with trips to Turkey and the Russian Taiga Forest.

Paul and Grace are devoted to 'their' otters.

'Why is it that wild mammals get so little appreciation?' asked Paul. 'Birds are always given priority. The RSPB has a membership of thousands. Big glossy magazines are published full of bird pictures. Why are there no big, glossy magazines full of pictures of *mammals*? Seabird cliffs are given Sites of Special Scientific Interest (SSSI) status. So why are otter haunts not declared SSSIs?'

A single disaster, such as an offshore oil slick, could be catastrophic for the 500–600 otter population of Skye. To safeguard areas of good otter habitat, the Yoxons have set up an International Otter Survival Fund with Julian Pettifer as patron.

Paul is assessing the habitat preferences of otters for his Ph.D. thesis. He is making a case study of one dog otter in particular. It makes regular visits to a sprainting site on a tidal islet in Broadford Bay. Once a week, Paul collects the spraint to monitor the otter's diet. His data suggest that it mostly feeds on bottom-living fish, such as five-bearded rockling, long-spined sea scorpion, viviparous blenny and common eel. But its diet changes through the seasons.

We waited patiently

Less often it will take plaice, saithe, butterfish, sand eels and gobies. Frogs and toads are eaten, and occasionally the remains of a bird or small mammal appear in the spraints.

'Remains of a mallard,' said Grace, tweaking out a blue feather from Paul's latest sample.

There was a time when they'd had to remember to lock the hens into the chicken house at night because of a certain rogue dog otter that used to sneak down the burn on the hillside opposite. It would cross by the culvert under the road and take a bird, returning in a few days for another. But, one night the otter grew too bold, used the road and was killed by a passing car.

The chicken house is sometimes raided for eggs and Grace has to explain to her guests that a thieving otter is the reason why they are not getting their free range eggs for breakfast! The empty shells may be found later, discarded and scattered on the beach, mystifying holiday-makers.

Grace and Paul share the chores: the cooking and the care of their two small children. With

Next day the weather had worsened. Sleety rain and bitter cold forced a change of plan. Instead of an exposed and open shore, Paul drove us to the Forestry Commission's otter haven at Kylerhea. We stopped on the way to view a golden eagle's eyrie half-way up a rocky ravine and again at Ord for a rainswept view of the high, jagged peaks of the Cuillins.

Motorists on Skye have to keep a constant watch for sheep. Island sheep seem to have no traffic sense whatsoever. They trot absentmindedly into the unfenced roads with

some local help, they cope, too, with the wardening of their small museum and with the nursing of sick animals in their wildlife hospital. That weekend the hospital patients consisted of a wood mouse with a broken leg and a hedgehog suffering from shock after being rescued from a dog. The Soay sheep in the outdoor pen were temporary residents in need of a new home, their owner having moved to the mainland. A special tank for wildlife victims of oil pollution, donated by the League Against Cruel Sports, was, thankfully, empty.

Grace said that the hedgehog was suffering from shock

never a look to right or left. We got used to Paul's sudden pressure on the brakes. 'Sheep ahead!'

Kylerhea was bleak and wet. But the sturdy hide at the end of the track offered shelter and there were wooden benches to sit on, and slat windows looking across to Glenelg on the mainland and the snow-capped mountains beyond.

The shoreline below is inaccessible and undisturbed, ideal for otters. Tumbled rocks serve as holts. There are freshwater pools and little streams. In the narrows, shoals of fish pass to and fro, and food is plentiful.

The rain eased. Once more the changing skies and the multi-coloured arch of an April rainbow. And there, at the edge of the water,

was our first otter. It was a young one, rolling in the kelp, bounding over boulders, running along the water's edge.

A second otter appeared, swimming fast towards the first. Both otters were diving now, only a few yards out. Plop! Rudder-tails disappearing last. Plop! And a big bound up again as if lungs were about to burst. Ten seconds of treading water – and plop! under again.

The two lively otters held us in thrall. No adult appeared; perhaps she was watching, hidden by boulders. Forty exciting minutes passed and then first one, then the other, began to swim purposefully into the Sound, trailing wide V-wakes of silvery bubbles, round the next headland and out of sight.

CHAPTER FIVE

Bats Need Friends

BATS
Robert Stebbings

•

Preston Montford Field Centre, near
Shrewsbury, Shropshire

'IMUST BE BATTY,' I thought, as I followed Bob along the long, dark tunnel.

We were in a cave in an abandoned limestone quarry. In the sunshine outside, small coppers and common blue butterflies flitted about the hawkbits and vetches. But Bob had led us up a slope and into one of the man-made tunnels that honeycombed the rock.

The floor was uneven and the air was chilly; there was a narrow ledge to edge along above a steep drop and now the roof was sloping downwards. We found that we would have to negotiate the next few metres crouching, with bent knees.

'Good territory for bats,' said Bob, once we were able to stand upright again. 'Passages and chambers at several levels like this offer a range of different temperatures.'

Warmer air in the higher chambers and cooler air in the lower, different flow patterns and humidities: each cave-using bat species has its own special preference. Bob suspected that more than one kind of bat might be making use of the tunnels: as roosts in summer and as hibernacula in winter.

Dr Robert Stebbings became interested in bats at a very early age. His first scientific paper was published in 1958 while he was still in his teens. Today, he and his wife, Sheila Walsh, work tirelessly, running their Bat Consultancy in Peterborough, promoting bat conservation, 'flitting from roost to roost, from mine shaft to attic, and even across our television screens' in defence of vulnerable bat colonies.

We moved on down the tunnel. The beam of Bob's powerful torch pinpointed a notch in the rock. He stopped to take a closer look. There were faint signs of yellow staining and tiny, muddy claw marks where a bat had been hanging free. 'Could be a horseshoe bat,' he said.

Not all bat species hang upside down in the open in this way. Most prefer to tuck themselves neatly into a niche or cranny.

Another stop; the torch beam had picked up a small heap of discarded moth-wings on the cave

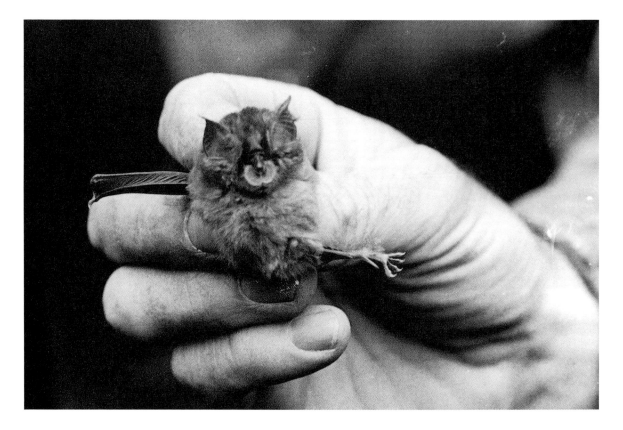

floor. Was it a sign of a long-eared bat?

The long-eared bat is a 'foliage gleaner'. It feeds by fluttering in the tree canopy with slow beats of its broad wings. Hovering expertly, it picks insects off the leaves. The high-frequency sounds it emits while foraging are faint; so faint as to be quite difficult to pick up on a bat detector. This is why the long-eared bat is sometimes called the 'whispering bat'. With its long ears and large eyes it is probably able to locate prey by sound and sight alone, and has less need of echo-location.

Any insect too large to be eaten in flight will be carried back to a regular perch. Moth wings, crane-fly legs, hard bits of beetle, bug and earwig are bitten off and flutter to the ground.

'Moths are a favourite food,' said Bob, as he examined the litter on the cave floor. 'What we have here are mostly remains of yellow underwings and silver-Ys.'

We took a closer look at the lesser horseshoe

Long-eared bat-litter is an entomologist's delight.

'At one traditional feeding perch in Yorkshire, 51 moth species were identified, including the first county record of a copper underwing.'

There were droppings, too. An experienced batworker can identify droppings to species by appearance and by the faint smell. ('Hint of Earl Grey, must be a...') Bat droppings crumble easily into fine fragments when rubbed between thumb and finger and so cannot be mistaken for mouse droppings, which are greasy and unpleasant-smelling.

A cave woodlouse was making an excellent job of recycling the long-eared bat droppings and was producing even smaller droppings itself.

A bat suddenly jinked out of the darkness ahead of us, swerved and vanished. We had reached the end of the tunnel. Time for the return journey, and this time Bob spotted a bat hanging from a toehold in the ceiling, its wings wrapped tightly around its small, furry body. It was a lesser horseshoe. To achieve this upside-down position, the bat must twist itself round in flight and clutch at a snag on the roof with its feet. It will hang, head down, for hours, in a sort of torpor. Bob held the horseshoe bat in his hand for us to have a closer look. It had wings like fine leather, pointed ears, silky brown fur, an odd little face with curious nose-flaps and a plump little body about the size of a teaspoon, compared to the tablespoon size of the greater horseshoe.

There are only two families of bats in the British Isles: the *Vespertilionidae* (12 species) and the *Rhinolophidae* (2 species, the lesser horseshoe and the greater horseshoe). Most *vespers* (the long-eared bat is an exception) 'shout' through their mouths. The *rhinolophids* emit sounds through the nose, modifying and directing the pulses by means of the curious horseshoe-shaped flaps.

Horseshoe bats, particularly greater horseshoe bats, are rare in Britain, having declined in numbers this century. They are probably the most cave-dependent of all our bats. In the damp conditions of a cave, soft wing membranes stay moist and supple.

A horseshoe bat will sometimes travel quite long distances to find an appropriate site for a hibernaculum. (The Leicester Bat Group made history with their discovery, in 1991, of a greater horseshoe bat in a county cave: the most northerly British record of this rare species.)

'Every tiny colony is important,' said Bob, returning the sleepy lesser horseshoe to its upside-down position on the cave roof.

Bat numbers are declining for a variety of reasons, the most serious being loss of habitat and the great reduction of suitable insects to feed on. Strictly protected in Britain, it is an offence to disturb or handle a bat without a licence.

Sometimes, to protect a vulnerable colony, English Nature will decide to fix a grille across a cave entrance. The precise design is important

A grille is sometimes fixed to protect a vulnerable colony

and this is when Bob may be consulted. The horizontal bars must be too narrow for humans to squeeze through, but wide enough to allow the bats to fly freely in and out.

Not all bats like caves. The pipistrelle, for instance, our commonest bat, seems to shun caves. It prefers to roost in the cracks and crevices of trees, brick walls, bridges, houses and the like. The spaces behind roof tiles, slates, barge boards and soffits in semi-detached houses on modern housing estates are very popular with pipistrelles.

It was not to a modern house that Bob took us at dusk that night, but to a splendid Georgian manor house where generations of 'pips' have utilized the spacious lofts as nursery roosts.

A new-born batling weighs a quarter of its mother's weight. (Imagine a human mother carrying a 13 kg (2 stone) baby in her womb!) It is usually born in June or July and suckled for up to 40 days. The female flies out at night to hawk for insects and, on her return, is able to recognize her infant, however large the colony and thick the clusters, by its scent and the little, individual squeaks it makes. In three weeks the batling has learnt to fly and will be ready to leave the roost.

On warm summer nights the owner of this lovely old house invites her friends round for a 'bat spectacular'. They sit in deckchairs on the lawn, sipping their drinks, and counting the bats as, wave after wave, the tiny winged mammals slip out from under the eaves.

But this evening, our hostess looked worried as she opened the door to us. 'I'm afraid you're too late,' she said apologetically. 'The pipistrelles have gone.'

Bob borrowed a ladder, propped it against the side of the house and climbed up to inspect one of the exit holes. No sounds of bat chatter came from within (bats are quite noisy in a nursery roost) and a spider had spun its web across the hole.

'I'm not altogether surprised,' said Bob. 'Pipistrelles are notoriously unpredictable.'

And it was September, the 'all change' time of the year. Bats are nomadic. Adult bats, in autumn, have mating on the mind. As the weather turns cooler, so they begin to think of hibernation. A suitably cold hibernacula has to be found in which to pass the winter.

The old manor house was surrounded by trees. Bob switched on his bat detector, and we walked slowly about the grounds, looking and listening for bats. A sudden, rapid staccato clicking – d-d-d-d-d-d-d-d – and a solitary pipistrelle fluttered over our heads, silhouetted against the sky. The microphone picked up the tell-tale buzzy 'burp' as the bat homed in on an insect, snapped it up, then flickered away over the rooftops to be lost to view. Bats navigate brilliantly, sending out high-frequency pulses that bounce back on hitting an obstacle: 'hearing' their way in the dark.

But no more bats appeared, it began to rain and we retreated.

All 14 species of bats resident in Britain are insectivorous. For decades, foresters in Scandinavian countries have taken advantage of this, putting up batboxes to encourage such useful predators of harmful pest insects. Conifer forests are almost devoid of natural roosts and a batbox to a bat is a good substitute.

As far as is known, the first batboxes in the UK were the 26 positioned by Bob Stebbings in a Dorset wood in May 1968. Bob made the boxes out of planks of roughened wood, designed to be draught and waterproof, and large enough to house a cluster. A bat likes to creep up the trunk of the tree and to enter the box through a slit in the floor.

Most bats are inquisitive. Any potential new roosting site is investigated and Bob soon began to find droppings. Within five months a colony of brown long-eareds was roosting regularly in one of his boxes.

This, to a naturalist, was very exciting. The research possibilities were obvious. By studying 'batbox bats', much more could be learnt of bat ecology and movements. In 1975, on television's *Nationwide* programme, Bob invited viewers to 'sponsor a box'. Perhaps 100 replies were

Bob inspected one of the exit holes

anticipated. To his delight, sufficient money was donated for 3,000 boxes. The World Wide Fund for Nature volunteered to arrange manufacture and delivery. The Forestry Commission selected suitable sites. Seven bat species have been recorded in batboxes since the scheme began and five species have so far bred: Leisler's, pipistrelle, brown long-eared, noctule and natterer's.

Some of the *Nationwide* boxes are situated in a conifer plantation on Cannock Chase in Staffordshire, and that is where Bob took us next day. Once a hunting ground for royalty, deer still roam free on Cannock: an area of rolling heathland, secluded valleys, sheltered woodlands, ancient oaks and new plantations of conifers.

Early experiments showed that most bats have a preference for high, south-facing boxes. But in very hot weather a bat might move round into a cooler box. Bearing this in mind, Bob provides a variety of aspects, several boxes to a tree.

Propping his ladder against the trunk of a

spruce, he climbed up to inspect the first clutch of boxes. Only one box was occupied, by a pipistrelle.

'Isn't it *tiny*?' is everyone's first reaction on seeing a pipistrelle in the hand. Bob held it in his palm, with his fingers curled lightly round the bat, his thumb preventing its escape. In this position the bat feels warm and safe, and stress is minimized.

He weighed it – 5 g (0.18 oz); and measured it – 40 mm (1.6 in) from head to tail. It was small enough to fit into a matchbox.

To give the pipistrelle an identity, he attached a loose-fitting, numbered ring to its forearm. Permission to ring bats is limited to a very few trained ringers and restricted to valid research projects.

Bats belong to the order *Chiroptera* (*cheir* = hand + *pteryx* = wing). The wing is a double layer of thin elastic skin, richly supplied with blood vessels; the skin heals quickly if torn. The forearm bone acts as a strut and the wing membrane is stretched over the frame of elongated finger bones, becoming taut and ready for flight when the 'hand' is fully extended. The clawed 'thumbs' are free of membrane and are made use of by the bat for grasping when climbing.

Bob's next occupied box contained a female Leisler's bat: a small, hairy hobgoblin with dark, shaggy fur, square ears, beady eyes and a bulbous nose. Her wings were long, narrow and pointed; Leisler's are fast flyers, pursuing prey high above the tree canopy. She was still suckling her baby, although it was late in the year to be doing so.

The batling's fur was grey and frizzy. It didn't take kindly to being disturbed and opened its mouth wide to scream in protest: a silent scream, inaudible to human ears. Bob stroked the batling, talked to it in his soothing way and it calmed down.

The Leisler's bat is nationally rare in Britain,

Opposite: *A loose-fitting numbered ring was attached to the forearm*

with the exception of Ireland, its main stronghold. A bat of forests, it was very seldom encountered before the advent of batboxes. Now there are reports of its presence every year. One individual ringed in Cannock Chase was found dead, four years later, in Exeter, 252.5 km (157 miles) away.

In September, a male will fly round and round a batbox tree at dusk: a slow, fluttery flight, accompanied by loud, emphatic squeaks clearly audible to the human ear. This is an autumnal 'songflight', performed to attract females to its batbox harem.

In the next occupied box, 13 brown long-eared bats clustered, huddling together to conserve heat. Long silky 'rabbity' ears, bright eyes and pinkish face... they are charming little bats and, after the pipistrelle, our most common species. Brown long-eared bats are particularly loyal to a site. Once they've found a batbox that suits, they keep returning, year after year.

Bob decided not to disturb the huddled colony – and it was time to go.

'Bats Need Friends' was Bob's message to us that batty weekend. 'I Love Bats' said the stickers on our luggage as we departed for home.

Leisler's bat: wings like fine leather

CHAPTER SIX

Secret Valley

WILDLIFE IN THE COTSWOLDS
Miriam Kelly

•

Woodchester Park Field Centre,
Nympsfield, Gloucestershire

A COTTAGE IN THE COTSWOLDS, bats flitting from a Gothic mansion, badgers in a bluebell wood, foxes on a floodlit lawn, the springtime chorus of birds.... Who could ask for more?

We arrived at the field centre for a May weekend jointly booked by my local Bat Group and Badger Group (affiliated to the Leicestershire and Rutland Trust for Nature Conservation). Woodchester Park offers both bats *and* badgers.

Miriam Kelly and her family have shared their home, The Cottage, for over 30 years: first as a school and now as a field centre. 'The Cottage' is a misnomer; it is actually a large, 13-bedroomed manse, part Elizabethan, with Victorian extensions. Miriam owns 14 ha (35 acres) of surrounding woodland and pasture, and has rights of access for educational purposes to the 'secret valley' below.

It was early evening when we arrived. A steep path zigzags down the wooded hillside from the field centre and, although tired after the journey, we couldn't wait to explore. May is bluebell time. The slopes were carpeted with bluebells and the starry white flowers of wild

ramson too: the air was pungent with the strong smell of garlic. We followed the path down, and emerged into a flowery meadow bright with buttercups and ox-eye daisies.

Dominating the long valley was the dramatically gabled, buttressed and gargoyled Woodchester Mansion: a gothic edifice with a strange history. Commissioned in the 1850s it was never to be completed and no one has ever lived there. But four species of bats roost in the extensive attics: pipistrelle, brown long-eared, lesser horseshoe and the very rare greater horseshoe.

The evening sky was darkening. Val stood ready with her bat detector directed towards the gables of the unfinished mansion. We waited expectantly. At dusk the bats fly out from under the eaves.

'KuWEET, kuWEET, kuWEET': that was the alarm call of a tawny owl. There was a soft flickering and from an attic roost the first bat emerged; twisting, weaving, hawking after insects of the night. Val picked up its ultrasonic pulse patterns on the detector: a rapid geiger-counter firing, 'd-d-d-d-d-d'.

'Pipistrelle,' she said.

More bats followed, some 'pip' size, some larger. Clive said that he could identify only two kinds of bats: 'Probably pipistrelles and probably-not pipistrelles.'

But Val had retuned the dial to 82 kHz and was listening intently to the characteristic warblings of a greater horseshoe.

'Wow-wow-wow': that was the staccato bark of a fox. A cool wind rustled the grass. Badger groupies decided it was time to return to the field centre. Bat groupies, armed with torches, stayed below.

Back in the common room, children were curled up in anticipation on cushions in front of the window. We settled ourselves in the armchairs. Spotlights fixed to the exterior wall of the house beamed on to the lawn outside. A peanut trail led from the edge of the wooded bluebell slope to a tray of kitchen scraps, tempting valley badgers on to the floodlit lawn.

Clouds raced across the full moon. Dark bat-shapes spooked out of the sky. Glow-worms sparkled in the daisied grass: tiny luminous beetles.

The child nearest to the window gave a little wriggle of excitement. From out of the shadows at the edge of the floodlit circle peered a distinctive black and white striped face. The head bobbed down and up again. Out padded a shaggy-coated badger. Nose to ground it moved across the lawn, audibly scrunching up each peanut in turn.

A flowery meadow bright with ox-eye daisies

Audibly? Sitting with us in the common room was Ray Goodwin, a professional sound recordist. At his side was his recording equipment. With the help of a microphone hidden in the grass outside, he was relaying noises back to the common room: the lip smackings of a badger 'hoovering' up peanuts, the hoot of an owl, the eerie scream of a fox, the rustle of the wind in the trees, the squeal of a frightened rabbit and the late night squawk of a pheasant....

When Ray unexpectedly lost his job as a farm worker, he resolved to turn his part-time hobby of recording wildlife sounds into a full-time living. He is now successfully doing what he enjoys most: watching, listening and recording. His wildlife tapes are in demand for natural history programmes on radio and for television

documentary films. Woodchester Valley is where he feels most at home; the location of many of his most sought-after recordings.

Something startled the badger. It paused in mid-scrunch, lifted its head, sniffed the air and, its paws pad-pad-padding the ground, trundled back into the shadows at a fast pace. This gave us the chance to shuffle a little in our seats.

'Ready for bed?' whispered the children's mother. 'No,' they pleaded, and were allowed to stay on, although by now it was past 10 o'clock.

Back on to the lawn came not one, but two badgers: an adult and a young one. Other badgers arrived, snuffling bear-like along the peanut trail. Scrunch, scrunch. We stayed mesmerized until midnight. There were five badgers on the lawn. But it had been a long day and we had promised ourselves an early start in the morning. So, one by one, we crept off to bed.

Sharing a room with Val, Jenny and me was a tiny pipistrelle bat. This didn't really surprise me. Jenny, like Val, is a licensed batworker and usually has a little bat-waif somewhere about her person. 'Stumpy,' she told us, had hurt its wing and would probably never fly again. She could not return it to the wild, but for the rest of its probably short but pampered life, Stumpy would play a useful PR role on visits to schools and interested groups. Children are captivated by the tiny creature; older people are helped to overcome any irrational fear of bats they may perhaps have inherited.

Jenny sat on the side of the bed feeding her bat with mealworms from a margarine tub before settling it for the night in its travelling box. 'I couldn't leave him behind...' she started to explain. But I had dropped off to sleep before she'd finished the sentence.

The alarm clock bleeped and woke us at 3.30 a.m. Pipistrelles would be returning to their roost in the old wooden bell tower. In drizzling rain we stood on the drive, peering upwards. Bats were wheeling against the grey sky, round and round. 'The bats their flighty circles make', as John Clare put it. One by one, they peeled off, sped towards the tower and vanished through a slit.

Val was counting them in. 'Thirty-seven...'

We waited, but the last gnat-satiated pipistrelle was home to roost.

We had breakfast and then it was time to explore Woodchester Valley, designated a Site of Special Scientific Interest (SSSI) for its wildlife value.

Miriam handed out identity disc permits to pin on our shirts. Wardens patrol the length of the private valley. Trespassers are escorted politely back to the gates and the outlying hippy colony.

The sun had broken through the clouds, sparkling the raindrops on petals and leaves. On either side of the woodland ride grew flowering plants: bugle, herb Bennet, bush vetch, wood forget-me-not, yellow archangel, sanicle, greater stitchwort, red campion, lily of the valley, Solomon's seal....

Trampled bluebells showed where badger 'brockways' criss-crossed, tunnelling through the undergrowth, leading to huge spoilheaps of ancient setts. We saw jewel-like, iridescent beetles on the umbels of cow parsley, orange-tip butterflies on cuckoo smock, small tortoiseshells on flowers of bramble and speckled woods in sunspots. Tiny red snails nibbled garlic-flavoured ramson leaves: 'badger's garlic' was an old country name for ramson.

And, resounding through the wood, the springtime chorus of birdsong: the trilling of the willow warbler's little down-scale tune; the repetitive notes – 'chiff-chaff-chiff-chaff-chiff-chiff-chaff' – of a chiffchaff; the melodic fluting of blackbird; the far-carrying phrases of a song thrush ('He sings his song twice over'); jumbled dunnock notes; bitter-sweet robin; and confident chaffinch ditty. Then the 'yaffle call' of a green woodpecker rang out: a clear laughing 'Kleu-kleu-kleu-kleu-kleu-kleu...'. (Was Ray hidden anywhere about with his microphone?)

I walked out of the wood and into the valley where the sun shone warmly down. Jackdaws spiralled above the tall chimneys and turrets of the Gothic mansion. Common spotted orchids and ragged robin grew in the long grass. Caddis flies 'disco-danced' in swarms over a hill bottom stream. And a buzzard soared across on broad, rounded wings.

The hawthorn copse on the slope of a hill was creamy white with may blossom. As I neared the top, a red fox trotted out from the conifer plantation at the far end of the valley, heading straight towards me. I froze on the spot, but it sensed my presence and stopped abruptly, beautiful ears pricked. Its eyes met mine, for a long moment it stared and then, in a streak of red-orange, it was gone.

I followed the fox into the plantation where goldcrests acrobated in the conifers, tiny, skippety birds, tweaking the needles in search of aphids and scale insects. 'Sree-sree-sree': that was the high thin contact call.

The track led to the first of the four lakes and there I met Clive. He'd sat down on the bank to watch mirror carp lolling in the shallows and he'd dozed off.

'I was awoken by something tickling my foot,' he explained.

Half-opening his eyes he'd seen a little chestnut-coloured bank vole creeping over his wellies. 'The next minute,' said Clive, 'a Land Rover trundled past and broke the silence, and the vole scampered away.'

A sharp-eyed warden had spotted him. He was just about to be extradited to the out-lying hippy colony, when he remembered in time the identity tag given to him by Miriam.

'Apologies,' said the warden, backing away.

'Peace, man,' said Clive.

After lunch, it was raining hard so Ray played some of the more curious of his tapes: the 'cork-popping' sounds made by courting capercaillies; the eerie scream of a sika stag in the rutting season; wing-fanning of a bumblebee ventilating its hive; noise of black grouse lekking; frantic buzzing of a fly caught in a spider's web....

But we wanted badger noises and Ray obliged with the shuffling sound of a badger edging backwards with its arms full of bedding, the snort it makes on emergence from the sett to clear its air passages of soil particles, whickerings of cubs at play....

And the rain had stopped.

That evening some of us decided to do some 'proper' badger-watching, at a sett, in the open.

'Dress dark and keep quiet,' advised Bill, heading for the most comfortable chair, 'and remember to stay downwind. If the badger sees you and becomes suspicious,' he added, settling himself back into the cushions, *'scratch hard –* like this.' And he demonstrated. 'Scratching to a badger means all's well.'

Bill, a founder member of the Badger Group, has experienced very many hours of badger watching and has fine photographs to prove it. We listen to what Bill says with respect.

Raindrops plopped through the leaves of the

Common spotted orchids in the long grass

trees as I tried to get comfy on a fallen tree trunk. The stench of wild garlic was overpowering. Midges landed on my head, their itching was intolerable.... It didn't take me long to see the error of my ways, and I joined Bill and the others.

In the common room, a drama was unfolding. Three adult badgers and a cub were scoffing peanuts, slowly making their way across the wet lawn to the scrap tray in front of the window. At the edge of the floodlit circle of light a red fox skirted warily, too nervous yet to quit the safety of the shadows. Another fox joined it, as wary and shy as the first. They were wonderful creatures, with foxy-red coats, pointed snouts, long, bushy tails and gleaming, laser-bright eyes.

It was after midnight when the foxes finally plucked up sufficient courage to trot on to the lawn. A badger took fright and padded back into the dark. But a cub stood its ground, with bristling fur and pugnaciously lowered head. The surprised fox stopped, swerved and gave the hostile, bristling cub a wide berth. It reached

GRHenckx

the scrap tray, snatched a chicken leg and gnawed at it in the way a dog does.

People were drifting off to bed. Bewitched, unable to move, I stayed on. The world outside was so still and quiet, dreamlike under the full, round moon: starry sky, silvered trees and long, black shadows. Animals came and went, ignoring each other's presence for the most part. The hours melted away and the sky began to lighten.

Dawn – and the chorus began. 'Kor-rok, kor-rok,' cried a pheasant. A robin tried a tentative few notes. Wood pigeons cooed. 'Belling' of a great tit...

One by one valley birds joined in the springtime crescendo of territorial song. Rabbits hopped from burrows as the rays of the sun crept up over the horizon, greening the grass. Colour spread like a wash. Mist rose from the damp ground and was dispersed by the sun's warmth. Foxes had long departed, but still the badgers fed. It wasn't until early risers, all prepared to bat-count once more, opened the creaky front door on to the drive that the animals took fright and vanished into the wood.

Miriam Kelly had arranged a conducted tour of Woodchester Mansion for those who were interested. The nineteenth-century Gothic edifice is now owned by Stroud Council and Stroud's conservation officer had agreed to act as guide.

Woodchester Mansion is built round a courtyard. The material used throughout is Cotswold stone, a warm honey-yellow oolitic limestone.

Wearing protective helmets, we were taken along passages, up winding staircases and into spacious rooms. We saw huge stone fireplaces, stone arches, stone vaulting on the ceilings and stone-traceried windows. Stone owls perch above the servants' quarters. Stone gargoyles peer from the stone-tiled roof. Stone carvings decorate the stone chapel. Even the bath is made out of a block of the mellow stone. It is a remarkable house and yet no one has ever lived in it.

William Leigh, a wealthy Catholic industrialist from the Midlands, and owner of The Cottage, commissioned a young local architect, Benjamin Bucknell, aged 21, to build the mansion in the valley below. The same Benjamin Bucknell had been responsible for the wings added to The Cottage.

Benjamin was the disciple of a Frenchman called Viollet-le-Duc who preached that 'the construction of a building should never be concealed but should be there for all to see'.

Work began in 1854. Sadly, after 14 years, Leigh's money ran out. Woodchester Mansion, which has been described as 'one of the best examples of Victorian Gothic in England', was never to be finished. Miriam Kelly and other local people would like to see a continuation of the long link between the Mansion and The Cottage, and a Trust has been set up to safeguard the future of this extraordinary building.

Miriam's field centre attracts many naturalists, and schoolchildren with their teachers too. Within easy reach is Frocester Hill, rich in limestone flowers, with glorious views across the River Severn. There is a fine arboretum nearby at Westonbirt. Hetty Pegler's Tump, the local long barrow, interests archaeologists. Further afield is the Wildfowl and Wetlands Trust Reserve at Slimbridge, which always has plenty to offer birdwatchers.

For more than 30 years Dr Roger Ransome has been studying the greater horseshoe bats of Woodchester Mansion. In 1986 he was awarded the Linnean Society's H. H. Bloomer Medal for his research work. He is author of *The Natural History of Hibernating Bats* (Christopher Helm, 1990).

Miriam persuaded Roger to abandon the greater horseshoes for a while and to talk to us about his bats.

'Woodchester Mansion,' said Roger, 'is ideal for bats. Attics differ in size, shape, aspect and draught patterns. There is a large cellar system, two underground tunnels, several wide chimney flues and an outside ice house.'

Such a wide range of suitable roosting sites allows occupation by greater horseshoes all the year round. Any flies or spiders that settle on the inside walls of the mansion are soon snapped up. Greater horseshoe bats are long lived. A 26-year-old male is on record. But the species has declined drastically this century. Colonies are almost entirely confined to the south-west of England and south Wales. One major cause of this decline is the lack of sufficient food at the 'right' time of the year.

Greater horseshoes feed on the cockchafers and large moths which are to be found in deciduous woodland. They hawk after the large dung beetles of permanent pastures in summer. A warm spring, with plenty of insects,

accelerates the time of birth and early babies have a greater chance of survival. But a cold, late spring can result in a lack of suitable insects at a time when bats are vulnerable: at their minimum weight on emergence from hibernation. If the young of the year do not put on sufficient weight in autumn, they may not survive the winter or be too weak to breed the following year.

And, in the last decade, many more pastures have been turned over to arable farming, which means fewer juicy dung beetles. But I was to learn more of the useful insect members of the cowpat community at Preston Montford Field Centre.

CHAPTER SEVEN

Life in a Cowpat

INSECTS OF A COW-DUNG COMMUNITY

Peter Skidmore

•

Preston Montford Field Centre,
Shrewsbury, Shropshire

A COW LIFTED HER TAIL – splat! – and moved on. Already, downwind, certain flies and beetles would be scenting this coveted new food source. Zooming in, the insects exploit to the full the warm, moist, sheltered habitat. Unpalatable grass is transformed, by bovine benefactors, into this superb cow-dung medium.

The insect colonizers, in their turn, help to convert the dung into a useful humus in which grass can grow. This is recycling at its most effective.

Peter led the way to the cow pastures on the banks of the River Severn. A yellow wagtail – yellow as butter – bobbed and flirted, snapping at flies that swarmed above the pats. Peter swished his net and caught some of the winged insects before they could touch down on the bouncy landing platform of dung. 'We'll identify them later,' he said.

Then he handed out buckets, trowels and rubber gloves. 'We need a selection of pats, from fresh to not-so-fresh.'

I found myself looking with distaste at a wetly-gleaming, freshly-steaming, greenish pile and quickly decided instead on a thickly-crusted model which had been around, drying out in the sun, for a few hours at least.

'Much less messy,' I thought.

The pat was honeycombed with galleries excavated by burrowing beetles and, as I lifted it into the bucket, it broke into large fibrous chunks.

Back at the centre the dung was tipped from the buckets into wire sieves and hosed thoroughly over an outside drain in the yard, leaving behind undigested plant debris and some of the insect members of a cowdung community.

But my cowpat was too old to sieve and hose in this way. I'd have to render it down first in a bowl of water. With rubber-gloved hands, I broke the coarse matrix into pieces until it could be hosed.

However, I was to have the last laugh.

In the laboratory, the contents of the sieves were tipped into white plastic trays. Under strong lights, we began to sort out the animals. And, because of its age, my cowpat turned out to be the most rewarding. Eggs had hatched into larvae. Larvae were shedding their skins and turning into pupae. Adult beetles and flies had emerged from the pupae. Parasitic mites clung to the hairy legs of beetles. Springtails were feeding on fungi. Earthworms had crawled up out of the soil... It was all go in my pat.

Peter Skidmore is keeper of natural sciences at Doncaster Museum. He is also author of one of the Field Studies Council's AIDGAP Keys: *Insects of the British Cow Dung Community* (FSC, 1991).

AIDGAP stands for the 'Identification of Difficult Groups of Animals and Plants'. Each of the series of AIDGAP keys are student-tested by amateurs, like ourselves. Revisions are made and the text amended in the light of student comments.

I tweezered up a fat grey grub for closer inspection. Only larvae of the insect orders Coleoptera and Diptera are commonly represented in dung. So, was my fat grub a beetle larva or a fly larva? I turned to the Key.

'Larva of beetle: three pairs of legs. Larva of fly: legs always absent.' My grub was legless. It was a fly.

But which fly? I scanned the Key. 'Dull, heavily sclerotized...' (Sclerotized? What did that mean? And I turned to the glossary: 'hardened body wall') '...and many conspicuous bristles.'

Yes, my grub had a leathery skin and was indeed very bristly. 'Conspicuous non-retractile head capsule.' That must be the odd brown knob at its front end.

A check with the drawing in the AIDGAP Key told me that the grub was a member of the family Stratiomyidae. After a few sluggish weeks, this unlovely slob would metamorphize into a handsome, metallic-green soldier-fly. It would spend its adult life visiting flowers for nectar and sunning itself on the umbels of hogweed.

'A superb fly,' said Peter enthusiastically.

Eight of the fifty species of soldier-flies are known to breed in cowpats.

Flies are usually the first colonizers, laying their eggs while the dung is still wet. Once a crust starts to form, the female's soft ovipositor cannot penetrate. Some fly species go to a great deal of trouble, oscillating their ovipositors to form a bubble cavity and arranging the eggs in neat rows around the inner walls.

'Can't think why they bother,' said Peter. 'No sooner have they finished than the beetles zoom in, tunnelling furiously through the fresh fluid dung, scattering all those neat little bubble-nests.'

All this tunnelling aerates the dung and permits entry to aerobic bacteria, fungal spores and other microscopic bodies of importance in the decomposing process. Despite the rough treatment of 'yobbo' beetles, most fly eggs have hatched by the end of the second day. The larvae congregate just below the surface where the oxygen supply is greatest. The crust forms, preserving the moisture and deterring further invasion.

'Within a day or two, a thriving metropolis of insect activity may be found beneath the now-firm crust,' says the AIDGAP Key.

Most inhabitants are coprophagous (i.e. dung-eating). But carnivores are also present: opportunist predators that fly in to prey on the early colonizers. There are parasites too. Certain species of parasitic wasps pierce and immobilize the larvae of cow-dung flies, then lay their eggs inside the soft bodies. The young wasps emerge and feed on the tissues of their – still living – hosts.

Now I was keying the larva of a fly that belongs to the Muscidae, a large family well represented in dung. The adults are never seen below the surface, but their larvae perform a leading role in the cow-dung community.

'Muscids are ferocious killers,' said Peter, 'able to devour their prey with astonishing rapidity. Downwards-slashing mouthparts, sideways-slicing... Incredibly elegant.' In a few seconds, only the scoured husk of the victim remains.

Back to the tray.

A slender, worm-like, dark-patterned grub keyed out to: the larva of the window gnat *Sylvicola punctata*. 'Often occurs in huge quantities in older cowpats.'

A beetle larva next. It had a well-defined head, antennae and several pairs of legs. The curled-up C-shape posture identified it as a member of the Scarabaeidae, the true 'dung beetles' which spend most of their lives in dung, only leaving to find a fresh cowpat or to pupate in the underlying soil.

I recognized the familiar 'wireworm', with its hard waxy body, and learned from the *Key* that it is the larva of a click beetle and feeds mainly on roots of plants, causing great damage to farmers' crops.

Tiny predatory rove beetles scuttled about, searching for other, even smaller, members of

the cow-dung community to feed on.

Mites, the minuscule relatives of spiders and harvestmen, seize their chance and cling to the hairy legs of a winged beetle or fly, hitch-hiking lifts to a fresh cowpat. Once in the dung, they lay their eggs and then, most ungratefully, seek out and consume the eggs and larvae of their 'good Samaritan' transporters.

In fresher cowpats people were finding newly laid eggs. Beetle eggs are typically oval, plain, smooth and shiny without fancy decoration. Fly eggs, on the other hand, are oval to cigar-shaped, often marked with a net-like pattern and sometimes (as with the sepsid fly) ornamented with a long respiratory horn which projects above the dung.

But Peter was showing us the black noon-fly *Mesembrina meridiana* that he'd caught with a swish of his net in the cow pastures. One of the most spectacular of the flies in the Muscidae family, a magnificent insect with bright orange wing bases and facial strips, it is 'a bluebottle-sized job'.

An individual female black noon-fly lays only five eggs (in contrast to the hundreds of eggs laid by most other flies). Each is laid singly in a different cowpat at intervals of two days. The eggs, which are large, hatch almost at once. Sometimes, perhaps because a suitable cowpat cannot be found in time, it may even hatch inside the parental oviduct and the fly deposits a first instar larva instead. The fully grown black noon-fly larva is the fattest, juiciest, yellowest maggot to be found in cow-dung in Britain and is much beloved by fishermen.

'Popular with anglers and rooks alike,' said Peter.

Another fly netted in the pastures was the yellow dung-fly, *Scathophaga stercoraria*, the fly most often seen buzzing to and fro over a cowpat. The males are furry, covered in golden hairs. The females are small and grey-green. They mate on the cowpat and lay their eggs. The larvae – 'filthy-looking maggots clothed in dense black spines' – hatch out and immediately begin to bury downwards.

G.R.HERICKX.

'A yellow dung-fly larva,' said Peter, 'is pathetic, falling an easy victim to every predator.'

Yet, once the larva has pupated and emerged as an adult fly, it turns into a voracious hunter. Tackling prey even larger than itself, it pierces the nerve cord and sucks out the body juices. Even crane-flies are not safe. Consuming, as they do, vast numbers of insects, many of them pest species, yellow dung-flies are probably of considerable economic importance.

More flies: the troublesome sweat-fly with its fondness for mammalian perspiration; a tiny, shining, ant-like sepsid fly with spotted wings; and a hover-fly, *Rhingia campestris*, the only syrphid to breed in cow-dung. With its orange abdomen and long, pointed snout *R. campestris* is unmistakable. Packed away inside the snout is the remarkably long proboscis with which it sips nectar from ground ivy, bugle and other tubular flowers.

'Casual visitors are also found in cowpats from time to time,' said Peter. 'Not true members of the cow-dung community, but predatory invaders from adjacent habitats.'

These include digger wasps, centipedes, hungry wolf spiders....

A female earwig will sometimes overwinter under an old cowpat, guarding her batch of eggs in early spring and caring tenderly for her 20 to 30 young. Woodlice and millipedes stray in from the surrounding soil to feed, primarily on decaying vegetable matter and, to a lesser extent, on the fungi, bacteria and moulds.

Réaumur (1738) was the first scientist to study the dipteran ('true') flies that breed in cow-dung. While doing so, he made the important discovery that the dung of different mammalian herbivores (cow, sheep, horse, goat) support different insect communities.

The next major worker was Portchinsky, who produced several articles between 1880 and

1913 on the role of predacious fly larvae. Since then a considerable literature on the cow-dung community has accumulated.

The crucial importance of the dung community in agriculture is spectacularly demonstrated in Australia where no native cow-dung-loving *(bucoprophilous)* fauna exists. It is estimated that the undegraded dung of five cattle removes from production 0.4 ha (1 acre) of land per year.

Considerable expense is being incurred in trying to establish a cow-dung community by introducing beetles and flies from elsewhere. The same problem is being experienced by importers of cattle to new ranching areas of South America.

A recent danger is the treatment of animals with drugs which render dung lethal to invertebrates. The implications, and the future viability of pastures where the drug is used, are extremely disturbing. Without the dung-converting skills of beetles and flies, our countryside would be a far less pleasant place in which to live.

In that short weekend, we identified 20 of the 80 or so possible species of 'cow-dung community' beetles and flies to be found in Britain: converters of dung into useful humus, and a valuable source of food themselves for many birds and mammals.

The yellow wagtail feeds regularly in cattle pastures; so do the starling, crow, jackdaw, magpie, lapwing, woodpecker, thrush, swallow, swift, house martin and meadow pipit.

A badger will turn over a cowpat with a swipe of its paw to scoop up the grubs beneath. Foxes, shrews, hedgehogs and moles forage at cowpats. Bats swoop low over the pastures at night. And where would the few remaining colonies of the greater horseshoe be without the fat dor beetles and dung beetles that buzz about on warm summer evenings?

CHAPTER EIGHT

Scarce Emerald

DRAGONS AND DAMSELS
Ted Benton

•

Flatford Mill Field Centre, East
Bergholt, Suffolk

'THE SCARCE EMERALD *Lestes dryas* is probably extinct,' announced the Nature Conservancy Council (NCC) in 1980.

But the NCC (now English Nature) was too hasty. Three years later the lovely damselfly turned up again at two sites on the east coast marshes. Dr Edward Benton is dragonfly recorder for North Essex. He was among those present at the rediscovery of the rarity. And *L. dryas* has bred at a few sites each year since.

Twenty-two of the thirty-eight species of dragonflies are known to breed in the local pools, rivers and reclaimed gravel pits of Essex. In July many species would be on the wing. With Ted to guide us, we could expect to see at least a few of them. Perhaps we might even see a scarce emerald?

On arrival at Flatford Mill I found I was sleeping in Willy Lott's House, painted so many times by the artist, John Constable. In National Trust ownership, the old farmhouse had changed little. Farmer Willy Lott was in residence when Constable was born in 1776 and

he was still there when Constable died in 1837. It was generally known as Gibson Gate Farm at the time, but Constable always referred to it as 'Willy Lott's House'.

From the window of my little bedroom I looked out on to the mill pond, scene of Constable's most famous painting *The Haywain*. Electric-blue damselflies danced over the surface. Beyond lay the weir, the millrace and the meandering River Stour that marks the boundary between the counties of Suffolk and Essex. Water, water, everywhere!

On the first morning we walked up the lane to Flatford Bridge, passing Valley Farm on the way, a fourteenth-century timbered house of wattle and daub lived in by Edward Jackson, warden of the field centre, and his family.

A little further up the lane, on the left, is the dry dock where Golding Constable, John Constable's father, oversaw the building of his barges. In 1985 the National Trust restored the site as nearly as possible to the scene depicted in *The Boat Builders*: one of the few '6-footers' that

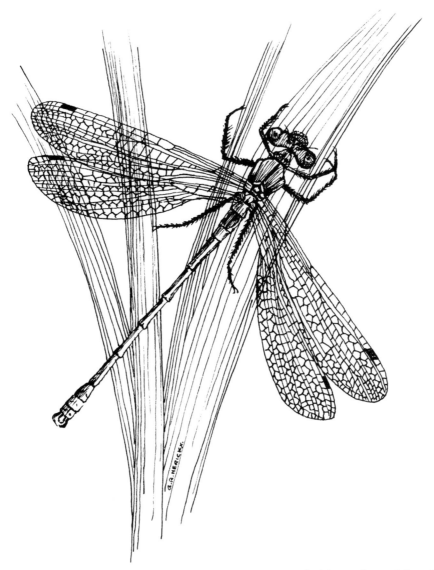

the artist finished on site and in the open air. Most of Constable's large canvases were painted many years later in his London studio, the early sketches being used as reference.

We crossed the bridge and followed the towpath that led to Dedham. Wide skies, pollarded willows, boats on the river, church spires, black and white cows grazing... 'These scenes made me a painter', wrote Constable, 'and I am grateful.'

Opposite were the water meadows, 'those sweet fields', where John Constable courted Maria Bicknell.

Tall riparian vegetation fringed the banks: hemp agrimony, great hairy willowherb, purple loosestrife, water figwort... good dragonfly habitat. And a banded demoiselle, *Calopteryx splendens*, zipped down river. It had an emerald body and Prussian blue wings. Easy to identify. No problem.

'Identification is not always so easy,' warned Ted Benton.

Flatford Mill, water, water, everywhere

A species may have several colour variations. Males and females differ. Newly emerged dragonflies go through an immature, pale, 'teneral' phase before taking on full adult coloration. Colours fade with age.

'Ignore the young, the old and the females, and concentrate on the contrasty males,' was Ted's advice to the beginners.

Wing venation is important, as is the small dark marking on the leading edge known as the *pterostigma*.

A fragile 'blue' damselfly rested on a blade of grass, wings folded along the slender line of its blue/black body. But, how do you tell the very similar 'blues' apart?

'Look closely at the long abdomen with its string of ten segments,' said Ted. 'You'll notice that two segments near the hind end – segments eight and nine – are bright sky blue. Diagnostic

of the common blue damselfly, *Enallagma cyathigerum*. And a tiny "mushroom" mark on segment two is also diagnostic.'

The common blue damselfly took off. It darted, hovered, darted. The sky blue 'tail light' was obvious in flight. (It was the same sky blue as Ted's shorts, we couldn't help noticing.)

A damsel clinging to a leaf of willowherb was identified as the blue-tailed *Ischnura elegans* by its all black abdomen and *single*-segment sky blue 'tail light'.

E. cyathigerum and *I. elegans* are the two commonest and most widespread of the damselflies that breed in Essex. They are present

Opposite: *Scene of Constable's painting* 'The Boat Builders'.

in ponds, ditches, flooded pits, reservoirs, canals, rivers and even swift-flowing streams.

Ted swooshed his net and caught a third damsel, the azure damselfly, *Coenagrion puella*, identified by the amount of blue on segments eight and nine, and the diagnostic U-shape mark on segment two.

But the river was crowded with boats; weekend trippers thronged the banks. Flatford Mill, with its Constable associations and National Trust cafe, museum and shop, is a great tourist attraction.

We stood for a while on Flatford Bridge, playing at being trippers ourselves.

'Carp,' said John, his eyes on the water below. 'And there's a dace. A big fellow.'

John had entered a Dragonfly Quiz featured in the pages of *BBC Wildlife Magazine*. He'd won first prize, a weekend with the Field Studies Council, but he denied being any sort of an expert.

'I know my mayflies,' he told us. 'Every fisherman does. But dragonflies, no. I shoot them mind,' he added rather alarmingly (until we realized that when John said 'shoot' he meant with a camera and not with a gun). So how come he'd won?

'I simply took a couple of dragonfly books down from the shelf,' he explained, 'blew the dust off them – and the answers were easy to find.'

And here he was, on Ted's 'Dragons and Damsels' course.

Dragons? Damsels?

Dragonflies, in the widest sense of the word, together make up the insect order Odonata: but are further sub-divided into two groups, Anisoptera ('unequal wings') and Zygoptera ('equal wings'). Anisopterans, the larger, more robust species are known as 'true' dragonflies; the differently shaped fore and hind-wings are spread to the side when at rest. Zygopterans, the generally smaller, more delicately built species are known as the damselflies; fore and hind-wings are similar in shape, and held vertically along the line of the body. In order to avoid

confusion, Ted calls the two groups 'dragons' and 'damsels'.

We retreated from the bustle of the riverbank to gravel pits behind Flatford Mill where willow herb, teasel and comfrey grew 1.8 m (6 ft) tall.

'Through the elephant grass,' muttered Paul, who had recently returned from a wildlife holiday in Africa. 'Look behind you,' he warned as we reached the edge of the pool. 'If you were on safari, you'd be dead by now!'

But there were no tigers about, only mallards and moorhens.

We swished with pond nets in the reeds in the hope of catching a 'nymph': the underwater larval stage of the dragonfly. After many months this ugly, mud-dwelling mini-beast crawls up the stem of a water plant into the air above, splits its skin for the last time and, miracle of miracles, emerges an aerial beauty.

Wriggling, hopping, burrowing, crawling, swimming, aquatic invertebrates were transferred from nets to trays: water fleas, snails, oligochaete worms, pond skaters, water beetles, larvae of stonefly and mayfly...

A 10 cm (4 in) long, pencil-slim, transparent elver plopped into the tray. 'Real Macfisheries stuff, this,' murmured someone as we released the young eel. It slithered back into the water – to complete its extraordinary life-cycle? An elver takes seven years to mature and then sets off on the 6,500 km (4,000 mile) return journey to its birthplace in the Sargasso Sea.

But even Ted couldn't net a dragonfly nymph. ('Every tutor's nightmare,' he murmured, swishing once again, 'not being able to come up with the goods.')

No dragonfly nymphs, but, to prove their presence, several cast-off skins (exuviae): almost exact replicas of the nymph itself. A cast-off skin is sometimes so close to perfection that the nymph can be identified to species. Even the highly specialized mouthparts are intact, with the extended lower lip ('labial mask') that shoots out to impale small prey animals and is then folded away, covering part of the face, when not in use.

Essex has no natural lakes. In their stead are man-made reservoirs, artificial fish ponds, gravel pits and excavated mineral workings. Fingringhoe Wick, on the west bank of the Colne Estuary, was once the scene of sand and gravel extraction. Today it is a superb 50 ha (120 acre) nature reserve, acquired by the Essex Naturalists' Trust in 1961. And that is where we went next.

Mineral working over a long period of time has left interesting pits of different outlines, depths and ages. Once the pits have filled with water, aquatic plants move in: water starwort, duckweeds, pondweeds, reedmace, bur-reed, common spike-rush and various other rushes. The resulting pools and open flooded stretches are wonderful dragonfly habitat. Fifteen species have been recorded at Fingringhoe so far.

Our first 'dragon' was the brown hawker *Aeshna grandis*. It zoomed to and fro across the yellow water lilies, negotiating neat turns at either side: amazingly agile in flight. Bronze wings rustled as it passed, each shimmering pair moving independently.

The brown hawker was patrolling its territorial backwater beat, warning off male rivals. It flicked the tip of its tail forward in mid-flight and repeated the movement several times: transferring sperm from the tip of its abdomen to an accessory sperm store between the second and third abdominal segment.

The bizarre mating strategies of dragonflies are unique in the insect world. On Kit's Pond a pair of ruddy darters clung to a reed stalk in the 'wheel' position. At the tip of the male's abdomen is a tiny pair of 'claspers'. Having transferred his sperm, the male is free to grasp, with his claspers, the female's head or neck. She curves her body upwards to collect the sperm, completing the curious wheel shape.

Claspers are particular to each species. As precisely as a front door key in a lock, each pair fits exactly the female's head (or neck): a guarantee that a male cannot mate with a partner of the wrong species by mistake.

More ruddy darter pairs were flying 'in tandem' over the water, dipping in unison, the male still grasping the female as she flicked her eggs on to the surface of the pond.

Both ruddy darter, *Sympetrum sanguineum*, and common darter, *Sympetrum striolatum*, breed in the reeds of the pool. Ted explained how to tell the difference between the males of the two small red dragons.

'The ruddy darter is a darker red and the abdomen is waisted. A narrowing of the segments two to five makes this dragonfly look as if it's wearing corsets. And the legs of a ruddy darter are completely black. Not striped like the legs of the common darter.'

We watched a darter (common) as it sortied out and back from its perch: a branch overhanging the water. It darted out on whirring silver wings to snap up a fly and darted back again.

The darter dragonfly was behaving surprisingly like a spotted flycatcher, a small migrant bird that flies to Britain to breed each year.

Norman Moore, author of *Dragonflies* (Collins New Naturalist, 1985) told how his favourite insect can be watched in the field 'much as a birdwatcher observes birds'.

Through close-focus binoculars (7 x 18 are best) dragonflies can very often be identified to species. Behaviour patterns vary (as with birds). Some male dragonflies even defend their territories and court their females.

'Dragonflies are the birdwatchers' insect.'

Our list was growing. Strong-flying hawkers, sortieing darters, and then there are the 'chasers' and the 'skimmers'.

A sedge warbler flew from the willow scrub. It swooped to snatch at a damselfly and narrowly missed. Mallard ducks were slurping duckweed. ('Reminds me of my children slurping cereal at breakfast,' said Ted.) A drake clapped his bill at a passing darter and it side-slipped in the nick of time.

Dragons and damsels, at their most vulnerable when absorbed in mating or egg-laying, have many enemies: birds, frogs, newts,

fish, even web-spinning spiders. But their huge faceted eyes, giving them near all-round vision, are extraordinarily sensitive to movement, as any photographer will tell you.

We left Kit's Pond and walked down a sandy ride between high banks. Sheltered from the wind, it was warm and the verges were bright with flowers: common centaury, sand spurrey, birdsfoot trefoil, hop trefoil, narrow-leaved vetch, red campion, field scabious, greater stitchwort, fleabane...

Flowers attract small insects. It is away from the water and in wide rides such as this that dragons and damsels spend much of their time, gliding up and down on the look-out for prey,

soaring up to snatch at a gnat, alighting on a bright flowerhead to pick off small aphids and beetles. A dragonfly's six hairy legs are well adapted for clinging and for scooping up prey in flight, but of little use for walking.

A southern hawker, *Aeshna cyanea*, a spectacular dragonfly with blue, yellow and apple-green markings, 'buzzed' us inquisitively as it zoomed past. Then it turned and flew back again to have a closer look. Unlike other hawkers (always on the move), *A. cyanea* will frequently settle for long periods, choosing a perch in a sunspot. Once known as the 'horse stinger' for its disconcerting buzzing habits, a hawker dragonfly is harmless, of course.

'Though, mind you,' said Ted, 'it can nip a bit if held in the hand.'

We reached the hide that looked out on to the central lake, once a gravel-washing reservoir. We saw tufted ducks with perky crests, moorhens swimming in their vigorous, jerky way, coots squabbling 'Kut, kut, kut', and taking off with much splashing and to-do and damsels dancing in swarms only centimetres above the surface of the shimmering water. A dazzling razzamatazz of electric blue: 'flying darning needles'!

Next day we drove to Old Hall Marshes, 13 km (8 miles) south of Colchester, and on the north shore of the Blackwater estuary. Old Hall Marshes is owned by the Royal Society for the Protection of Birds, the largest area of coastal grazing marsh in the county. Thousands of brent geese winter on the mudflats. Bewick swans, eider ducks, goldeneye and red-breasted mergansers turn up regularly. Waders fly in. Short-eared owls and hen harriers hunt the rough grassland.

The RSPB warden was there to meet us, more used to being quizzed by ornithologists than odonatists. But, although reserves are principally acquired and managed for birds, the RSPB is sensitive to the needs of all the wildlife on its properties. Excluding butterflies, no other insect group has been better recorded than the dragonflies. Vulnerable wetland habitats are protected and water quality is monitored with dragonflies in mind.

Eleven species breed on the marshes including the scarce emerald, *Lestes dryas*. Was the rare damselfly, a 'threatened species' in the *Red Data Book*, still present on the lonely Essex marsh? Or had its transient breeding pools dried up in the summer heat? We wanted to find out.

The sun beat relentlessly down as we trekked across the scorched terrain. Criss-crossed with a network of drainage ditches and wider 'fleets', the land has been reclaimed over time from estuarine mud and saltings. More recently, sea walls were built to withstand flooding and the excavations have left borrow dykes on the landward side.

It was the hottest day of the year. Butterflies fluttered across the wild flowers which grew in such profusion: knapweeds, thistles, vetches, trefoils.... There were common blue butterflies, wall browns, skippers, commas, gatekeepers 'and lots of meadow browns, typically pottering along at knee height above the grass,' said the warden.

We stopped often, at each rush-filled borrow dyke and shallow pool. A scarce emerald lays its eggs singly in the tissue of submerged or marginal water plants. As one brackish pool dries out and becomes unsuitable, so the damselfly, if it survives, moves on to colonize a new pool. Scarce emeralds have been described as 'wanderers' in the literature because of the transitory nature of their habitat. Sometimes they even seem to disappear altogether, as happened in 1980.

Ted swept once again with his big kite net and was called a 'red-faced chaser' for his pains.

We saw two dead water shrews: victims of the heat. A brackish ditch choked with sea club-rush... another sweep of the net. And this time an emerald green damselfly, a male, clung to the black gauze, wings half open in a resting posture typical of the emeralds.

Both species breed at Old Hall Marshes. Was this the 'national rarity' *Lestes dryas*? Or the almost identical, but less rare *Lestes sponsa*?

The shape of the inner claspers at the tip of the abdomen is diagnostic. Inner claspers that are 'more or less straight' identify the emerald damselfly, *Lestes sponsa*. Inner claspers 'curved obliquely inwards' identify the scarce emerald, *Lestes dryas*.

Even without a hand lens it was plain to see that the inner claspers were curved obliquely inwards: powder-blue bloom on segment two of the green abdomen, blue eyes and blue 'tail-light'. Off it flew, the exquisite scarce emerald, to settle again in the sea club-rush.

Hot, tired and very, very thirsty, we trudged back across the sun-baked marsh.

CHAPTER NINE

Appley Dappley, Little Brown Mouse

SMALL MAMMALS
Rasik Bhadresa

•

Flatford Mill Field Centre, East
Bergholt, Suffolk

Trees uprooted by high winds in the great October storm of 1987 lay where they had fallen, and there was a smell of damp and decay in the air. Autumnal leaves scrunched beneath our feet as we carried the boxes of Longworth live-traps into the privately owned wood: one of 20 plus woodland sites monitored twice yearly for the National Small Mammal Survey.

To find out more about trends in mouse and vole populations, volunteers are asked by the Mammal Society to live-trap small mammals for three days in May/June and again in November/December. Flatford Mill Field Centre incorporates the live-trapping into its programme of 'small mammal' courses, offering a chance for students to get hands-on experience

of wary little animals that are virtually unapproachable in the wild.

Dr Rasik Bhadresa had already explained to us the mechanics of a Longworth live-trap. Made of metal, it comprises two sections: a nest box and a tunnel. A hinged door at the entrance is held open by a small wire trigger which is attached to the treadle on the floor. When an animal enters the tunnel it walks across the treadle, releases the trigger and the door swings shut.

We had practised setting the traps: adjusting the strut, locking it into the groove at the top and connecting the rear of the tunnel to the stop on the nest box floor. Now we were in the wood and ready to place the 98 traps into position on the 1 ha (2.5 acre) survey site. But first each trap must be furbished with warm bedding and plenty of food so that the small captive comes to no harm: dry hay for bedding, porridge oats for cereal-loving mice and voles, and blow-fly pupae in case an insectivorous shrew gets caught.

Small mammals are innately curious and will usually investigate any strange object that appears on their patch. Some even become 'trap happy', returning again and again to this new source of food and shelter.

'The trap entrance must be flush with the ground,' said Rasik. 'Preferably on a runway or next to a natural feature such as an old tree stump. And make sure that the nest box is sloping downwards so that water drains away if it rains.'

The plot had been laid out in 7 x 7 gridlines with 15 metres (50 ft) separating the trapping points.

'Two live-traps at each trapping point,' reminded Rasik.

But, after the terrible battering of the storm, very few of the original bamboo canes put into position to mark the trapping points were still standing. Whole trees had been uprooted, leaving deep cavities filled with water. Heavy branches had fallen across the paths. Tops of conifers were snapped off like matchsticks. The wood was in a terrible mess.

Longworth live-traps revolutionized the study of small mammals

It was dusk before we'd opened up the grid-lines, worked out where all the trapping points should be, replaced the canes (if we could find them) and put the live-traps into place.

The invention of the Longworth live-trap in the 1940s has revolutionized the study of small mammals. 'Small mammals' are defined, rather arbitrarily, as 'mammals weighing less than 120 g (4.2 oz)'.

'Perhaps,' said Rasik with his big smile, 'the definition of a small mammal ought to be "a mammal small enough to get caught in a Longworth live-trap"!'

Back at Flatford Mill, Rasik suggested that we should each 'choose an animal' and read up about it in the library, later presenting our new-found knowledge to the others. But first he would introduce us, with the aid of slides from his collection, to the mice, voles and shrews native to mainland Britain.

There are four species of mice: the wood mouse, the harvest mouse, the house mouse and the yellow-necked mouse. There are three species of vole: the bank vole, the field vole and the water vole, although the latter, 'Ratty' of *Wind in the Willows* fame, is too large to be classed as a 'small mammal'. There is one species of native dormouse; but the dormouse stays in the tree canopy and does not let itself be caught in Longworth live-traps. And there are three species of shrew: common shrew, pigmy shrew and water shrew.

Then he packed us off to research further in the well-stocked library and to report back in an hour. My choice was the bank vole.

The bank vole (I was to report back later) has much in common with the wood mouse. Both are ground-living, mainly seed-eating little creatures. They scamper along tunnels in the undergrowth, weave nests, sleep in their burrow systems and produce several litters a year. Widespread and common, bank voles and wood mice are to be found in all types of woodland, scrubland, hedgerow, grassland, and even in areas of marsh and fen if there is sufficient cover. Diets are similar; mainly seeds, grain, leaves, buds, grass, roots, fruit, nuts, fungi and (particularly the wood mouse) soil invertebrates. Rarely seen, they leave signs of their presence: gnawed-open hazel-nuts, holed acorns, cracked cherry stones, nibbled toadstools, chewed ash keys, torn bark and stripped cones. Both will climb trees and both cache food in the autumn.

But the wood mouse is mainly active by night. The bank vole is active by day as well, with peaks at dawn and dusk. Perhaps by dividing up the 24 hours in this way the two animals, sharing similar lifestyles, avoid unnecessary competition.

The bank vole, *Clethrionomys glareolus*, is also known as the 'wood vole' or 'red vole'. The wood mouse, *Apodemus sylvaticus*, is sometimes called the 'long-tailed field mouse'. As alternative names for the field vole, *Microtus agrestis*, include 'short-tailed vole' and 'short-tailed field mouse', it is all rather confusing. This is why, in any scientific survey, animals are referred to by universally accepted Latin names.

The following morning we assembled for the first trap round of the day. A pale sun sparkled the yellowing leaves and, in a crack in the gate post, a dozen ladybirds had hidden away for the winter, waxy wing-cases a good waterproof against the weather. Scarlet hips and darker red haws cheered the hedgerow. The shocking-pink berries on the spindle tree were split to reveal the bright orange seed capsules within. Blue tits flicking over leaves on the woodland floor flew off at our approach. But a robin continued singing its melancholy little song from the branches of an ash.

We worked along the first gridline. Traps one to four were empty. Number five was occupied. Rasik picked the trap up and, holding it inside a large polythene bag, unclipped the tunnel. He gave the nest box a gentle shake. Out tumbled a mouse with large brown eyes, big ears, sleek, yellowish-brown coat, fleck of yellow on the white fur of the chest, long white whiskers and a long, long tail. It was a wood mouse. Very Beatrix Potterish.

Rasik gripped the mouse gently but firmly by the scruff of the neck close behind the ears.

'Never hold a mouse by the tail,' he warned. 'In its efforts to escape, it may shed the skin.'

With a pair of nail scissors he clipped a snippet of fur from the right flank of the mouse. The hairs would grow again, but for a short while the animal, an adult female, would be identifiable by the fur-mark if recaptured. It is possible to make an estimate of the size of a colony by recording the number of mice recaptured over a period of time.

With a pair of Pesola scales, Rasik weighed the wood mouse, still in its polythene bag: 21 g (0.74 oz). A good weight. It was fattening up for the winter.

Rasik weighed the wood mouse

We set it free on the spot where we'd found it. Appley Dappley – sorry! – *Apodemus sylvaticus* leapt away in a trice and disappeared into the undergrowth.

The next trap held a male bank vole: weight:18 g (0.63 oz). It had a chubby face, small, rounded ears, small eyes, shorter tail and shaggy, reddish-brown fur, as compared to the 'Brylcreem sleek' fur of a mouse.

The vole-in-a-bag began to groom itself, licking its front paws, titivating its whiskers, bowing forward to smooth the fur on top of its head. Grooming is a small mammal's way of calming itself in a stressful situation.

With a fur-clip mark on the right shoulder, *Clethrionomys glareolus* scampered away, paused for a brief glance back, then vanished from view.

Ashley was sifting soil, counting and identifying soil invertebrates: spiders, slugs, millipedes and beetles. Mice and voles are mainly seed eaters, but will take soil invertebrates when the opportunity offers. Shrews, on the other hand, are totally dependent on meat.

One after-effect of storms is a bonanza of wood-boring beetle grubs for insect-eating mammals and birds. Fallen trees rot and decay, and the beetles assist the process. Shrews, badgers and foxes home in. Woodpeckers hack at the rotten timber with powerful bills, flicking their long tongues into the maze of insect galleries.

On the trunk of a silver birch tree, the razorstrop polypore had taken hold, like a plump cushion. Black forks of leathery candlesnuff, tipped with white spores, sprouted from an old log. A little pile of cracked open, tooth-marked beechnuts on the same log was the work of a mouse or a vole.

We found more occupied traps: two more bank voles, one wood mouse. Rasik found an owl pellet beneath a tawny owl's tree roost. 'I'll add it to my collection,' he said.

Small mammals are threatened by many predators. The tawny owl is perhaps their worst enemy, particularly in winter when vegetation is sparse and ground-living creatures have fewer places to hide – and are consequently easier to catch.

In the daytime the tawny owl roosts in the cavity of a hollow tree or perhaps behind a curtain of thick ivy. At night it hunts by sitting very still on a perch. The asymmetrical ears, one higher than the other, are so sensitive that an owl can get a fix on the tiniest squeak or rustle from the woodland floor below. The stiff feathers of the round facial disc collect and amplify sound. With its binocular vision, it watches for the slightest movement and pinpoints its prey. Swooosh! Silently it swoops, talons at the ready for a swift kill. The wavering call – 'Hooo, hu huhuhuhoooo' – must strike terror into every small creature.

Owls usually swallow their prey whole. The indigestible fur, feathers, teeth and bones are regurgitated as compact lumpy pellets, grey and matted. These pellets take around 6 to 8 hours to form from the time the prey is eaten. The owl will cough up two a day. Because small mammals can be readily identified from their skulls, the analysis of skeletal material in owl pellets is a valuable tool for the naturalist and another useful method for finding out which species of small mammals are present in a locality: detective work of a rather gruesome kind.

So, back in the laboratory, fortified by Rachel's ginger wine, we dissected owl pellets from Rasik's small stock, soaking them first in hot water so that the woolly-like matrix began to soften and disintegrate. (Are owl pellets what clothes moth larvae ate before woollen socks were invented?)

Using forceps and mounted needles we teased the pellets apart, separating out the tiny undigested bones. With the help of a microscope, and the Mammal Society's Key *The Analysis of Owl Pellets* by D. W. Yalden and P. A. Morris (Mammal Society, 1990), it was possible to identify the bones to species.

Vole skulls are often found intact. A splintered hole in the back of the skull indicates where the owl has dealt the killing blow. Mouse skulls are more fragile and are not usually found intact.

The easiest way to differentiate mice, voles and shrews is by their teeth, so we put any jawbones to one side.

The teeth of an insectivore are arranged in continuous rows: useful for scrunching up beetles. Teeth of the three shrew species found on mainland Britain are tipped with red. Size distinguishes the pigmy shrew. The front incisors of the common shrew are notched; the larger incisors of the water shrew are unnotched.

A gap between the incisors and the cheek teeth identifies the jawbone of a gnawing rodent (mouse or vole).

Zigzag surfaces, deep grooves and brown stains on the biting surface of the cheek (molar) teeth? *Vole.*

Rounded tops and shiny white-enamelled cheek teeth? *Mouse.*

And with the help of the microscope, it is possible to identify the mouse or vole to species.

Ashley glued his owl pellet finds on to white card to add to his collection. Jawbones and tiny limb bones: pelvis, humerus, tibia-fibula, femur. By grading the minuscule vertebrae, he reconstructed the spine of a mouse.

But now it was time for the afternoon round of the traps. Twice a day for three days we visited the wood and monitored the small mammal population on our survey site. Records would be sent to the Department of Zoology, University of Cambridge. Dr John Flowerdew, coordinator of the National Small Mammal Survey, collates the findings and sends out updates to his volunteer surveyors. The project began in 1982 and is scheduled to continue well into the 1990s.

Already the regular biannual live-trapping is shedding light on the seasonal fluctuations of mice and vole populations.

Small seed-eating mammals are profoundly affected by the amount of seed crop produced each year by our native tree species. Some trees, especially oak and beech, are very irregular seed producers, varying from one year to the next: a phenomenon known as 'masting'. There are 'good' and 'bad' masting years.

Wood mice seem to follow a fairly regular annual pattern. It is believed that early summer numbers are largely determined by the size of the previous autumn's acorn (or beechmast) crop. A good crop followed by a mild winter results in more mice surviving to the following spring. If numbers are high at the start of a new breeding season, older males may become aggressive and chase 'adolescent' males out of the home territory. But in a poor crop year, many young mice will die over winter. For those that survive there is less competition, more food available and numbers will build up quickly again to the late summer peak.

A female wood mouse normally produces several large litters. If the weather is mild, breeding may begin in February and extend into December. But early-born young suffer a poor rate of survival. Late-born litters help to boost the population at a time when the 'old' generation is dying: few mice live longer than 15 months.

The ecology of bank voles is more complex. Annual fluctuations tend to be puzzlingly unpredictable. Voles, remember, are related to the lemmings. Populations of voles in northern European countries (but not so much in Britain) will increase to plague proportions and then, as suddenly, crash.

Our total of bank voles and wood mice trapped on the survey site was rising. It was exciting to 'recapture' a marked individual. And there was another species of small mammal present in the wood.

'This trap's heavy,' commented Colin on the second morning.

Twins? A late, very pregnant female? A *weasel*? It has been known: a very rare occurrence. But no, the trap was not heavy enough for a weasel. ('If you suspect you've caught a weasel,' advised Rasik, 'open the trap

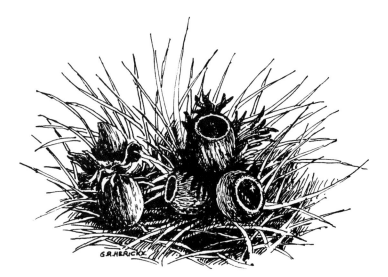

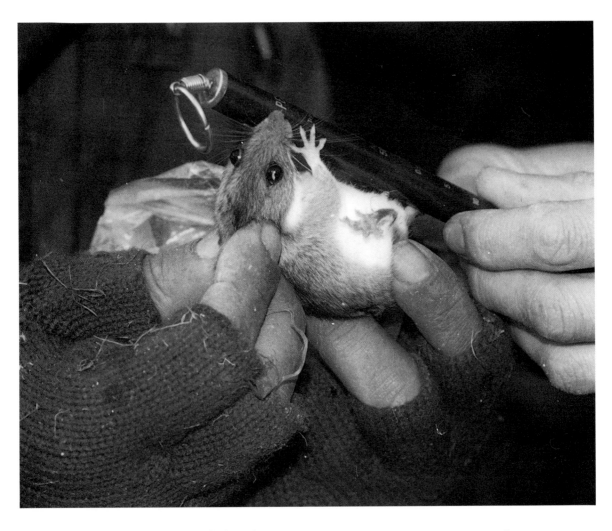

door with a stick – and stand well clear!')

The door was released and into the polythene bag rocketed a *giant* of a mouse.

'Yellow-necked mouse. That's nice!' said Rasik, looking pleased.

We were to catch four more yellow-necked mice over the three survey days. *Apodemus flavicollis* is rather locally distributed: confined, with only a few exceptions, to mature deciduous woodlands in the south of England and in the border counties of Wales. Its diet and lifestyle are very similar to that of the wood mouse. Why are they not more common? It's a mystery.

Rasik weighed the giant mouse, and it

The yellow-necked mouse was a whopper

wriggled and squeaked loudly in protest. It really was a whopper, a male, weighing 37.5 g (1.3 oz). Across the white chest stretched a broad yellow collar reaching the dark fur on either side. The colours are richer in comparison to the wood mouse, more orange on the back and the pale belly fur is more contrasty.

'A yellow-necked mouse jumps like a springbok, just you watch!' said Rasik.

And it did. It leapt away in enormous great bounds, back into the brambles. It was a very handsome mouse.

CHAPTER TEN

Thou Has Tamed a Curst Shrew

SHREWS – AND OTHER SMALL MAMMALS

Sara Churchfield

•

Rogate Study Centre, The Red House, Rogate, near Petersfield, West Sussex*

T HE COMMON SHREW is a small mammal with an unenviable reputation.

Since ancient times shrews have been the source of many different myths and superstitions. In the Middle Ages, antidotes and charms were invented to protect people and their domestic animals from the 'diabolical' shrew. Topsell, the seventeenth-century natural historian, described the shrew as: 'A ravening beast, feigning itself gentle and tame, but being touched it biteth deep, and poisoneth deadly. It beareth a cruel mind.'

Our common shrew, *Sorex araneus*, is named after the spider (*Araneus* = Latin for spider), for both shrews and spiders were considered to possess a venomous bite. Do shrews really deserve their bad reputation? If Dr Sara Churchfield, author of *The Natural History of Shrews* (Croom Helm, 1990) couldn't enlighten us, then no one could.

We arrived at the study centre to find that Sara had already put 100 Longworth live-traps into position. She had selected two very different kinds of habitat. Fifty traps were set in rough, tussocky meadow and fifty in mixed woodland. In the traps was cotton wool bedding, oats for mice and voles, and plenty of blow-fly pupae for the insectivorous shrews we all hoped we'd catch.

A common shrew must eat around 550 invertebrates a day if it is to survive. It can die of starvation if deprived of food for more than 4 hours. And it is illegal to use live-traps *without* making provision for the hungry shrew.

*King's College has closed its Rogate Study Centre. However, Dr June Chatfield and Dr Sara Churchfield continue to tutor their popular courses at several other field centres.

'Shrews,' said Sara, 'are immensely inquisitive creatures. If a shrew sees a trap it will shoot – vrooooom – straight up the tunnel.'

In pairs, we worked the gridlines. Mine was on the outer edge of the grid square and I got stung by stinging nettles in the hedgerow bank. 'But,' said Sara, 'you'll probably catch more animals; the so-called "edge effect".'

We checked the traps, one by one, releasing any trap occupant into a polythene bag.

Mice have a smart habit of jumping out of the bag when you least expect it, as I soon found out.

'Help! It's run up my sleeve and escaped ... again!'

'Relax, gently does it,' advised Sara. 'Take it slowly, it's not going to savage you!' And once more she demonstrated. 'Manipulate your animal into a corner of the bag. Run your fingers along its spine. Take a firm grip just behind the ears where the skin is really loose. Then lift it out – without losing it.'

On our first round of the day we caught seven wood mice (four in the meadow and three in the wood); three bank voles (one in the meadow and two in the wood); and one yellow-necked mouse (in the meadow). But no shrew.

'There's plenty of time,' said Sara.

It wasn't until we were on our second woodland round the following day that we caught (row four, trap seven) a tiny, restless, pointy-nosed, velvet-furred... 'ravening beast'?

An intensely active little creature, the shrew (for that was what it was) did not stay still for a moment in its polythene prison. But Sara has handled hundreds. Grasping it firmly with one hand, supporting it with the other, she lifted the shrew out of the bag.

'*Sorex araneus*,' she said. 'Common shrew.'

The little animal was calm now, cradled in her hands: only its snout still wiffling. We were very impressed. To misquote Shakespeare, 'She'd tamed a curst shrew'.

Its eyes and ears were small and inconspicuous, its tail bristly, its whiskers magnificent and its teeth red-stained like the teeth of all *Sorex* ('red-toothed') shrews.

'Blob-shaped and whiskery with flat feet.'

G.R.HERICKX.

Plantigrade feet are a primitive characteristic that the shrew shares with its close relations, the moles and hedgehogs, i.e. they run along with the sole of the foot placed flat on the ground. Shrew, moles and hedgehogs are in the most ancient order of Insectivora.

'Are shrews poisonous?' we asked.

'No,' said Sara, 'not unless you count the mildly narcotizing saliva of some species, including our water shrew, which has the effect of immobilizing prey.'

The shrew's fur was as short, dense and velvety as the fur of its closest relative, the mole. It felt very soft to the touch with dark brown fur on the back, lighter brown on the flanks and lighter still on the belly.

'A breeding female,' said Sara.

A small, bare patch on top of the shrew's head showed where fur had been yanked out during the brief mating. 'Rough treatment by the male.'

The male takes a tight grip of the female's skin with his teeth and this quite often leaves a mark, usually on the head or the neck. Courtship is a very rudimentary affair. The female is only receptive for a few hours in every 3 weeks of her reproductive cycle. At all other times she will fiercely rebuff the male's persistent advances.

Sara weighed the shrew (9.5 g (0.33 oz)) and let her go, to resume its round-the-clock quest for food.

'Part the grass to find runways of small mammals and their droppings,' said Sara.

The droppings of voles and mice are generally smooth in texture, consisting in the main of chopped up grass. Shrew droppings are dark and granular. Faecal analysis identifies beetle bits, snail shell chips, earthworm bristles, centipede legs, wing fragments and chitin from the plated backs of woodlice. A shrew scurries along runways and furrows through leaf litter, snapping up any invertebrate in its path. Sara has counted more than 30 different prey items, but beetles and earthworms make up the major part of the common shrew's diet.

'Shrews show a remarkable ability for locating prey,' said Sara.

Its tiny eyes are probably of little assistance, but a shrew's sense of smell is well developed. A combination of smell, touch and hearing, and a very thorough searching is the shrew's key to success. Bouts of frenzied foraging alternate with brief rest periods, day and night, winter and summer.

'Sometimes, if you keep very quiet and still, it is possible to observe shrews in the wild. I remember one shrew foraging busily in the short grass and, while I watched, it devoured a fat earthworm, a crane-fly larva, a large caterpillar and a slug. All within 10 minutes.'

A shrew has a short life; it is unlikely to live for much more than a year. Between May and September, the relatively short breeding season, a pregnant female builds a complex, dome-shaped nest of woven grass and leaves. She will probably bear one to three litters (each of three to nine young).

Naked and blind at birth, the young grow rapidly and are independent by 4 weeks. She is a good mother, staying close to her babies, suckling them and calming them with little twittering noises. If one baby wanders, she responds quickly to its distress calls and rushes out to carry it back to the nest.

'Is there any truth in the old stories of "shrew caravans", a mother shrew leading her babies, each one holding on to the next one's tail?'

Sara nodded. 'There are reports from reliable witnesses. The female is probably moving her litter to a new nest for some reason.'

Approximately a third of the young will survive the weaning period. Those that overwinter successfully will start their own families the following year, dying soon after.

Insect-eating tree shrews may have been the early ancestors of the insectivorous bat. Bats have been likened to 'shrews with wings'. A shrew shares with a bat the ability to echo-locate. 'But,' said Sara, 'the shrew's echo-location skills are *very* rudimentary as

Opposite: *Part the grass to find the runways of small mammals*

compared to the bat and not used in the location of food.'

At dusk we went in search of 'winged shrews' along the banks of the River Rother. Bat shapes flickered across the calm surface of the water, visible in silhouette where the water gleamed white in the last rays of the setting sun. In the black shadow of overhanging trees, bats disappear from view.

Shirley Thompson switched on her electronic bat-detector. It clicked away, picking up ultrasonic pulses and converting them into audible sounds.

'Short, sharp clicks. On the correct wave-length for Daubenton's,' she decided.

Sara's search for shrews, under logs and around the roots of trees, proved fruitless. But water voles were present. Two holes in the riverbank were entrances to tunnels dug out by the long incisor teeth of a 'Ratty'. Close to the holes were little 'lawns' of grazed grass where a water vole had been feeding.

On the way back to Red House we stopped on the bridge for more bats: pipistrelles flitting to and fro, snapping up the midges that swarmed in clouds over the water.

Shirley is an active member of the Kent Bat Group and a licensed bat worker. A convalescing Leisler's bat, brought to her at the last moment, was with us at Rogate. It had been picked up by the roadside, apparently unable to fly, and taken to a vet. Unfortunately its finder had neglected to leave her name and address or any details.

'We can't release the Liesler's without knowing the whereabouts of its likely roost site,' said Shirley.

The local radio had promised to send out an SOS. Meanwhile, 'Lucy' the Leisler was being cosseted with mealworms in her own special travelling box.

One of Shirley's earliest charges, a noctule, was named 'Norah Batty'. She became quite famous, appearing on TV, even meeting her namesake.

'Noctules and Leisler's are remarkably tame and good-tempered,' said Shirley, 'not touchy, like some pipistrelles!'

Lucy, perched on Shirley's lap, began to 'purr' gently. She shivered, vibrating her body muscles to produce heat as if to prepare for flight. Suddenly she took off, circled round and round the room above our heads, and finally settled high on a curtain rail. No coaxing could induce her down, so Shirley resignedly went off to fetch a ladder.

Next day most of us were up early. A walk through the forest failed to find fallow deer, but hares raced across the misty morning fields. At the live moth trap in the grounds, moths caught overnight were identified. Dark-arches, magpie, snout, heart and dart, yellow underwing, scalloped oak: at dusk they would all be released.

After breakfast it was back to the Longworth live-traps and another round. We found more bank voles and wood mice, and, in the meadow, a second common shrew.

Shrews are found worldwide, surprisingly robust and hardy, able to withstand a wide range of temperatures. 'New' species are still being identified. Some 260 species have been recognized so far. You find shrews in semi-desert scrubland, close to icy mountain torrents, on the strandline of seashores and even in the freezing arctic tundra.

In the laboratory freezer was a dead shrew that the cat had brought in. Strong scent glands in the skin, associated with social organization, make a shrew's flesh obnoxious to most predators. But owls will eat shrews and so, on occasion, will stoats, weasels and foxes. Cats will catch a shrew but, disliking the taste, will not normally eat it.

Sara decided on a dissection. 'A parasitologist's dream!' she said, picking up the scalpel and making the first delicate incision. Shrews are host to a great variety of internal parasites: roundworms, tapeworms and flukes.

When Sara had finished dissecting the shrew, and identifying the flukes, she passed the skin over to Shirley. Starting at the head and sprinkling it liberally with borax powder, Shirley rolled the skin carefully on to a strip of cardboard, as if pulling on an inside-out stocking. Arranging it to look as 'natural' as possible, she secured it with a few dabs of glue. Now the mounted skin would be left in the press for 24 hours, by which time it would be fit for her collection.

Out in the meadow, wild flowers were growing in profusion: red campion, milfoil, meadow buttercup, germander speedwell, greater stitchwort, tufted vetch. Butterflies flitted from flowerhead to flowerhead: meadow brown, small tortoiseshell, ringlet, orange-tip. On a grass stem a broad-bodied chaser dragonfly had settled: shimmering wings and a powder-blue abdomen. A huge male wolf spider, brandishing clubbed palps like boxing gloves, stood guard outside its tunnel-web in the tussock grass. 'Tussocks are particularly enticing to small mammals,' said Sara, 'with gappy roots to nest in, and an abundance of seeds and resident invertebrates to eat.'

It was time to eat ourselves and we settled in the flowery meadow with our packed lunches. But Sara stayed tuned to signs of small mammals.

A blade of meadow-grass began to tremble and slowly disappear downwards.

'Field vole,' said Sara. 'If you listen very hard, ear to ground, you'll hear it chomping.'

Voles have a preference for the softer grasses, such as Yorkshire fog. Any hard bits are discarded in little heaps on runways and in nests. Grasses are at their flowering best in May: meadow-grass, cocksfoot, foxtail, rye-grass, sheep's-fescue.

'Listen!'

From a tussock close by came a thin, belligerent squeaking.

'Shrews,' said Sara.

Shrews are solitary animals. Most of the time they avoid encounters by keeping out of each other's way. If two shrews meet unexpectedly, they will utter a shriek of alarm and move off quickly in opposite directions. But sometimes –

two males with courtship on the mind perhaps – they meet and neither will give way. A momentary freeze is followed by loud, staccato shrieks. If this shouting match doesn't work, and neither shrew retreats, then battle will commence in a tooth-and-claws scuffle. Up on their hind legs, the two shrews lash out at each other, kicking and biting, still squeaking loudly, locked in combat, until, eventually, one breaks free and rushes off into the undergrowth.

Anti-social? Fiercely aggressive? Is a shrew's 'diabolical' reputation deserved? Should we arm ourselves with charms and antidotes?

'No,' says Sara (who, in spite of her devotion to her favourite study animal, is not in the least 'shrewish', but rather jolly, in fact).

Shrews, she says, are highly beneficial. Their voracious appetites help to regulate pest insect populations. A shrew's state of health acts as a biological barometer: an early pollution warning to humans that something is wrong.

The tiny shrew has a valuable role to play in the ecosystem. And, as if to prove the point, British shrews are legally protected by the Wildlife and Countryside Act 1981.

'Listen, you guys,' whispered Sara.

'Chee-chee-chee-chee-chee': the squeaking of a tiny 'bustling benefactor'.

CHAPTER ELEVEN

In Search of the Hairy Cheese Snail

LEAF LITTER ANIMALS
June Chatfield

•

Rogate Study Centre,
near Petersfield, West Sussex

THE SHREW BUSTLES along runways in the leaf litter, locating prey with its sensitive whiskers, probing with its mobile snout, and gobbling up thrips, beetles, earthworms, centipedes, woodlice and any other leaf litter invertebrates that happen to be in its path. Leaf litter invertebrates are nature's recyclers: getting to work in the autumn of each year, turning all those fallen leaves into useful humus and releasing minerals into the soil.

Gilbert White, a country curate living in Selborne, was referring to leaf litter animals when he wrote to his friend Daines Barrington on 20 May 1777, 'the most insignificant of insects ... are of much more consequence, and have much more influence in the economy of Nature, than the incurious are aware of' (Letter XXXV).

He knew that, if it weren't for the tiny recyclers, we'd be knee-deep in leaf litter. He was intrigued in particular by the humble earthworm: the most efficient recycler of all. He noted, in the same letter, how worms perforate and loosen the soil; how they draw into it leaves, twigs and stalks; and how they throw up 'infinite numbers of lumps of earth called worm-casts, which being their excrement, is a fine manure for grain and grass'.

'A small and despicable link in the chain of Nature,' wrote White, 'yet, if lost, would make a lamentable chasm.'

Dr June Chatfield, zoologist and tutor of our 'leaf litter' course, is a former curator of the Gilbert White Museum. She told us, 'White took delight in noting and recording every observation, however slight, that might be of interest to a naturalist. He was, in fact, a pioneer field worker, the first British ecologist.'

'My remarks are the result of many years' observation,' he wrote, 'and are, I trust, true in the whole, though I do not pretend to say that they are perfectly void of mistake, or that a more nice observer might not make many additions, since subjects of this kind are inexhaustible.'

The part played by leaf litter animals is still an 'inexhaustible' subject. And amateur naturalists still take delight in noting and recording: not least, the group of British Naturalists' Association (BNA) members who had booked for the weekend course. Old BNA hands travel well equipped. Out of BNA haversacks came glass pooters, knee pads, hand lenses, test tubes, sieves, paintbrushes, field guides, notebooks ...

The Rogate Field Centre is on the West Sussex/Hampshire border. Within easy reach are both Wealden woods of the acid greensand and chalk woods of the South Downs. We were to sample the leaf litter of each and make comparisons.

First we headed for nearby Tullecombe Wood with its acid-tolerant trees: beech, silver birch, rowan and Scots pine. In the wide rides and sandy clearings grew common heather (ling), bell heather, sheep sorrel, tormentil and gorse.

June used a simple indicator test – the 'fizzical' test – to verify the acidic conditions. She poured a little dilute hydrochloric acid on to a sample of soil. If any calcium carbonate is present, it will effervesce. Nothing happened. No 'fizz'. A meter reading in the laboratory later confirmed the pH value of 4.5.

Inside the wood, the ditches were full to the brim with leaf litter. We got down on our knees and scrabbled through the shroud of decaying leaves in search of the tiny animals that had so intrigued Gilbert White.

Leaves of beech are 'hard' leaves with a persistent waxy epidermis. They had lain in the ditch since last winter and were only just beginning to rot down. Leaves of birch and pine also stay intact and waterproof for a considerable length of time. ('Soft' leaves, of trees such as elm, ash, alder, sycamore and rowan, rot down much more readily.)

Hard leaves provide useful air spaces through which minuscule moisture-dependent invertebrates can roam. It may take up to 3 years before the leaf litter animals are able to complete their work, assisted in their decomposing task by rain, bacteria, protozoa and fungi.

It was a sweltering hot August day. Yet, surprisingly, despite the heat, the friable litter and crumbly humus beneath the top layer of leaves felt damp to the touch. There was no sign of movement at first; the natural reaction of many small creatures when disturbed is to 'play dead'. We waited patiently and after a minute or two there were stirrings: a centipede speeding too fast to count the legs; tiny metallic-black rove beetles; pseudoscorpions with claws extended lobster-like; thrips with feathery wings; springtails that leapt high into the air... The leaf litter was coming to life.

An artist's paintbrush is a handy tool and most leaf litter animals can be picked up quite easily on its fine hairs. But the pooter, a tool designed specifically for the entomologist, is even more efficient. By sucking, as if with a drinking straw, the specimen is drawn up the rubber tube and into a glass bottle.

A tiny springtail is a definite challenge. Disturb a springtail and it releases a spring, shaped like a tuning fork. The spring flicks down and the springtail shoots up. At a single bound – flea-like – it is gone. Springtails are present in great abundance in litter. Less than 2 mm ($\frac{1}{16}$ in) in size, they belong to an order of primitive wingless insects, the Collembola.

Insects, however primitive, invariably possess six legs as adults. But what was *this* strange creature with a rotund, one-piece body and *eight* very long, thin, gangly legs, looking like a spider, but without the spider's narrow waist?

'A harvestman,' said June, 'close relation of the spider.'

The black, zigzag saddle-marking that ran from its head to the tip of the grey abdomen identified it as *Mitopus morio*.

A red-spotted *M. morio*? No, the red spots turned out to be mites hitching a ride. And there was another species of harvestman, entirely

black, except for two pale gold dots on its abdomen and distinctly shorter legs, *Nemastoma bimaculatum*.

With only 25 species of British harvestmen, recognition in the field is not too much of a problem. (By contrast, there are 994 British species of rove beetles, 300 springtails, 40 centipedes and 70 woodlice.)

The harvestman, unlike a spider, has no silk to spin or venom to inject. It hunts at night, catching prey by forming a sort of mobile web with its eight tactile legs. The second pair of legs, the longest, are used as feelers to scent the air. On top of its head is the ocularium: a little 'turret' with two simple eyes perched back to back, each eye staring out sideways.

Like the harvestman, the pseudoscorpion, only 2 to 4 mm (0.08 to 0.16 in) in size, is also an arachnid relation of the spider: a predator that paralyses its prey with tiny, fearsome poison claws. But the 'false scorpion' lacks the tail-sting of the 'true scorpion'. Pseudoscorpions are easily recognized by their habit of going into reverse gear when threatened; they can run as fast backwards as they can forwards.

June led the way to several more sites in the same Wealden wood, to scrabble through more leaf litter and to add more animals to our lists: scuttling woodlice, pincered earwigs, two-tailed bristletails, wriggling potworms, many-legged millipedes, 'lucky' money spiders, red velvet mites, and the grub-like larvae of beetles and flies.

'Leaf litter is an under-recorded habitat,' she said, 'and new species still turn up from time to time.'

June is co-author, with Dr V. Pfleger, of Hamlyn's *A Guide to the Snails of Britain and Europe* (1983). She is also vice-president of the Conchological Society of Great Britain and Ireland. Snails are her first love....

There are about 100 different species of terrestrial snail in Britain (including introduced species). Snails come in a variety of sizes. The

Opposite: *June identified a tiny door snail*

tiniest is the pygmy snail with a shell only 2 mm (0.08 in) high. But there are many other species almost as tiny. Snails, on this hot day, would have burrowed deep to escape desiccation, plugging up their shells with solidified slime, and moving upwards only at night when conditions are cool and damp. We could not expect to find live snails on the surface, but only dead and empty shells.

Searching for shells involved the painstaking sifting of handfuls of soil through the fine wire mesh of a sieve. In such a calcium-poor habitat, we did not expect to find many. To a snail, calcium is vital for shell growth. So it was no surprise that the shells trapped in our sieves in this acidic woodland were mostly delicate, thin-walled, almost transparent specimens, identified as 'glass snails'. Waxy glass snail, *Aegopinella nitidula*; rayed glass snail, *Nesovitrea hammonis*; cellar glass snail, *Oxychilus cellarius*; tawny glass snail, *Euconulus fulvus*; hollowed glass snail, *Zonitoides excavatus*: flat, whorled and glossy, fragile and easily broken.

Glass snail shells are pretty. Worth keeping: to clean, mount and label for a collection. We wrapped them carefully in cotton wool and slipped them into glass tubes to carry back in our rucksacks.

Delicate glass snails are able to survive by utilizing the calcium to be found in vegetation. They will feed on empty snail shells, egg shells and animal bones if need be. In a calcium-stress situation, glass snails will even resort to rasping the shells of other living snails.

When a young snail hatches out, it is already equipped with a tiny shell, the *protoconch*. Absorption of calcium allows the mantle to secrete new material.

'The main shell growth,' June explained, 'occurs at the collar, a fleshy ridge of tissue at the edge of the shell lip.'

The shell grows to the appropriate size for the species and the irregular growth lines are part of the shell pattern.

More snails: hardy species, virtually ubiquitous throughout the country, as we saw later by referring to the distribution maps. Brown-lipped banded snail, *Cepaea nemoralis*, the garlic snail, *Oxychilus alliarius*, and the pitted and lack-lustre shell of the garden snail, *Helix aspersa*.

A ribbed shell, 7 mm (0.28 in) across, and tightly coiled, like a miniature coil of rope, was that of the rounded snail, *Discus rotundatus*, one of our commonest species. It lives happily in leaf litter, under logs and in almost any damp, shady locality.

When no new shells appeared in our sieves, we drove on to a calcareous wood at South Harting, at the edge of the South Downs. Gilbert White loved the South Downs, referring to them, in a letter to Thomas Pennet, as a 'vast range of mountains'.

'There is somewhat peculiarly sweet and amusing,' he wrote, 'in the shapely-figured aspect of chalk-hills in preference to those of stone, which are rugged, broken, abrupt and shapeless.'

On the slopes grew flowers of the chalk: lady's bedstraw, mouse-ear hawkweed, wild thyme, clustered bellflower, birdsfoot trefoil, eyebright, fairy flax, mignonette and common spotted orchid.

Here, hydrochloric acid fizzed satisfyingly when dropped on to the strongly alkaline soil: pH 7.5.

We followed the open path into beech woodland, seeing wild privet, dogwood, wayfaring, wild rose, hazel, field maple and ash. And in the leaf litter beneath were snail shells galore.

Snails! To a conchologist, that's what chalk country is all about!

We saw more brown-lipped banded snails and white-lipped banded snails, striped pink and yellow, and brown and cream. And there were more glass snails, and the solid, periwinkle-shaped shell of the uncommon and local round-mouthed snail, *Pomatias elegans*. The round-mouthed snail is also known as the 'land winkle'. It is one of only two species of terrestrial snails in Britain to possess, like the marine

snails, an operculum: a little 'door' that closes tightly as the snail retreats into its shell.

Other finds were the three-toothed snail, *Azeca goodalli*, a warmth-loving snail; the long-toothed herald snail, *Carychium tridentatum*, a characteristic snail of leaf litter; and Rolph's door snail, *Macrogastra rolphii*, local in south-east England and the Midlands.

Whorled shells, lipped shells, spired shells. Flat, matt, glossy, globular, ridged, smooth and hairy shells.

The common hairy snail, *Trichia hispida*, was an interesting find. Looked at through a hand lens we could see its shell was covered all over with short, curved hair-like projections. More sifting revealed the hairy shell of a juvenile strawberry snail, *Trichia striolata*; as it grows, the hairs will erode away, leaving tiny, dimpled scars. But more exciting than either of these was the hairy, almost bristly, shell of the juvenile cheese snail, *Helicodonta obvulata*.

At the edge of its range in Britain, the cheese snail is a 'national rarity', confined to chalk on a very few ancient woodland sites. Fortunately small colonies are present, in Sussex and Hampshire, on land owned by the Forestry Commission. Aware of their responsibility, commission ecologists have included the protection of *H. obvulata* in their conservation management plan. The position of each cheese snail colony is mapped. Old logs are left where they fall to avoid disturbance. And timber is hauled out on routes devised with the protection of the nationally rare cheese snail in mind.

Chalk country is the preferred habitat of snails, and also of woodlice and millipedes.

Woodlice are land-living relations of the lobster and crab. These 14-legged little scuttlers utilize lime from the chalk to strengthen the tough cuticle plates of their exoskeleton armour.

Out came the sieves again. *Oniscus asellus*, large, flat, oval and grey, is the commonest British woodlouse; it clings tightly to any surface like a true louse. *Trichoniscus pusillus* is small, shiny, reddish-brown and fairly common. *Philoscia muscorum* is medium-sized, slim-bodied, long-legged and fast-moving. *Armadillium vulgare* is the familiar 'pill' woodlouse with its many folk nicknames: 'Tiggyhog', 'Grammar Sow', 'Woodpig' and 'Bibblebug'.

A. vulgare rolls itself up, armadillo-like, into a tiny tight 'pill'. But there is also a millipede, *Glomeris marginata*, that rolls itself up in the same way and is known as the 'pill millipede'.

We were extremely fortunate to find the two animals side by side at the same site.

G.R. HERICKX

'When the pill woodlouse and pill millipede are scuttling around,' said June, 'you can tell the difference by counting the legs. The woodlouse has seven pairs, the pill millipede has far more. But identification is not so easy when both are curled up tight. You have to look at the tail, which is segmented on a woodlouse.'

A centipede scurried across the leaf litter and, as quickly, vanished. Millipedes and centipedes are superficially similar. But millipedes are herbivores, feeding mainly on dead plant material. With two pairs of legs to a body segment (dozens of legs in all), millipedes cover the ground in a ripple-wave motion. Centipedes are carnivores with poison claws. They are flatter in shape, more brightly coloured, with fewer legs – one pair to a body segment – and they are faster movers.

Back in the laboratory we attempted to identify, to family if not to species, the 'difficult' invertebrates in the leaf litter samples. The litter was spread out on trays and kept damp. What could we find?

A small beetle with a prominent snout? One of the weevils.

Yellowish-brown slug with a prickly mantle? The hedgehog slug, *Arion intermedius*.

Harvestman with a three-spined 'trident'? *Paroligolophus meadii*.

Gilbert White would have envied us our microscopes, illustrated field guides and FSC *AIDGAP Keys*.

'Nothing would recommend entomology more than some neat plates that should well express the generic distinctions of insects according to Linnaeus,' he wrote to Thomas Pennant in 1771 (Letter XXXIV). 'I am well assured that many people would study insects, could they set out with a more adequate notion of those distinctions than can be conveyed at first by words alone.'

It was time for a break and we picnicked on the lawn. Like Gilbert White, June is very fond of her tortoises. She had brought her six pets with her; they trundled about the lawn, and we fed them slivers of lettuce leaf and cucumber. White's tortoise 'Timothy' appeared in the pages of his book, *The Natural History of Selborne* (now published in an illustrated edition, introduction by June Chatfield, by Thames & Hudson, 1993). The Greeks, he noted with interest in his diary, used the same word for 'snail' and 'tortoise'.

So, what happens when a leaf falls from a tree? First it is attacked by the leaf litter invertebrates. Then other invertebrates feed on the droppings: secondary decomposers. Bacteria and fungi move in. Earthworms go into action, ploughing through the damp, dark, decaying mass, refining the particles still further. Opportunist predators, like the spider, lie in wait, ready to pounce, chase, hunt down, seize, trample upon, inject with venom, wrap in silk, kill and devour....recyclers of a macabre kind.

Predators and prey are all grist to the mill to badgers, foxes, mice, voles, moles, hedgehogs, shrews and insectivorous birds.

All this burrowing and digging in search of food loosens the soil, lets in the air and releases essential chemical elements. An organic compost rich in nutrients is the result, providing a source of renewable energy to be absorbed by the roots of plants, and used again and again as the recycling process continues, with the help of the leaf litter animals.

'Mighty in their effect,' wrote Gilbert White, 'from their minuteness which renders them less an object of attention; and from their numbers and fecundity.'

CHAPTER TWELVE

Safari into Somerset

DISCOVERING MAMMALS
Penny and Warren Cresswell
•
Leonard Wills Field Centre,
Nettlecombe Court, Williton,
Somerset

NETTLECOMBE COURT, an impressive part-Elizabethan mansion, is perfectly placed for discovering mammals: standing as it does in a secluded valley between the Bristol Channel and the Brendon Hills. There are badgers in the valley, bats in the old church tower, dormice in local woods, wild red deer on Exmoor, otters on the Somerset Levels and Moors and small mammals in the grounds.

A patch of rough grassland was open to the drive on one side, and bordered by hedges and the trees of a small wood on the other three sides. 'Good small mammal territory,' said Penny. 'We'll plot out a grid and set Longworth live-traps.'

Long measuring tapes ribboned out and got caught up in the cow parsley and thistles; or twisted into knots as we hurled them over hedges. To complete the grid, Amy struggled with the secateurs, clipping away at briars. She squeezed through the thorny gap and emerged, scratched but triumphant, on the other side.

Bamboo poles were pushed into the ground at carefully measured intervals. Trapping points were paced out in the knee-high grass.

'Prime the traps with hay and oats, and a little cat food for the shrews. And look for their runways in the long grass.'

At last all the traps were in position. There was just time for a cup of coffee before setting off to the Somerset Levels, one of the few remaining strongholds for otters in England.

Penny drove the minibus along winding Quantock lanes, down into the urban sprawl of Bridgwater, across the River Parrett with the hump of Brent Knoll in the distance, and into the arable plains of the reclaimed Levels to follow the River Brue. Having lived for a while in a cottage on West Sedgemoor, she is familiar with the coastal Levels, and the inland valleys and flood plains of the five rivers that make up the peaty Moors.

As arable fields were left behind, the landscape began to change in character. Long,

straight ditches dissected the water meadows. Pollarded willows marked out the rhynes (ditches). Road verges were frothy with creamy meadowsweet. Fishermen lined the banks. Cows grazed in lush pastures. Lapwing took off in floppy flight.

There is nowhere else in Britain quite like this ditch-dissected landscape. Below sea level for part of each day and flooded in winter, it has a rather special flora and fauna. In summer the pools, hollows, hummocks and ridges are home to breeding waders: snipe, redshank, curlew and the black-tailed godwit. In autumn and spring, passage migrants fly in to feed on earthworms, plentiful in the moist, peaty soils. And, in winter, ducks and swans settle on the 'silver meadows': wigeon, teal, shoveler, pintail and Bewick's swans from Arctic Russia.

'We'll plot out a grid'

'Westhay's Peat Moor Visitor Centre is worth a visit,' said Penny, slowing down and turning the minibus into the car park. 'It's an English Heritage museum, built in the grounds of the Willows Garden Centre.'

Inside the museum, displays and re-constructions told us a little of the history of the area.

Eight thousand years ago the whole of the Somerset Levels was a freshwater swamp. Peat began to accumulate as *phragmites* reeds died back and sank beneath the water-logged surface. Early hunters and gatherers began to visit the area in dugouts and rafts, which allowed them to move across the watery landscape from island to island.

Around 6,000 years ago, the first farmers arrived in Britain. They cultivated crops, kept cattle, caught fish, gathered wild fruit and berries, and trapped wildfowl. In the Somerset Levels, these ingenious settlers began to construct wooden tracks across the marshes to connect areas of higher land. Walkways made of wattled hurdles and bundles of brushwood linked farmsteads. Some led in the direction of the prehistoric 'lake villages' of Glastonbury and Meare.

At Westhay Museum is a replica of a section of the Sweet Track, named after Ray Sweet, the peat cutter who discovered it in 1970. Archaeologists have traced it over a distance of 1,500 m (1,640 yd). Built from oak planks, and supported by coppice poles and angled wooden pegs, the track was laid down some 5,000 years ago: the oldest known example of a timber causeway in the world.

Peat cutting, for fuel and for building blocks, may have begun in Roman times. Until relatively recently, peat was cut by hand using a peat-saw and spade.

Peat bogs preserve evidence of the activities of prehistoric man: flint axes, bows and arrows, spears, knives, broken pieces of pottery, ornaments and remnants of clothing. Wild animals such as deer, boar and otter would have been hunted for their skins.

Otters still frequent the Levels: seldom seen, and mainly restricted to an area north of the Polden Hills. Bridges across the drains are favourite sprainting sites and this is where we looked first.

Penny slithered down the bank to inspect a new stone bridge, built to replace an older bridge which had become unsafe. A ledge incorporated into the old bridge had been much used by otters. The architect of the new bridge had included a similar ledge in his design. Were the otters using it? But, 'No sign of spraint,' Penny called up from below.

Along the riverbank, gatekeeper butterflies flickered across the grass. Goldfinches tweaked the mauve petals of tall teasels and sent them fluttering to the ground. A reed bunting wheezed from the cover of phragmites reeds.

At a second bridge, Penny found positive signs of otter: droppings and a paw print. The third bridge proved inaccessible. At the fourth, she reported spraint of otter and scat of mink.

The scat contained part of the jawbone of a water vole: proof that a mink is more catholic in its diet than the otter.

Leaning on the parapet, we watched swallows skim across the water: flying close enough to show off their red throats and the white spots on deeply forked tails. A pair of banded demoiselles 'in tandem' darted on shimmering Prussian blue wings. On long stems, the three-petalled flowers of arrowhead swayed above the water, each white petal marked with a purple 'eye', and arrow-shaped leaves, used as landing platforms by emerging insects: mayflies, damselflies, alder flies.

The Romans were probably the first to attempt to control the winter flooding of the

'No sign of spraint,' said Penny

Moors and Levels. They dug ditches and channels to protect their scattered farmsteads. In the twelfth and thirteenth centuries, the Glastonbury monks took steps to tame the rising waters by diverting the River Brue into an artificial channel. During the enclosure years, 1770–1840, rhynes were cut to drain and divide the land into small rectangular fields, laying out roads and farms in the form in which we still see them today.

Traditional farming practices continued until the early 1970s. Since then big new pumping machines have drained thousands of hectares of land for agricultural use. Peat extraction became a major mechanized industry. Large areas of wetland began to disappear, and so did many of the characteristic wetland birds and flowers.

Something had to be done. The Somerset Moors and Levels was designated an Environmentally Sensitive Area (ESA). With the help of grants, some farmers returned to the old way of managing the land. Many hectares have been acquired by conservation organizations and managed for the benefit of wildlife. The Royal Society for the Protection of Birds owns several reserves. By controlling water levels, nesting birds have been encouraged to return and numbers are on the increase. Wetland plants are showing signs of recovery. And otters are hanging on.

It was time to return to Nettlecombe Court to monitor the Longworth live-traps. We found bank voles, including twins, young ones, which somehow had managed to enter the trap together; wood mice, a common shrew which gobbled up a proffered beetle before we let it go, and a tiny pigmy shrew. It was thrilling to see small mammals at such close quarters. We went batwatching that evening and then rounded off the day in the Nettlecombe Court bar.

Nettlecombe Court was probably built as a manor house by Hugh de Ralegh at some time between 1154 and 1165. The building was developed and enlarged by his successors. John Trevelyn added two new wings in 1599 and rebuilt the great hall. Between 1703 and 1707 more alterations were made, giving part of the hall a Georgian look.

Off the little courtyard is probably the nicest bar of any FSC centre. There was a blazing log fire and Penny played her guitar.

But we were up early next day: 4 a.m. The walk from East Lynne to Watersmeet is a favourite one for holidaymakers. To avoid the crowds we set our alarms and were following the riverside path soon after dawn: ancient woodland, splashing waterfalls, leaping salmon, bobbing dippers, soaring buzzards.

Time to monitor the live-traps

Later we drove to Porlock and picnicked on the beach. Behind Porlock are the Withy Woods, on the edge of the great Horner Woods complex, and it was here that we hoped to see signs of wild red deer. Wizened sessile oaks with corkscrew twisted branches grew on the sides of steep, sea-facing slopes. Poor soil and winter gales had stunted the trees, and made walking upright difficult.

'To see deer at close quarters,' said Warren, 'you need to be in the wood either at sunrise or at dusk. And preferably alone.'

Red deer were originally animals of the forest. Woodland is still the best place to look for tracks and signs. The deer take cover in the trees at night and move on to the moor when daylight comes. For most of the year, apart from the time of the rut, they move around in large single-sex groups, stag parties and hind herds. They graze on grass, bilberries, holly, hazel, heather, bramble, lichen and mosses.

Warren was finding his first 'signs': the slot markings of cloven hooves and the shiny black droppings of a hind. He pointed out a bare

G.R.HERICKX.

patch of earth where a great stag had stamped and thrashed at the time of last year's rut: scraping it bare of vegetation, urinating upon it to saturate the soil with odours, smearing the surrounding bracken with a secretion from the scent glands just below the eye, making the territory his own.

Nothing will grow on a rutting stand after the harsh treatment a stag metes out each autumn. Aggregates of these bare depressions are spaced out all the way to County Gate: black scars, part of the Exmoor landscape.

But it was still only July, too early yet for a stag to be thinking of the rut. In midsummer its main concern is getting rid of the itchy, soft velvety skin that covers the fully grown, still sensitive antlers. A low branch scrubbed free of moss and bark showed where a stag had drawn his antlers down hard, frenzied by the itching of the velvet.

Once the velvet has been worn away, the exposed white antler bone soon darkens and hardens. As the weeks pass, the blood supply to the nerve endings cuts off. The antlers become insensitive to feeling and the stag finds himself equipped with an efficient pair of fighting weapons, to use, if necessary, in defence of the hinds in his autumnal harem.

Red wood ants streamed from huge, domed twiggy nests to nip us and squirt formic acid,if we were foolish enough to stand still long enough to let them. Midges plagued us in their swarms and we swiped at them with bracken fronds. It was a relief to leave the trees and to move out on to the open moor.

Heather was coming into purple bloom... mewing of young buzzards and the wheezy notes of a yellowhammer in a gorse bush... yellow tormentil, blue milkwort and the delicate pink of common spotted orchid....

We drove to Dunkery Beacon, Exmoor's highest point. Streams flow down from The Chains, a flat, desolate watershed. Below are beautiful wooded valleys, spectacular cliffs and picturesque villages. Much of it is National Trust land. And between Dunkery and the sea are to be found some of the greatest concentrations of red deer in the West Country.

In single file we trekked across rough hummocky ground – tough on the ankles. Scratchy heather, boggy patches, splashy streams. Skylarks flew up in a twittering flock. A merlin shot across, jinking over the bracken. We dropped down low, advancing with care as we approached the steep-sided coomb.

A small herd of hinds grazed on the slope opposite. Two had young calves, born in late May and still with their dappled coats. Four more deer appeared on the skyline; young bachelor stags with short antlers. Another hind rose suddenly out of the bracken in the combe bottom and set off at a brisk trot, a lovely bouncing gait. The young stags on the high tops moved down out of sight. The hinds had settled to chew the cud with their dappled calves beside them.

We crept quietly away. It was nearly time to check those live-traps again. And hadn't Warren said something about stopping on the way back for a clotted cream tea?

CHAPTER THIRTEEN

Dormouse in a Hazel Wood

DISCOVERING MAMMALS
Doug Woods
•
Leonard Wills Field Centre,
Nettlecombe Court,
Williton, Somerset

G.R.HERICKX.

VERY FEW OF US have ever met a dormouse.
But that's not surprising. Dormice are
tiny, arboreal, nocturnal creatures. They
live in the tree canopy and only come out at
night. More of their life is spent asleep than
awake and to see one in the wild is a rare event.
And yet, with its 'Alice in Wonderland'
associations, everyone has a soft spot for
Muscardinus avellanarius.

Doug Woods, area chairman of the Somerset
Trust for Nature Conservation, decided to
survey his local woods for dormice. First he put
up food tables, hoping that any animal coming
to feed on his apples, nuts and grain would
leave droppings behind. Dormouse droppings
are distinctive. But, if there were dormice in the
vicinity, they failed to materialize. (A tea-party
without a March Hare? What could you expect!)

Elaine Hurrell, the organizer of the Mammal
Society's Dormouse Survey 1975–79, advised
him to look for 'signs' of dormouse presence.
With a little practice, it is easy to recognize a

hazel-nut opened by a dormouse. By this
method, Doug was soon able to establish which
of his woods had dormice.

In her Devon garden, about that time, Elaine
('a naturalist of the old brigade') was
experimenting with dormouse nest boxes. So
Doug decided to put up 20 boxes of his own.
Dormice take readily to boxes, regarding them
as superior-grade tree holes. In the first year,
five of Doug's boxes were occupied. He has
been monitoring nest box dormice ever since.

Children from local schools sometimes
accompany him on his rounds. And the
Cresswells had arranged a visit during their
Nettlecombe Court 'Discovering Mammals'
week.

We met at the edge of a coppiced hazel wood
on the steep slope of a limestone gorge. Nettle-
leaved bellflower, enchanter's nightshade and
marjoram, all flowers of the limestone, grew on
the verges. The narrow, twisting path through
the wood was wet and slippery, and the going

was tough with dangling honeysuckle vines, gnarled tree roots, thickets of bramble and snagging briars.

With Dr Pat Morris and Dr Paul Bright, Doug radio-tracked 'his' dormice at night in difficult conditions such as these. He is a member of the Dormouse Research Project Team, based at Royal Holloway and Bedford New College, and sponsored by English Nature, the Vincent Wildlife Trust and the World Wide Fund for Nature.

Very little was known about the habits of this tiny elusive animal at the beginning of the 1980s. What makes a dormouse tick? What does it eat (apart from cucumber sandwiches at Mad Hatter's tea-parties)? How dependent is it upon honeysuckle and hazel? How can we manage woods in a dormouse-friendly way?

Eight of Doug's nest box dormice were fitted with radio collars, each pea-size transmitter weighing less than 2 g (0.07 oz). ('Collar that Dormouse,' the Queen screamed. 'Off with his head!')

Dormice get up as the sun goes down and return to their nests in the small hours of the morning. Paul, Pat and Doug (but mostly Paul) had to creep about the precipitous wood, often in pitch darkness, keeping track of any dormouse feeding in the tree canopy.

It wasn't easy. 'A hands and knees job.' With a protective helmet on his head, a red light torch in one hand and a 'whacking great aerial' with loops of leads in the other, the radio-tracker had still, somehow, to make notes as he followed the bleeps. Data were fed straight into the computer kept in a caravan on site. Seven years on, the

radio-tracking team now knows a great deal more about the highly complex ecology of a very fussy little animal.

By now, we had reached the first of Doug's boxes, deep in the hazel wood. Very similar in design to a blue tit nest box, it was tied to the tree trunk 2 m (6.5 ft) above the ground and the entrance hole faced the trunk, a 'back to front' nest box, making access easier for the dormouse and discouraging bird 'squatters'. But the box was empty.

A second empty box, then a third... The fourth was occupied. Doug, with the palm of one hand covering the entrance hole, carefully unhooked the box. 'If he's awake, he may hop out in a hurry,' he said.

But the dormouse was curled up inside, sound asleep, its bushy tail wrapped around its body like a furry blanket.

'Aaaaaah,' we all sighed. Dormice are irresistibly *twee*.

In Doug's cupped hands, it stirred, opened its huge dark eyes and peered at us sleepily. (Had it been dreaming happily of 'twinkle bats' and 'treacle wells'?) Before it could wake fully, Doug tucked the dormouse back into its nest and hung the box up again.

Box number six contained a nest, but no occupant. Dormice nests are domed, about the size of a grapefruit: a woven structure, fashioned out of stripped honeysuckle bark, grass and leaves.

'Compare the neat, domed nest of a dormouse with the untidy, careless "bachelor" nests of mice and voles,' said Doug.

Wood mice and bank voles collect withered leaves from the woodland floor as nesting material. The dormouse uses fresh green leaves, nipping them off the branches. Often the nest is sited in a tree hole, an old bird's nest or squirrel drey. One individual may use several nests, both natural and man-made, moving around from one to the other.

The wren's nest can be mistaken for a dormouse nest for it is also domed, but made of grass and moss, and with a distinct entrance hole, 'doorstep' and, maybe, feathers inside.

'Ouch!' said Doug. The wide-awake dormouse in the next box had bitten his thumb.

It was the first time he'd been bitten by a dormouse. The sharp chisel-teeth had left a pin-prick impression. 'Chisel dormouse' and 'hazel dormouse' are country names for the common dormouse.

Gilbert White, curate of Selborne, wrote in his journal in October 1781:

> There are three creatures, the squirrel, the field-mouse and the bird called the nut-hatch, which live much on hazel-nut; and yet they open them each in a different way. The first, after rasping off the small end, splits the shell in two with his long fore-teeth, as a man does with his knife; the second nibbles a hole with his teeth, so regular as if drilled with a wimble, and yet so small that one could wonder how the kernel can be extracted through it; while the last picks an irregular ragged hole with its bill.

But Gilbert White makes no mention of dormice.

Elaine Hurrell was the first to recognize that the difference in nut-opening techniques can be made use of by dormouse surveyors.

Voles, mice and dormice gnaw a hole in a hazel-nut, then scoop out the flesh with their teeth. The bank vole bites across the top of the nut and leaves radiating tooth-marks on the cut face of the hole's rim, but not on the shell surface. The wood mouse and the dormouse open the nut from the side. A nut opened by a wood mouse has tooth-marks on both the rim of the hole and the outer shell surface. A nut opened by a dormouse has a rounder hole with a smooth-cut rim and faint tooth-marks on the shell surface.

Doug produced a handful of gnawed nuts from his pocket to demonstrate.

'This nut has been hacked open by a squirrel,' he said, passing it round. 'This is a vole-opened

nut and here is a nut opened by a mouse.'

The corrugated rims of the nuts opened by the wood mouse and the bank vole nut felt rough, like the edge of a 10p coin.

'Now here is a nut gnawed open by a dormouse. The rim of the hole is smooth.'

The 'chisel' dormouse is the neatest little carpenter.

We had got to the end of the round. Inside the last box, the final dormouse of the day was sound asleep. It did not stir, even when Doug held it in his hand. It felt cold to the touch.

'It may not be getting enough to eat,' he said.

July can be a 'hungry' month: a midsummer pause between the flush of insects and flowers in spring, and the abundance of fruit and nuts in autumn.

Dormice (and grey squirrels too) have been known to die of starvation in July, especially when a shortage of food coincides with wet and windy weather. Rain will send a dormouse scurrying back to the nest; its soft fur soaks up water like a sponge. To conserve energy it lowers its body temperature and sinks into a deep sleep: 'summer torpor'. This is a defence against the harsh conditions outside.

No other British mammal sleeps as soundly, and for such a long period, as the hibernating dormouse. ('The Dormouse is asleep again,' said

the Mad Hatter, and he poured a little hot tea on to its nose.) When it wakes in late April or early May, it will weigh only 12 g (0.4 oz). If the weather is clement, an energy-rich, sugary diet of pollen and nectar soon fattens it up, and it will reach its normal summer weight of 15 to 22 g (0.5 to 0.8 oz).

The dormouse is very particular in its requirements. It is a 'specialist' feeder, ill-adapted to eating 'bulk' food, like leaves.

It hangs upside down by its toes to reach the pollen-smothered stamens of sycamore flowers. It nibbles hazel catkins and nips off the nectar tubes of honeysuckle. It pokes its little head into hawthorn blossom to get at the nutritious red anthers.

As summer progresses, so its diet changes from flowers, sweet sticky honeydew, aphids and small caterpillars to berries, fruit, seeds and nuts. A dormouse seems to prefer hazel-nuts while they are still quite soft, picking them off the tree as they turn from green to ripe golden brown. To reach a nut, it will run out to the very tips of twiggy branches. Hazel-nuts are fattening and, by the end of October/beginning of November, a dormouse might weigh 35 to 40 g (1.2 to 1.4 oz).

'So fat it can scarcely roll itself into a ball,' said Doug.

'Sometimes,' he said, 'on a quiet night, a

A dormouse nips off the nectar tubes of honeysuckle

member of the Project Team might hear the pitter-patter of discarded shells dropping from the canopy.'

Dormouse watchers find cracked kernels of wayfaring berries on the woodland floor, jagged edges on chewed florets of honeysuckle and gnawed ash tree keys, stripped of their seeds.

But if the limited, high quality food it depends upon is not present in a rather small area, a dormouse can find itself in difficulties.

A dormouse prefers ancient woodlands and particularly mixed coppice. *A Practical Guide to Dormouse Conservation*, written by Paul Bright and Pat Morris (Mammal Society, 1989), is intended for woodland managers and reserve wardens. It suggests ways of improving habitat for dormice, such as coppicing trees sensitively, a small area at a time, so that a continuous sequence of flowers, fruits and nuts is maintained from April to November. As one food source dies away, there has to be another to take its place.

Doug told us that he finds some very surprising occupants in his boxes from time to time. No matter how carefully designed and

Opposite: *...and cracks open the kernels of wayfaring berries*

positioned, sooner or later 'squatters' inevitably move in. A nuthatch pair raised five youngsters in one box, plastering up the entrance hole (in the way of nuthatches) to make it smaller. Blue tits make their nests, weaving animal hair, perhaps horse or badger, into the structure. When Doug cleans out the boxes at the end of the summer, he finds a variety of invertebrates: centipedes, millipedes, moths, slugs, earwigs, spiders, beetles and 'even an earthworm, though it's a mystery how it got there'.

Once he disturbed a nest of irate bumble bees. A cluster of nine long-eared bats was a nice find, as were bank voles, a yellow-necked mouse, even a pigmy shrew.

'It amazes me,' said Doug, 'the number of small mammals that climb trees. The yellow-necked mouse was sitting on top of a heap of acorns! I counted 196 acorns, together weighing 0.82 kg (1 lb 13 oz). The mouse must have been using the box as a winter larder, carrying the nuts one at a time up the tree.'

West Country ornithologists, who regularly put up boxes for pied flycatchers, sometimes find a dormouse occupant instead.

All through the summer a dormouse stays in the tree canopy or in the shrub layer. It so hates coming down to ground level, that it will make a long detour to reach a favourite blackberry patch. Rather than take a short cut across a ride, it crosses by aerial bridge where tree branches meet.

'Gaps between trees are bad news to a dormouse.'

Woodland managers create wide rides to encourage an interesting ground flora. Trees are cleared to entice in butterflies and dragonflies. Open glades are left in certain woods to attract nightingales back. But management policies such as these ill-suit the dormouse.

'Don't get the idea that dormice *only* live in hazel woods,' said Doug. 'Banks of willowherb, holly thickets, the edges of conifer plantations, even reedbeds are sometimes home to a small colony of dormice.'

Dormice are long-lived: up to five years. The female produces one, occasionally two, litters a year of three to five young. The babies stay in the nursery nest for 6 to 8 weeks.

Compare this to the several large litters a year of mice, voles and shrews; offspring are independent in less than 3 weeks but the lifespan is short, perhaps 12 to 15 months.

The dormouse stays in the tree canopy all summer. It is not until the autumn, when the weather begins to turn cold, that the animal descends to the ground. It may choose to hibernate in a coppice stump, a mouse hole or a small crack in a tree. But researchers were surprised to find that it will often prefer to scrape out a small hollow on the woodland floor, weave the tiniest of nests and go to sleep there, its sandy-gold colouring a good camouflage among the autumn leaves. ('Curiouser and curiouser,' as Alice would have said.)

'I sometimes feel that each of my dormice has its own personality,' said Doug, as we walked back along the track. 'One will scoot as soon as it hears me coming. Another stays put in the box. One goes easily into torpor at the first drop in temperature. Another is hyperactive and keeps on the go whatever the weather.'

Early in the year, several dormice will sometimes share a nest, living amicably together in 'happy harmony'. But once into breeding condition, they become solitary and territorial. However, there are instances of the same male and female cohabiting in a box for several weeks and even continuing to do so from one year to the next. A lasting 'pair bond'? This would be very unusual for a small mammal.

All recent evidence, decided the Dormouse Project Team, points to a decline in the numbers and range of the dormouse. It is now considered quite a rarity in Britain and is fully protected by the Wildlife and Countryside Act. Intentional capture, handling and disturbing of dormice or their nests are illegal without a licence from English Nature or the Countryside Council for Wales.

Yet a century ago the dormouse was said to be 'widespread and common'. In 1885, G. T. Rope, a Victorian naturalist, reviewed its status in England and Wales by noting all references to dormice appearing in the natural history columns of *The Field* the previous year.

The Zoologist published Rope's findings. Dormice were 'common' in the southern counties, from Cornwall to Kent and from Shropshire to Essex; and described as 'present' in most of the Midlands, Wales and as far north as Yorkshire. They were sometimes kept as pets and a boy living at Nettlebed in Oxfordshire was said to have taken 'scores' of dormice to school.

'This is no exaggeration,' comments Rope. 'Woodmen frequently find dormice as they thin the trees in winter, so common are they.'

Today dormice show a distinctly southerly distribution pattern: present in certain woodlands south of a line from the River Thames to the River Severn and in the Welsh borders. Exceptions are isolated colonies in Cumbria and Northamptonshire. Even within the favoured counties, distribution is patchy.

'Anything north of Watford is not really dormouse territory any more.'

The dormouse is poorly suited to our maritime climate. A late spring can delay breeding and young dormice born after the end of September are unlikely to survive the winter. But its arboreal lifestyle keeps it safe from most predators and typically 50 per cent of adults may survive from one year into the next.

As part of its Species Recovery Programme, English Nature is funding 'The Dormouse Initiative': a practical programme aimed at increasing numbers of dormice. Working with the Vincent Wildlife Trust, and using sites where dormice were once common, carefully monitored reintroductions are being attempted.

The common dormouse, *Muscardinus avellanarius*, is not the only dormouse in Britain. The fat (or edible) dormouse, *Glis glis*, was introduced in 1901. Approximately ten times the size of the common dormouse, and fairly numerous, it is confined to woodlands in the Chiltern Hills.

The Romans kept edible dormice in special jars called *gliraria* to fatten them up for the table. Was Lewis Carroll, when he wrote of a dormouse in a teapot, thinking of *Glis glis*?

Alice sighed wearily. 'I think you might do something better with the time,' she said, 'than wasting it in asking riddles that have no answer.'

'If you knew Time as well as I do,' said the Hatter, 'you wouldn't talk about wasting *it*. It's *him*.'

(NOTE: The quotations in this chapter are taken from *Alice in Wonderland* by Lewis Carroll.)

CHAPTER FOURTEEN

Newts are Nice

AMPHIBIANS AND REPTILES
Chris Mattison

•

Losehill Hall, Castleton, Derbyshire

I N A CORNER of the pond, a male palmate newt was displaying amorously to his female. Whiplashing his spiked tail, flicking it from side to side, he sent currents of water perfumed with pheromones (a sexy scent) rippling towards her. He darted, braked, darted. The female stayed immobile, as if mesmerized by his antics.

'He's going to deposit a tiny packet of sperm, then entice her into a position to pick it up with her body,' explained Chris.

Chris Mattison was introducing us to the amphibians and reptiles of the Peak National Park. It was early spring, the best time of the year to search for frogs, toads and newts: the time of the great 'splash-down'. Reptiles, too, are emerging from a winter spent in hibernation.

In Britain, there are 12 native species of amphibians and reptiles. There are six amphibians: common frog, common toad, natterjack toad; smooth newt, palmate newt and great-crested newt. And there are six reptiles: common lizard, sand lizard and slow-worm; the grass snake, smooth snake and adder.

Nine of the twelve are present in the Peaks. The exceptions are the natterjack toad, sand lizard and smooth snake: confined to sandy sites and lowland heaths in a very few counties.

How many 'herptiles' would Chris be able to introduce us to in one short weekend?

'I can't make any promises,' he warned. 'If it's wet and cold, it could be a wasted two days.'

The Peak National Park covers 1,440 km^2 (555 miles^2) and offers two contrasting landscapes: the 'Dark Peak' and the 'White Peak'. Losehill Hall is conveniently central and within easy reach of both. The high tors, dramatic escarpments and bleak gritstone moors of the north, east and south surround, in a horseshoe shape, the gentler, greener, limestone country.

Losehill Hall, set in 11 ha (27 acres) of garden, park and woodland, was built in 1882. With its steeply pitched gables, tall chimney stacks and long, narrow windows, the house is a good example of Gothic architecture, so fashionable in Victorian times. The Peak National Park acquired the Hall and opened the Study Centre, the first of its kind in a National Park, in 1972.

On our first evening we located frogs and spawn in the small pond behind Losehill Hall.

The common frog, *Rana temporaria*, and the common toad, *Bufo bufo*, are easy enough to tell apart. Frogs are the moist smoothies. Toads are the dry, warty fellows. With its longer back legs, a frog can leapfrog high over the waddling toad.

Early in spring, frogs and toads begin to stir from their winter's sleep. It's time to return to spawning ponds. The frogs usually arrive first. The toads, jostling together in their hurry to 'a-wooing go', follow a little later. With much commotion – croaking, wrestling, struggling,

fighting – each male attempts to leap on to the back of a female. Front legs around her chest, he clasps her in a tight embrace. In this position (known as 'amplexus') the female lays her eggs for the male to fertilize and the spawning may go on for several hours.

Frogs lay globular, jelly-blob masses (remember tapioca pudding?) that float on the surface. Toads produce strings of jelly and, in deeper water, entwine the jelly necklaces around the stems of aquatic plants. The tiny black eggs, well protected by the transparent jelly, hatch into wriggling tadpoles. They grow

Frogs are the moist smoothies

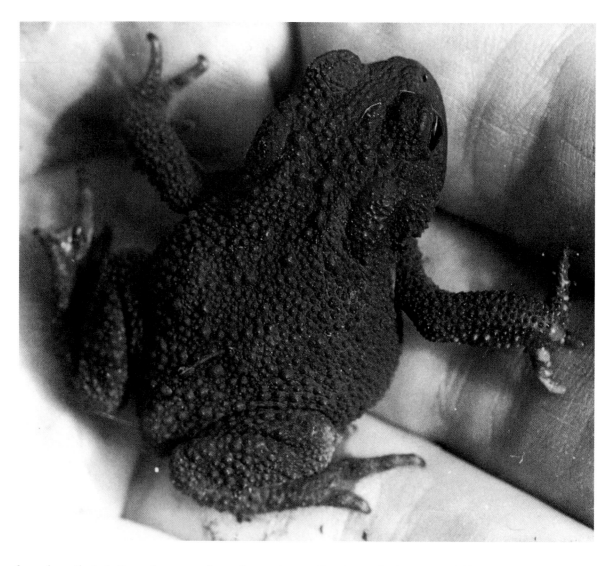

legs, lose their tails and emerge from the water to disperse across the surrounding countryside.

To track down elusive newts, we travelled north into the millstone grit. In a man-made pond, not far from the road, was a palmate newt hungrily guzzling frogspawn, the favourite food of many aquatic creatures. (Toadspawn is unpalatable, nasty tasting and escapes predation.)

'Here!' said Chris.

He'd found the courting palmate pair and we watched fascinated as the male whiplashed its

Toads are the dry, warty fellows

spiked tail to entice the female. What would happen next? But the newts moved into the weeds and out of sight.

Each newt species has its niche and the palmate newt has a preference for acidic water. The smooth newt – the commonest and most widespread of our newts – prefers shallow, alkaline pools. But it is not too particular and can be found almost anywhere; it is the one most likely to turn up in a garden pond.

Chris took us to a pond in the millstone grit

The favourite habitat of the great-crested newt is deeper, more open water. It tends to avoid pools that are highly acidic. This handsome and rather rare newt is protected by the Wildlife and Countryside Act and a licence is required to handle it.

But Chris knew of a pond inhabited by all three newts: situated in border country where the gritstone of the north meets the limestone of the south. The mix of acidic and alkaline water in this curious pond is such that it can be tolerated by all three species.

We half expected a picture-book pond with golden kingcups and water lily pads. Instead,

Chris led us to a steep-sided concrete tank on the site of an old lead mine. The rough concrete floor was strewn with bricks, rubble and bits of old piping. Paddling about in this grotty pond were smooth newts, palmate newts and great-crested newts.

Chris fished with his net, transferring the newts he caught to water-filled trays. Newts are not too difficult to identify in the courtship season of spring. Males are attired in their new breeding finery: a frilly crest along the back and gaudy black-blotched bellies.

The palmate newt, *Triturus helveticus*, is the smallest: smooth-skinned, velvety, dark brown above, straw-yellow below. Its tail is extended at the square-cut tip by a fine black filament ('spike'). Sooty-black webs separate the toes of the hind feet.

The smooth newt, *Triturus vulgaris*, is very similar, but slightly bigger. Its belly is orange, and it lacks the spike to its tail and the webs on its feet.

The great-crested newt, *Triturus cristatus*, is a splendid creature. It is nearly twice the size of the palmate newt and smooth newt. A high jagged crest ripples down its warty back and along its silver-streaked tail. On the belly are orange and black blotches. Great-crested newts can be individually recognized by the pattern of these belly blotches.

Female newts are dull in comparison with no breeding adornments even in spring, apart from a modest tail crest. Large size identifies the female great-crested newt. But you have to look closely at the female smooth and palmate newts to differentiate the spotted throat of the former, and the pinkish and unspotted throat of the latter.

'Newts are nice,' we all agreed as we tipped them gently back into the grotty pond.

Once the newts' breeding season is over the males will lose their finery. Eggs, each wrapped individually inside the leaf of an aquatic plant, will have hatched into tadpoles. Newt tadpoles look like miniature versions of the parents, except for the large feathery gills behind the head. A newt tadpole's legs form soon after hatching, much earlier than in the case of frog and toad tadpoles.

Most adult newts leave the water in early summer. They move discreetly into some damp, dark place, not too far from the water's edge: under a log, or in a crack between stones or in the long grass.

To see lizards, we drove north to the Upper Derwent Valley in the Dark Peak. The building of the three reservoirs – Howden, Derwent and Ladybower – created a 9.5 km (6 mile) long expanse of water, established for long enough now to appear natural in its wooded valley. Above Howden, a path led us through a conifer plantation of larch, pine and spruce, across the stream at Slippery Stones, and on to the boulder-strewn, grassy lower slopes of the heather moors.

'Lizard territory,' said Chris. 'Ideal spot to start looking. Warm boulders for sun basking. Lots of crevices in which to hide. Plenty of insects and spiders. And it's south-facing to catch the early morning sun.'

He'd already caught sight of the first little sun basker. A common lizard was soaking up the heat, its body pressed against the hot stone. It was a beautifully spick and span lizard, newly awakened from hibernation. Tiny dry scales patterned its mail armour skin with geometrical precision: a mosaic of grey, green and brown. Its tail – as long as its body – tapered to a narrow tip. A miniature dragon; did it breathe tiny flames of real fire?

But someone's shadow fell on the mini-dragon and it vanished in a trice.

A well-drained moor with heathland vegetation is typical lizard habitat. It offers warmth, plenty of cover and lots of small invertebrates to feed on.

The lives of reptiles are controlled by temperature. Being cold-blooded, they must 'recharge their batteries' by absorbing heat through solar-sensitive skins; the sun is their source of energy. Once warmed up, the lizard, or snake, can become active again, and is able to

pursue, catch and digest its prey.

Another lizard. And another... Basking in the sun. Soaking up energy.

'That lizard's not got a proper tail,' observed the youngest member of the group, 8-year-old Mark.

'You're right,' said Chris.

It was growing a new tail from the stump. Perhaps it had lost its old one in a fight? In April, with mating on the mind, rival males can become aggressive. Sometimes they will fight in defence of their territories. Or perhaps the damaged lizard had escaped from a predator by leaving part of its tail behind? In time the tail would regrow, but it would never be quite as good as new.

The lizard blinked its eyes, to show that it *was* a lizard and not an eyelid-less snake.

'What happens in winter when it's cold all the time?' asked Mark.

Most reptiles live in hot countries. British reptiles have had to evolve ways of coping with the lower temperatures of a cooler climate. In winter, they hibernate between September and March, retreating into a dry underground hole. In summer, they can survive on very little food.

Reptiles generally lay eggs. But eggs, in our fickle summers, run the risk of chilling. The common lizard, our only viviparous lizard, has adapted by bearing its young alive; the embryos develop within the female's body and are born, fully formed, in July or August.

Young Mark, we decided, was a herpetologist in the making. He was nearly as quick as Chris at spotting slight movements in the twiggy heather and had already wheedled a promise from his mother to buy him an iguana for his birthday.

Chris admits to having been 'obsessed', his own word, with amphibians and reptiles since he was a young lad of Mark's age. He came to the decision that animals which are universally feared must be the most interesting – to the consternation of his parents. He still finds pleasure in studying spiders, leeches and scorpions, as well as amphibians and reptiles. In recent years, he has travelled the world in search of snakes, lizards, frogs and toads to write about, and to photograph, for his Blandford books.

That night Chris introduced us to some of his reptilian pets and then, from the comfort of armchairs, we 'globe-trotted' as he showed us some of his slides. The tropical rainforests of Africa, Australia and South-east America are the richest – and most vulnerable – habitats on earth. In rainforests, frog evolution seems to have run riot: burrowing frogs with spade-like hind feet; torrent frogs clinging to wet and slippery surfaces with suckered feet; tree frogs that glide from high branches with the aid of webbed toes; mouth-brooding frogs; frogs that whistle like birds; barking frogs; horned frogs; frogs with red eyes.

Wearing old canvas sneakers and armed with a waterproof torch, a stick for flipping over dead leaves and, most importantly, plenty of mosquito repellent, Chris would set off just before dusk. Swamps resounded with the full symphony of frog chorus....

But back to the Peaks and Losehill Hall.

We wanted to find a slow-worm. It's not a 'worm', of course, but a legless lizard. A drystone wall is a favourite spot for basking slow-worms. So we drove to the White Peak with its gently rolling hills, spectacular dales, stone barns and drystone walls, and followed the limestone track leading down to Lathkill Dale.

'Walk slowly and quietly', reminded Chris. 'Don't let your shadow give you away.'

But the weather was steadily deteriorating. Mist rose from the valley and, to a slow-worm, cold and damp are anathema. The legless lizards had abandoned all thoughts of sun basking and hidden themselves, out of sight, probably in the dry spaces between stones.

Chris smiled in sympathy at our disappointed faces.

'Herpetologists have to get used to disappointments,' he chided. 'So take your blinkers off – and look around you.'

He stooped to pick up a chunk of limestone and pointed out a fossil brachiopod: a marine shellfish dating from Carboniferous times.

Dippers and grey wagtails on slippery boulders in the splashing River Lathkill, newly arrived willow warblers singing from the alders, buds bursting open on ash, hazel and hawthorn, and early spring flowers, wood anemone, primrose, violets and celandines growing on the banks: we discarded our 'herpetological blinkers' and enjoyed the day.

CHAPTER FIFTEEN

Rowan Tree and Red Thread

HEDGES: THEIR HISTORY AND NATURAL HISTORY

Robert Cameron

•

Preston Montford Field Centre,
Shrewsbury, Shropshire

SNOW-WHITE MAY BLOSSOM smothered the hawthorn hedge: flat-topped creamy umbels on elder; laburnum with drooping yellow petal-chains; tiny, waxy-green flowers on spindle; milky cymes of rowan.

'Hedgerows are at their loveliest in spring,' said Robert. 'I always pick the May holiday weekend to go hedge dating, if I can.'

We were dating hedges high up on the bracken slopes of Stiperstones. Not a place where one would normally expect to see hedgerows, particularly of such surprising diversity. But here, close to the border of Wales, we were in squatters' country.

After the discovery in the middle of the eighteenth century of rich deposits of minerals in these Shropshire hills, itinerant labourers had moved in. Illegally, more often than not, they would grab a piece of land on the open hillside, build a house and sow seeds for crops. To protect their staked-out smallholdings they planted hedges, using whatever woody species they could find. As more labourers arrived, so squatters' hedges appeared higher and higher up the slopes.

Hedges planted by those Shropshire squatters defy Hooper's Law which says:

The number of shrub species per 27.5 m
(30 yd) length x 100 = the approximate age
of hedge in years

The story behind this 'rule of thumb' method for dating hedges is well known. In the 1960s Dr Max Hooper, a senior scientist with the Nature Conservancy, surveyed thousands of hedges, mostly in the midland and eastern counties. He found a striking correlation between the known date of the hedge and the composition of its shrub flora. New species appeared to move in at roughly the rate of one per century as seeds are blown in, or deposited by birds or mammals. Hooper went on to develop his formula (explained in *Hedges*, Collins New Naturalist, 1974).

A 2-species hedge, according to the formula, is likely to be between 100 and 300 years old; and a 10-species hedge between 900 and 1,100 years old.

Species counting can distinguish an Enclosure Act hedge from a medieval hedge, or a hedge of Stuart or Tudor times.

Roughly speaking, 'the younger the hedge, the fewer the number of shrub species; the older the hedge, the greater the number of shrub species'.

But (we are warned) the confidence limit is wide. Colonization of hedges also depends on such factors as available seed sources, climate, soils and planning policies. And all over the country people have been busily dating hedges, proving – or disproving – the formula ever since.

Professor Robert Cameron and colleagues from Preston Montford set about testing Hooper's Law in the county of Shropshire. With the help of field centre students, hedges were sampled in several different parishes and the results compared with their known history. It did not always match up. They concluded that, although subsequent work in other counties (Kent, Sussex, Devon and Huntingdonshire) has amply confirmed Hooper's age/species relationship, 'Shropshire's hedges are rather different.'

And now we were hedge-dating ourselves with Robert Cameron.

Our first survey hedge, on the Montford Estate, was long and straight, and ran down the side of a huge field of oilseed rape.

Montford Estate is the home of the Clive family of 'Clive of India' fame. During Queen Victoria's reign Robert Clive had reorganized the old field systems several times; the changes are well documented. The final enclosure layout was in 1881: so the hedge is a little over 100 years old. Like other forward-looking, late Victorian landowners anxious to improve their land, he replaced a patchwork pattern of many small fields with fewer and larger regular-shaped fields. And he planted 'quickset' hedges around their perimeters.

Contemporary agriculturalists considered these hawthorn hedges to be 'very modern' by the standards of the day. The single-species Montford hedges were atypical of Shropshire as a whole.

We divided into pairs and prepared to pace 30 yd (27.5 m) lengths. How many species had colonized the Montford hedge in the 100 years since it was planted?

'To avoid bias, approach a point in the hedge without prior inspection,' directed Robert. 'Walk 10 paces and *then* pace out the 30 unseen yards (27.5 m).'

He reminded us to count the shrubs on one side only, and not to include climbers such as ivy, honeysuckle or bryony in the final total.

So we paced a dozen sample lengths between us, counting species. This was a monotonous task, for the hedge consisted almost entirely of hawthorn, interspersed with planted holly trees and some wild rose, averaging out at 2.3 woody shrubs in each 30 yd (27.5 m) length. If we allowed for the landowner's penchant for planting holly trees in his 'enclosure' hawthorn hedge, then wild rose was the one additional shrub acquired in the first 100 years and Hooper's Law worked well.

'Wild rose is often an early colonizer,' said Robert. 'Birds feed on the hips and disperse the seeds.'

In counties other than Shropshire, elder or blackthorn might be the first colonizing species to arrive in an enclosure hawthorn hedge.

Beneath the hedge were spring flowers of arable land: shepherd's purse, mayweed, poppy, field pansy, chickweed, fumitory, scarlet pimpernel, yellow charlock, white campion, red dead nettle, Jack-by-the-hedge and germander speedwell.

The word 'hedge' is from the Anglo-Saxon *hege* or *haga*. The first hedges, before man began to plant them, would have originally self-seeded along the line of ditches or banks close to trees.

The Roman writer Cato's advice to Roman landowners was: 'Around the borders of the farm, and along the roads, plant elms and some poplars, so that you may have leaves for your sheep and cattle, and the timber will be available if you need it.'

Planted hedges were probably very few in early English times. Labour was plentiful and cheap, and Little Boy Blues and Bo Peeps kept the cows out of the meadow and the sheep from the corn. Perhaps hedges came into fashion in the post-plague labour shortage days after the Black Death (1348–50 and 1361–2). Villages were abandoned, fields left derelict. Suddenly there was more land than was needed, but fewer people available to work on it. A new class of yeoman farmers emerged. By private arrangement, abandoned common-field strips were often enclosed with hedges and turned over to sheep.

John Fitzherbert, in his *Book of Husbandry* of 1523, writes, 'Get thy quickset in the wood country and let them be of whitethorn and crab tree for they be best, holly and hazel be good.'

'Buy quickset at market, new gathered and small, buy bushes and willow, to fence it withall,' wrote Thomas Tusser in his *Five Hundred Points of Husbandry* (1573).

In the late eighteenth and early nineteenth centuries, enclosure reached a peak. During the reign of George III (1760–1820) 5,000 separate parliamentary Acts were passed. Hedges were planted at an average rate of 2,000 miles a year; this process, however, probably only affected one-fifth of the country. Parliament specified that: 'Plots of land allotted by virtue of this act shall be inclosed and fenced round with ditches and quickset hedges....'

This reorganization of the British countryside was intended to encourage greater efficiency. Food production was on the increase to feed an expanding population. For the poor, parliamentary enclosure often meant the loss of common land and of traditional rights. Much hardship resulted and it was a period of considerable social upheaval and protest. As John Clare wrote in the late eighteenth century:

Inclosure, thou'rt a curse upon the land
And tasteless was the wretch
Who thy existence plann'd.

The account books of the great nursery firms of the day recorded the sale of thousands of plants of 'quickset'. All over the Midlands and the eastern counties, long, straight, drawing-board lines of hawthorn hedges divided the land into regular rectangular enclosure fields: planned landscapes.

But, with a very few exceptions, the eighteenth- and nineteenth-century enclosure Acts affected the Shropshire countryside very little.

The west Midlands differs from the east in many ways. The climate is wetter, soils are generally poorer and there are substantial upland areas merging with the mountains of Wales. There were fewer people, and much woodland and waste survived until the late medieval and early Tudor times. Woodland clearance in Shropshire was gradual and piecemeal, and land was usually enclosed by private agreement, an amicable affair.

In 1803, J. Plymley wrote in his *General View of the Agriculture of the County of Shropshire*: 'I enclosed a small common a few years ago, without the expense of planting hawthorns by taking what grew on the waste already and planting it in a line.'

Shropshire's small farmers share a long-held tradition of enclosing their small and irregular fields and allotments with whatever shrub species they can find. Trees are added for future timber sales. Mixed-species hedges are the rule rather than the exception. Local traditions of planting often give particular villages a characteristic pattern; as, for example, the laburnum-rich hedges of Pennerley.

From the Montford Estate we travelled to Bicton Heath.

'Here we'll find,' said Robert, 'typical examples of mixed-species hedges planted by smallholders.'

We divided up again. I joined Ted and Sally, and we picked a random spot in our chosen hedge. Ted was studying the flowers in the hedge bottom. He identified an umbellifer. 'Pignut,' he said, with some excitement.

'Stop botanizing,' scolded Sally, his wife. 'We're not here to sort out umbellifers. You have the longest legs so *you* can do the pacing.'

Ted obediently walked 30 measured treads and put his walking stick down as a marker. Now we had to sort out the species. It was an interesting hedge, with some curious shrubs to identify with the help of a field guide.

Midland hawthorn or common hawthorn? 'Deeply indented leaves and a single style in the centre of the red stamens.' It was common hawthorn and not the twin-styled Midland (or woodland) hawthorn.

Pedunculate oak or sessile oak? Two small 'ears' at the base of the almost stalkless leaves: pedunculate oak.

Beech or hazel? Beech leaves are shiny, prominently veined and silky on the underside. Hazel leaves are soft and downy, saw-edged with a small point.

Common elm or wych elm? We had to seek Robert's help for this one. 'Both have a lopsided "toothache" bulge at the base of the leaf,' he said. 'But the abrasive sandpapery feel of the surface, the larger size and sharp point at the tip of the leaf identifies wych elm. However,' he added, 'what you have here is a hybrid. Elms hybridize easily.'

We compared results. Samples varied widely from 4.35 species per 30 yd (27.5 m) length to 6.42 species: ash, sycamore, holly, elder, blackthorn, crab apple, gooseberry, damson, raspberry... These typical mixed-species

enclosure hedges dated from the mid-eighteenth century. They couldn't be more than 200 years old. It was obvious that they did not conform to Hooper's Law.

'Have you noticed the number of shrubs that are *useful*?' asked Robert. 'These farmers were poor. Some had to eke out their income with a second job. They deliberately planted shrubs that would be of practical economic value.'

A hedge was regarded as more than a stock-proof fence. It was there to be harvested for its wild fruits, for firewood or as a cash crop.

We moved on now to survey ancient 'assart' hedges. Assarting is the piecemeal whittling away of a wood: for firewood or to clear and enclose a space for crops; a common practice from Celtic times up to the seventeenth century.

During the reigns of King John and Richard I, assarting of the royal forests provided a source of income for the royals who rented out the cleared land to local farmers. The original wood might disappear, but often a woodland edge would be left behind to mark a boundary. Such 'woodland relic' hedges are generally rich in flora and fauna.

The hedge at Ford is thought to be the oldest in the Montford area. Perhaps it marks the boundary of a Norman lord's demesne. But, as with so many of Shropshire's hedges, there is a dearth of documentary evidence. No border disputes and no legally contentious incidents appear in the records to give a clue to age or history. Ford hedge is a double hedge with a narrow trackway running between. Beneath the canopy of foliage it was cool and shady. We counted 17 species of shrub, averaging out at 7.3 species each 30 yd (27.5 m) length – dating the Ford hedge back to medieval times, c.1200 – if Hooper's Law applied.

Four of the shrubs were species indicative of ancient woodland: hazel, field maple, wych elm and dogwood. All these are poor colonizers and unlikely to be found in a young hedge unless planted and nurtured by man.

It was an interesting hedge

The range of woodland plants growing in the lane was firmer evidence still: dog's mercury, wood anemone, wood sorrel, dog violet, yellow archangel, primrose, bluebell and wood melick. All of these are flowers with poor powers of dispersal and indicator species, in the county of Shropshire, of ancient woodland. Old 'woodland edge' hedges are often refuges for such indicator plants: 'historical signposts'.

'Certain snail species can also indicate the age of a wood or hedge,' said Professor Cameron, author of *Land Molluscs of Britain and Northern Europe*.

Snails colonize new territory so slowly, moving less than 10 m (11 yd) in a lifetime, that some species have the potential to date a hedge. (Another 'law' waiting to be formulated?)

On the following day, we drove to Stiperstones and parked the cars at Perkin's Beach.

A winding dirt track led past a nineteenth-century chapel and past a cottage with beehives in the garden. Beyond was the open heather moorland. New shoots of heather were pushing up through the twiggy brown. Gorse was aglow with sunny yellow flowers. Tiny pink buds were opening on bilberry bushes. And the wind was blowing white petal confetti from the stunted and wizened 'bonsai' hawthorn trees.

Stiperstones was probably cleared of the last of its woodland in medieval times. For centuries people grazed their sheep on the open common land, collected firewood and foraged for food. But, with the discovery of minerals in the eighteenth century the miners moved in: a lost way of itinerant life described in Mary Webb's novel *Gone to Earth*, published in 1917.

When the lead ran out in the 1890s, squatters and their families left. The signs of their presence are still there to be seen on the steep slopes: ruins of cottages and neglected gappy hedges.

An invisible cuckoo was shouting at us: 'CU-ckoo, CU-ckoo'. And, once more, we began to list the shrubs and trees: hazel, field maple, wych elm, dogwood, common hawthorn, blackthorn, elder, wild privet, mahonia, holly, crab apple, gooseberry, damson, raspberry, red currant... We counted 24 species in all. Totals varied widely from 4.35 species to 7.00 species per 30 yd (27.5 m) length. And what useful hedges they were!

Berries, nuts and fruit would have gone into the larder. Damsons could be turned into jam or sold to a manufacturer to colour ink and dyes. (Damson dye was used to stain sailors' trousers the correct nautical blue right up until the beginning of the twentieth century.)

Hazel was coppiced for useful poles. Holly leaves served as a winter browse-food for grazing stock. Pigs were let loose to forage on beechmast and acorns. The stems of blackthorn made good walking sticks. Spindle yielded wood suitable for carving into pegs, skewers and spindles for spinning wheels. Willow could be woven into baskets. The bark of oak produced tannin to be sold as a cash crop to the leather trade.

But what was the economic value of such shrubs as snowberry, wild privet and laburnum?

'Perhaps they were planted simply because they were pretty.' suggested Robert, 'purely for their decorative qualities.'

Paradoxically the hedges highest up the hillside – despite the thinner, more acidic soil – were among those with the most species. Shrubs of the uplands, such as willow, gorse, broom, silver birch, alder and rowan, produce vast quantities of light, wind-blown seed that sets in abundance and germinates with ease.

Hedges on Stiperstones were generally more species-rich than in the more fertile lowlands. But why did a rowan tree so often stand sentinel outside the front door of a ruined cottage? What was the reason for its obvious popularity?

Rowan tree and red thread
Hold the witches all in dread.

On the summit of Stiperstones is a formation of quartzite rocks called locally 'the Devil's

The humps and hollows of an old lead mine seemed a good place to stop for a picnic. We had climbed high enough up Stiperstones to be able to enjoy the tremendous views across the vale to the Long Mynd. In the grass of our chosen picnic spot grew bugle, navelwort, greater stitchwort and herb Robert, and the vanilla scent of broom hung in the air.

Blackcap, whitethroat, dunnock, chaffinch and blue tit sang from their songposts in the lush green hedges. Small family parties of long-tailed tits – blurs of pink and grey – slipped in and out of willows, trilling softly, balancing delicately with their rocket-stick tails. Butterflies sheltered in sun spots on the lee-side, and sipped the nectar of bramble and periwinkle.

Hooper's intriguing formula has made people look again at old hedges, particularly the woodland relic hedges. It is impossible not to notice their special importance to birds, small mammals, insects and other invertebrates; and their value as a refuge for woodland flowers.

A. E. Housman (1859–1936) appreciated Shropshire's green copses and diverse hedgerows. In his book of poems, *The Shropshire Lad*, he wrote:

Give me a land of boughs in leaf,
A land of trees that stand;
Where trees are fallen, there is grief;
I love no leafless land.

Chair'. Perhaps the squatters quailed at the thought of the Devil looking down upon their settlement. It was said that every time he stirred in his chair, thunder crashed and lightning flashed. Rowan trees have the reputation of keeping evil spirits at bay, so it is likely that the 'magic' tree was planted for superstitious reasons.

CHAPTER SIXTEEN

As Good as a Tonic

PLANTS AS MEDICINES,
FOOD AND DYES

Patrick Harding

•

Losehill Hall Study Centre,
Castleton, Derbyshire

MILLER'S DALE, in the Peak National Park, is a botanist's paradise. Uncommon flowers of the limestone bloom on the slopes: pyramidal orchid, grass of Parnassus, rock rose, mountain pansy, carline thistle and Nottingham catchfly.

So why were we botanizing happily in the rubble and weeds of old railway lines at the disused Miller's Dale station, instead of rhapsodizing over rarities on the limestone slopes?

'*Weedy* species are the wild flowers most likely to have been made use of by our ancestors for medicinal purposes,' Patrick explained.

Dandelion, he said, was once used as a diuretic: called 'wet-a-bed' by country folk. Eyebright is still used as a remedy for eye disorders. An infusion of the leaves of ribwort plantain can ease a sore throat. Coltsfoot makes a soothing syrup for a tickly cough.

It was the month of August and the sunny yellow flowers of coltsfoot – a plant that thrives on disturbed ground – had long since disappeared. Only the distinctive leaves, shaped like a 'colt's foot', were present in abundance on the waste patch.

'Feel the downy underside of the leaf,' said Patrick. 'Feel how soft and velvety it is.'

He broke off a piece of stalk and it oozed a gel-like substance. Coltsfoot is high in mucilage: said to protect the lining of the gut and airways, reducing irritation. Its generic name is *Tussilago*, meaning 'cough dispeller'.

Patrick picked a sprig of St John's wort, *Hypericum perforatum*. He held a leaf up to the light. It appeared perforated: dotted with tiny pinprick holes. But the 'holes' are actually translucent oil glands. An ointment made from the oil is said to be a wound healer. Absorbed into the body it has a calming effect. Early Crusaders had faith in St John's wort, making use of its properties on the battlefield, superstitiously likening the red juice which exudes from the stem to the blood of the beheaded disciple, St John the Baptist.

Another plant believed to 'heal wounds' is yarrow (or milfoil), *Achillea millefolium*. There is a reference to yarrow in the Anglo-Saxon version of Apuleius Platonicus's *Herbarium*: 'It is said that Achilles, the chieftain found it; and he with this same wort healed them who were stricken and wounded with iron.'

Self-heal, valued for its antiseptic oils, was one of the two 'wound herbes' of which John Gerard (1545–1612) wrote, 'In the world, there are not two better, as hath been often proved.' (Bugle was the second.)

And what about speedwell, herb Bennet, pilewort, mullein and purging flax?

The history of herbal medicine dates back thousands of years. In the Bible we read: 'He causeth the grass to grow for the cattle, and herbs for the service of man' (Psalm 104:12). And '...the fruit thereof shall be for meat, and the leaf thereof for medicine' (Ezekiel 47:12).

Old herbals are fascinating. But how many thousands of people must have died as the result of trial and error experimentation?

Hippocrates (*c.* 300 BC) was the first of the Greeks to leave a list at his death of some 400 simple remedies; among the plants he prescribed were mint, poppy, mugwort, sage, rosemary, rue and verbena.

Pliny the Elder, Dioscorides, Galen, Turner, Gerard and Culpeper are all remembered for their herbals.

But sixteenth and seventeenth-century healing became increasingly suspect as the writings of herbal practitioners propagated the risible theory of the 'doctrine of signatures'. For every disease (they wrote) there is, in nature, a herb to cure it: signposted by God by some likeness indicative of its special use.

'[God] hath not only stamped upon them a distinct forme, but also given them particular Signatures, whereby a man may read, even to legible Characters, the use of them,' wrote William Coles in *The Art of Simpling* in 1656.

The blotched leaves of lungwort were likened to 'unhealthy lungs' and prescribed for chest complaints. Lettuce leaves, exuding a milky juice, were given to nursing mothers to 'propagate milk'. The kernel of a walnut was said to resemble a brain inside the hard 'skull' shell and 'signified' a cure for all 'troubles of the head'.

Nicholas Culpeper (1616–54) went even further. He linked diseases and healing herbs to the movements of the planets. Astrological medicine!

His preposterous tracts enjoyed huge sales, in spite of being condemned by medical practitioners of the time. And *Culpeper's Herbal* is still widely read today.

'Forget Culpeper!' was the advice of Dr Patrick Harding, professional botanist and tutor for the University of Sheffield's Division of Adult Continuing Education. 'You wouldn't dream of repairing your car with the aid of a car maintenance manual of the 1880s, would you? So why consult a 300-year-old book to find out about *modern* herbal medicine?'

Culpeper's works are interesting as history and eminently quotable. But they are of little real scientific value. It was quite a relief to metaphorically throw his *Herbal* out of the window.

Research into the properties of medicinal plants is taken seriously in the 1990s, not least in the research laboratories of the Royal Botanic Gardens. Plant analysts at Kew confirm scientifically what our forefathers 'knew' intuitively: that plants produce many complex chemicals, including chemicals of proven therapeutic value. Some of these, it seems reasonable to assume, must have evolved as a defensive response to attacks by plant-eating insects.

So, pausing at each new flower to consider its chemical properties in the light of modern knowledge, we followed the Miller's Dale trail. And Patrick continued to pepper his observations with pleasurable snippets of lore from the old books.

MEADOWSWEET: cools the blood; contains salicylic acid, a pain-killing and anti-inflammatory ingredient – the original 'aspirin'. 'The smell thereof maketh the heart merrie, delighteth the sense,' was Gerard's rather curious observation. Was he referring to the sweet smell of the flowers or the cucumber smell of the leaves?

LADY'S BEDSTRAW: contains an enzyme that curdles milk and so is sometimes called cheese rennet. 'Excellent good to bathe the feet in hot weather.'

WILD THYME: antiseptic properties. 'Cures headaches and giddiness and disposes to sleep.'

WILD GOLDEN ROD: a diuretic, cleanser of the blood. 'A sovereign wound herb, inferior to none.'

We nibbled the aniseed-tasting seeds of sweet cicely, chewed the nutty leaves of salad burnet and relieved the pain of stinging nettles with a cool dock leaf.

Hedge woundwort, herb Robert, daisy, bittersweet....

We journeyed by coach to Hardwick Hall, 9.5 km (6 miles) north-west of Mansfield. Hardwick Hall was built by Bess of Hardwick in the 1590s, after the death of her fourth husband had left her a wealthy widow. The National Trust, now owners of Hardwick Hall, recreated the herb garden in the 1960s, planting over 60 different culinary and medicinal herbs: varieties likely to have been cultivated for domestic use in Elizabethan times. A nuttery was added with walnuts, cobs and filberts.

Squashy ripe mulberries plopped from mulberry trees as we walked the length of the

mulberry avenue. The herb garden was full of bright colours and fragrant perfumes, with plants like lovage, rue, skullcap, horehound, dill, alkanet, good King Henry, vervain, catmint and coriander.

They are wonderfully evocative names and it is tempting to quote from those old herbals again.

BORAGE: 'Of known virtue to revive the hypochondriac and to cheer the hard student.'

FENNEL: 'The stomach it doth cleanse and comfort well.'

FEVERFEW: 'For them that are giddy in the head.'

PENNYROYAL: 'Tis good for Coughs, for the Gripes, the Stone, Jaundice and Dropsie.'

MOTHERWORT: 'For them that are in hard travail with childe.'

CATMINT: 'For those that are meek and mild ... and would be forceful.'

BETONY: 'A very precious herb, that's certain and most fitting to be kept in a man's house.'

MARJORAM: 'A remedy against the bitings and stingings of venomous beasts.'

SOLOMON'S SEAL: 'Taketh away in one night, or two at the most, any bruise gotten by falls or women's wilfulnesses, in stumbling upon their hasty husband's fists, or such like.'

Aromatherapy is an ancient art that has been practised for thousands of years. The aromas of the volatile oils of such scented plants as rosemary, lavender, marjoram and peppermint are used to promote physical and emotional well-being.

The National Trust recreated the herb garden

121

Sweet woodruff, high in coumarins and 'smelling of new-mown hay' was used as a strewing plant on the floors of dwellings. Camomile helped rid medieval homes 'of the foulness of offending odours'. Rosemary was often burnt in sick rooms for its aromatic vapours: 'a comforter of the brain and a strengthener of the memory'.

When illness strikes, most of us, sensibly, pop round to our friendly neighbourhood doctor. But, for a mild ailment, we may fall back on the tried and tested 'natural' remedies remembered from childhood: the vapours of steaming balsam that clear a stuffy nose; mint tea for indigestion; eucalyptus oil to rub on a wheezy chest; a camomile infusion for a sweet night's sleep; wintergreen embrocation for minor aches and pains; or a clove to relieve toothache.

We visited Chesterfield and explored the coach park just a stone's throw away from the crooked spire.

Wormwood and mugwort grew side by side; strong-smelling shrubby plants, with deeply-cut leaves and tiny, inconspicuous flowers. Both featured prominently in medieval magic and medicine, and were used as strewing plants, and as a deterrent against fleas and lice.

> While wormwood hath seed get a handful
> or twain
> To save against March, to make flea
> to refrain
> Where the chamber is swept and the
> wormwood is strewn
> No flea for his life dare abide to be known.
> (Thomas Tusser, *Five Hundred Points
> of Good Husbandry*, 1573)

An essential oil (thujone) extracted from the flowerheads of wormwood, *Artemisia absinthium*, was once the key ingredient of absinthe, the notorious alcoholic drink. If taken in excess, it acted as a slow poison and caused brain damage. (Van Gogh's problems were not helped by drinking absinthe.) Its use as an ingredient is now banned.

There are species of plants growing freely in the British countryside that contain some of the deadliest poisons in existence: henbane, monkshood, deadly nightshade, foxglove, thornapple, hemlock....

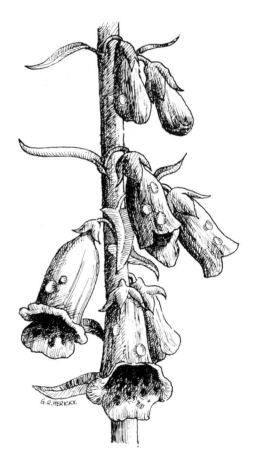

G.R.HERICKX.

'Never take risks,' Patrick warned us. 'Experimenting with herbs can be dangerous. Consult the professional herbalist.'

High on Stannage Edge in the Dark Peak next day, the heather was in full bloom, a glorious expanse of purple stretching across the moorland as far as the eye could see.

'Heather produces soft browns and beiges for dyeing,' said Pauline. 'A few sprigs will not be missed. We have to be very conservation conscious these days, and only pick wild flowers where they are growing in profusion.'

Pauline Hinchcliffe keeps rare breeds of sheep on her smallholding. She dyes their homespun wool with natural dyes, and uses it for weaving and tapestry.

In among the heathers were low-growing dwarf shrubs, identified as bilberry. The purple berries that escaped going into our mouths (for bilberries are delicious) were added to Pauline's collection of natural dyestuffs. Back in the dales, we stopped to pick snowberries and elderberries from the hedgerows. And from a patch of waste ground (where a healthy plant of cannabis was a somewhat unexpected find!) we gathered clover, weld and toadflax.

Liz Cole reiterated Patrick's warning words as she talked about the preparation of edible plants for a 'food for free' supper.

'Always make certain of your identification when gathering herbs,' she said. 'Better still, take a botanist along. Avoid roadside verges – almost certainly polluted with lead. And don't pick flowers from cultivated fields; they may be contaminated with chemical sprays.'

Down in the meadow behind Losehill Hall we picked wavy bittercress, *Cardamine flexuosa*, and spikes of common sorrel, *Rumex acetosa*. John Clare wrote of the parched fieldworker who chews a sorrel leaf to 'slake his thirst': 'The mower gladly chews it down/And slakes his thirst the best he may.' The arrow-shaped leaves taste cool, sharp and peppery.

That night we dined on potato, onion and sorrel soup followed by a rose petal salad with bittercress and nasturtium leaves. There were large helpings of bilberry pie for dessert, blackberry ice-cream from Liz's freezer and elderflower champagne. Liqueurs followed: sips of home-made tinctures, rose geranium in vodka and may blossom in brandy. Decidedly merry, we reassembled in the kitchen for a demonstration on how to dry and store herbs.

'Spread the plantstuff out thinly on mesh trays in a warm, well-ventilated room,' said Liz. 'It must dry quickly if natural colour and the active ingredients are to be preserved. Once the herbs are completely dry and crunchy, you can crumble them up and store them in tightly closed jars.'

Liz showed us how to prepare a soothing ointment made from beeswax, sunflower oil and leaves of marigold. We brewed herbal teas, infusing leaves and stems of lemon balm with honey as a sweetener. And we sampled yarrow and elderflower tea, and golden rod and meadowsweet. We slept very well that night!

Medicine, food *and dyes*.

Pauline Hinchcliffe had brought a selection of soft white skeins of wool: bouclés, worsteds, thin plies and thick plies. She filled three large stainless steel pans with water and put them to heat on the gas stoves. Into each pan she lowered a different skein of wool, plus a 'mordant'.

Mordants, she told us, are chemicals used to 'fix' the dyes. The original mordant (*mordre*, from the French 'to bite') was ammonia in the form of stale urine, easily available and easy to collect.

'Fermentation was part of the elaborate dyeing process,' said Pauline. 'The stench was so appalling that Queen Elizabeth I issued a decree: no dyeing must take place within five miles of a royal estate because of the "foul odour".'

Fortunately for us the technique of dyeing and the range of mordants available has advanced since Elizabethan times. In the workroom at Losehill Hall we used modern mordants: alum, chrome, tin, iron and copper.

'A mordant fixes the dye and, at the same time, exerts a subtle effect on the range of final colours,' explained Pauline.

Tin 'sharpens'. Alum 'brightens'. Iron darkens or 'saddens'. Chrome produces a richer, warmer tone. Copper helps to enhance the greens.

The skeins of wool were simmered for an

hour and were then hung up to dry. Now the fun of preparing the dyestuff began. Our gathered material was boosted by plants from Pauline's wild flower garden and a few 'exotics' she'd purchased from her local chemist. Leaves, flowers and stalks were torn into pieces. Clover, ling, hemp agrimony, weld, horsetail... 15 dyestuffs in all.

Taking a strand of wool from each of the six differently-mordanted skeins, we tied them together into a little bundle. The pans were put on to boil and a different dyestuff went into each. When we had sufficient bundles of mixed strands, we added them to the pans and watched as the dye seeped into the water and the wool slowly began to change colour.

Elderberry gave purple; snowberry, lemon-yellow; camomile, green; toadflax gave brown. The mordants in the wool affected the dyes, producing a range of tones from very pale to very dark, from sombre to bright.

The dyestuffs simmered for an hour. Then we gave the multi-coloured strands a thorough rinsing. Draped on wire coat hangers, they were hung up to dry in the drying room. The colours were lovely, soft natural tones: nothing harsh or abrasive. Now the process was repeated all over again with a fresh lot of dyestuffs: St John's wort, horsetail, yew berries, and the medieval favourites, madder and weld.

'A preponderance of plants yield yellows and browns,' said Pauline. 'Remarkably few give red, blue or green. Madder, weld and woad are the exceptions.'

Madder is related to the bedstraws. Lady's bedstraw, hedge bedstraw and goosegrass all give a red colour.

Weld (or dyer's greenwood) is probably the

Camomile dyes green

oldest known yellow dye. Dyer's broom was added to produce Kendal green and Lincoln green.

Woad, another ancient dye plant, produces blue. It was used as body paint by British warriors, according to Caesar's report in *De Bello Gallico*. At first imported from abroad, woad was probably grown commercially by medieval times.

Foreign dyes were imported in the seventeenth and eighteenth centuries, and animal and mineral substances gradually supplanted vegetable dyes. 'Royal' purple, for instance, was extracted from dog whelk; red from the cochineal beetle.

The first synthetic dye was discovered, purely by chance, in 1856. William Henry Perkins, a chemist's assistant, was hoping to find a substitute for quinine. He boiled a black coal-tar derivative in alcohol and the resulting bright violet fluid stained everything with which it came into contact. The dye was marketed and proved a commercial success. Other manu-

factured dyes, so much simpler and easier to use than natural dyes, followed fast and the practice of dyeing with natural materials has almost died out. It continues still, as a cottage industry, in a few areas of the Highlands and Islands of Scotland. Lichens, mosses, crottles and orchils thrive in the damp, pure air of Scotland; bruised and boiled they give tweed its typical 'tweedy' aroma and colour.

We knotted strands of our lovely soft-coloured wools on to 'sample' cards, over 90 different colours in all. There was sufficient wool left over to take away, perhaps to highlight a design motif in a knitted garment or to add to an embroidery. In such a short period of time Pauline had, of necessity, stuck to basic procedures, omitting refinements. But we had learned enough to experiment for ourselves at home.

Pick yourself a pick-me-up. Savour the flavours of food for free. Learn to dye in the dales. A natural break in the Peak National Park is as good as any tonic.

CHAPTER SEVENTEEN

Focus on Nature

WILDLIFE PHOTOGRAPHY
Tony Wharton

•

Malham Tarn Field Centre,
Settle, North Yorkshire

'BLOODY CRANESBILL,' I muttered, squinting at it through my camera lens, 'why won't it stay still? Blowing about like that, how can I get a good shot?'

Geranium sanguineum is a flower of the limestone and Malham Tarn is in the limestone country of the Upper Craven. There was a splendid patch of it behind Miss Hilary's Cottage. If only the swaying stems would stay still long enough to allow me to take a photograph.

The wind swept across the tarn, rippling the water into crested waves, and switch-backing the mallards and coots. Wind movement is a major problem in close-up flower photography. So how does the *professional* photographer cope when faced with less than ideal conditions?

'Use as fast a shutter speed as possible to stop movement,' said Tony Wharton.

But on a dull day a fast shutter speed requires a wide open lens. And a wide open lens allows only a narrow depth of field. With a narrow depth of field, there is a risk of much of the picture being out of focus. It's a vicious circle. What to do?

Faster film? Such as ASA 200 or even 400? To permit a greater depth of field and in-focus sharpness? But the faster the film, the more likely it is that the final pictures will be grainy, less than perfect. The slower the film, the sharper, more finely detailed and grain-free the image.

'The professional,' said Tony, 'intent on selling his work, rarely uses other than a slow Kodachrome 25 or 64 film. Or a Fuji 50.'

Flash?

Flash is only used as a last resort. Natural light is almost always preferable when it comes to photographing flowers.

'The answer is to use a tripod,' he said. 'A tripod cuts out the camera shake which is almost unavoidable with a hand-held camera.'

The best is a tripod designed to adjust to a low level for close-up work, and with a ball-and-socket head.

'And it's not much use going to the trouble of

setting up a tripod, if you then forget all about using the cable release.'

A sturdy tripod plus a cable release should make it possible to work at a slower speed and with a smaller aperture.

'Close-up photography,' said Tony, 'magnifies the image – and magnifies the problems.'

As the camera goes in close, so any movement is exaggerated. A tripod is crucial and is used by 99 per cent of the professionals, whatever the weather.

Tony Wharton is a Fellow of the Royal Photographic Society, a member of the RPS Distinctions Panel in Nature and a full-time professional, so he should know.

Owners of tripods were by now pulling them out from cases. Putting up a Benbo tripod, the first favourite of most pros, has been described as 'like wrestling with a set of demented bagpipes'. Tripods are awkward things, being heavy to carry, and all unwieldy legs and finger-pinching joints. But once the camera is fixed securely, something magical happens. You start to think about the picture: its composition, place in the frame, suitability of background. Tripods slow you down, make you take your time. And you end up with a better picture.

We looked again at the lovely spread of bloody cranesbill.

'Choose a flower that is sheltered from the worst of the wind. Pick a "typical" specimen, but one in as near perfect condition as you can find,' said Tony.

'There is a "law"', he added, 'which guarantees that a better specimen always turns up a couple of yards further on and after you've taken the photograph!'

'Move around, try different viewpoints, different perspectives.'

After the showers of the morning, flowers looked fresh and cool and 'dewy'. I focused on a specimen facing into the light and sheltered from the wind by a sturdy tree trunk. Raindrops glistened on the deeply-cut leaves and satin-like petals. The colour was not blood-red at all, but a

bright magenta-pink. Radiating veins on the petals lead nectar-seeking bees to the bright yellow stamens in the centre.

The light was about right. Bright sunlight casts harsh shadows, which is why professional photographers avoid the midday sun. Even a dull or hazy day is to be preferred. Diffused hazy sunlight often gives the best results. Alternatively, for good texture and soft shadows, take photographs in the early morning or late afternoon.

Format? Most of us were holding our cameras at the horizontal, but 'Don't forget the vertical,' said Tony. 'Often the best format when photographing flowers.'

I hastily turned my camera round: an Olympus 35 mm SLR OM20 camera with a 90 mm Tamron tele-macro lens for close-up. The film I was using was Kodachrome 64. The automatic meter read: f.8 at 1/30. What did Tony think?

The dark background (he said) is biasing the reading. Underexpose slightly for punchy colour and fine detail.

There is never any guarantee that the exposure given by through-the-lens (TTL) automatic metering is correct for every occasion. A TTL meter is not geared to cope with all possible light conditions, but rather to give the reading for an 'average' tonality scene. If you follow the meter reading slavishly, the picture can be either under or overexposed in a high contrast close-up situation. A professional must know how and when to interpret meter readings, and learn to compensate by exercising manual control.

'Learn to think in "stops",' said Tony.

Bright flower against a dark background – stop down. Dark flower against a bright background – open up.

Thinking in stops requires an understanding of basics: the secret of getting quality pictures. Stopping down, by going to a smaller f.stop, reduces the amount of light reaching the film. Opening up does just the opposite. A stop is defined as a doubling or halving of the exposure value.

Check the TTL meter reading by focusing the camera on a middle-tone area. A mid-brown camera bag will do, or a patch of grass, a tree trunk, a stone wall, anything as long as it is 'mid-tone' and in the same light as the subject. Use the palm of your hand: depending on your skin colour, your palm is probably one stop brighter than a middle tone, so take a reading and open up one stop. Or buy a purpose-made grey card from your photography shop and pack it with the rest of your equipment, as Tony himself does.

Placing his grey card next to the flower, Tony first focused on the cranesbill, using my camera.

He took a reading, then moved the camera to point at the grey card and read the meter again. He stopped down one stop, as it 'told' him to do. Now the camera was set manually at the correct exposure for the bright flower.

'For maximum depth of field get square on,' he reminded. 'And don't forget to use your preview button.'

Many cameras possess a preview button: invaluable for close-up photography. A preview button permits you to see how much of the subject will be in sharp focus in the final shot. It usefully highlights any distractions in the background: cigarette ends, small white pebbles, plastic bags, ring-pulls...

I flicked away a dead leaf and tugged at a shiny blade of grass. There, that was enough. Mustn't overdo the 'gardening'. To get 'square on' I had to kneel on the wet grass. ('Proper photographers must expect green knees.') Focusing on the yellow stamens, I aligned the flower with the back of the camera so that the two were parallel.

'Learn to anticipate that split second when the wind drops and the flower is still,' said Tony, 'even if it means waiting until next Thursday. Then – shoot!'

Malham Tarn Field Centre stands at an altitude of 366 m (1,200 ft) in the Yorkshire Dales National Park. Malham House itself, made famous by Charles Kingsley and his *Water Babies* (published in 1863), was leased from the National Trust by the Field Studies Council in 1947, along with some 160 ha (400 acres) of land. The Pennine Way passes close by and continues through magnificent limestone scenery: miles of soft green uplands, criss-crossed with grey stone walls and dotted with ancient stone barns. The lawn in front of the field centre slopes down to the tarn. Within walking distance are the famous landscape features of Malham Cove and Gordale Scar.

Old hay meadows in limestone country are a mecca for botanists and for wild flower photographers. Fairy flax, marjoram, wood cranesbill, rock rose, salad burnet, horseshoe

Above: *Otter country*

Right: *Vole in the hand*

Above: *The dormouse is asleep again*

Left: *Small mammal trapping at Nettlecombe*

Right: *The legally protected great-crested newt*

Left: *Plant dyestuffs simmering in the pan*

Right: *Common heather and gorse*

Below: *Lovely soft colours, wool dyed with natural dyes*

Right: *Broad Haven Youth Hostel*

Left: *Spiders, bugs and beetles tumbled down into the beating tray*

Right: *Iron pyrite (fool's gold) on a fossil bivalve.*

Above: *Artic terns bear sand eel gifts*   **Below:** *Rotund little puffins*

G.R.HERICKX

vetch, sheep's fescue, milkwort, birdseye primrose, pyramidal orchid....

Where the flat surface of exposed limestone has become eroded and dissected along vertical lines then limestone pavements occur: weathered blocks (clints) separated by deep fissures (grykes). The tops of the clints are usually bare. But hidden away in the grykes, wherever a little soil has accumulated, are such flowers as baneberry, rock hutchinsia, wall whitlow grass, rue-leaved saxifrage, burnet saxifrage, slender bedstraw and small scabious.

In moister places on the moors grow globe flower, grass of Parnassus, great burnet, saw wort, melancholy thistle, water avens, birdseye primrose and Jacob's ladder.

Trees are predominantly ash, and ash woods in the dales are the habitat of herb Paris, giant bellflower, lady's mantle, monkshood, lily of the valley and Solomon's seal.

Spring sandwort and mountain pansy are the specialities of old abandoned lead mines....

But in one short weekend of instruction in close-up camera technique, there would be little time for botanizing expeditions. Besides, there were flowers enough on the doorstep.

Below the field centre the limy waters of the natural spring-fed tarn are fringed by fen, mire and raised peat bog. The tarn itself is of great interest. There is no other comparable lake in the uplands of Britain. Limestone is normally porous, allowing water to seep through, which is why so many streams in the Craven district disappear underground into water sinks and swallow-holes: a characteristic of limestone. But the shallow basin of Malham Tarn is lined with non-porous slate, marine muds laid down 440 million years ago.

We followed the path down from Miss Hilary's Cottage, through alder and willow carr, yellow iris, purple moor grass, tussock sedge, to Tarn Moss, ticking off meadowsweet and marsh valerian. The path led to the peat bog: a soggy sponge of accumulated sphagnum moss that had developed on a site originally occupied by open water; the Tarn was once twice the size it is today.

Over the centuries, human interference – peat cutting and drainage – has altered large areas of this acid peat bog. In 1791 the level of the Tarn was raised by 1.2 m (4 ft) north of the inflow stream, flooding the surface with base-rich water so that the soil and associated vegetation changed from bog to fen.

Earlier this century, drains were cut and regular burning was introduced to dry out part of the bog. The purpose was to increase the growth of young heather, an attempt to turn peatbog into grouse moor.

A boardwalk led across the remaining peatbog and we were soon kneeling on the slats and photographing the specialized bog flowers: common sundew and bog asphodel.

Common (or round-leaved) sundew is a carnivorous plant. Its roots are too short to make contact with the limestone-rich ground-water beneath the peat and there is little nutrient in rain water. So the sundew has adapted to living in a low-nutrient habitat by trapping tiny insects like midges, gnats and thrips. A small spike of closed white flowers grows on a single stalk from the leaf rosette. Tiny red hairs on the spatulate leaves glisten as if beaded with dew; these hairs are sticky, and turn inwards at a touch to trap and ingest the living protein.

Bog asphodel has flowers like small stars: six yellow petals and crimson-red anthers. The stem rises from a flattened fan of sword-shaped leaves.

'Think the picture through before you take it,' Tony reminded. 'Decide on lens and viewpoint. Plan the composition. Get in really close for maximum effect. And take your time.'

I changed to a wide-angle 24 mm lens. A wide-angle lens matches the plant to its surroundings: a picture with a background spread; a 'habitat shot'. Click! Click!

The lovely marsh cinquefoil in its peaty pool made another tempting subject with its narrow, sultry purple petals and broader maroon sepals. By using my 200 mm lens, I could isolate the flower, throwing the cluttered background out of focus. But there was insufficient light for this demanding lens. The wind was blowing across the peaty pool, rippling the water, and I changed back to the more accommodating 90 mm macro.

Tony was using flash. He was stalking a very active beetle with a flash gun attached to his camera. Insect photography is where electronic flash comes into its own.

'It's next to impossible to get cracking results of an active insect without flash,' he said. 'Move in slowly with your camera, then fire the minute the insect is in focus...'

Click!

Tony uses a single, small flash gun on a 'butterfly bracket' positioned 10 cm (4 in) above the filter ring. He designed the bracket himself, angling it to light the insect from above. The speed of the flash – about 1/1000 of a second – effectively freezes both subject and camera movement. To soften shadows, he will sometimes use a smaller 'fill in' flash with a slave unit on a second bracket fixed to one side of the camera.

'It's essential to run a series of tests before you start,' said Tony. 'Position your flash, shoot using each f.-stop in turn, and write down what you've done. When the film comes back from the processors, you will see which shot is best. Jot down details on the back of the camera body so that you don't forget,' he said. 'You want to be able to control and repeat your successes, and you can only do that if you run tests and keep records.'

Cameras are as idiosyncratic as their owners. Everyone has to get to know their own model, its quirks and eccentricities.

Tony first became interested in photography when he took up angling as a young man and wanted pictures of his catch. It wasn't long before he was 'hooked' himself. His pictures were soon winning prizes and earning him money. After some years, he was able to take early retirement from his position as deputy headmaster to work full time as a professional photographer. He now runs courses, workshops and phototours to places as far away as India, Kenya and the Falkland Islands.

By now we were repeating to ourselves, as if learned by rote: 'The smaller the lens aperture, the greater the depth of field. The larger the aperture, the shallower the depth of field.'

Depth of field? The amount that looks sharp in a photograph from near to far. In close-up work, magnification increases and depth of field decreases. Focus is critical.

We had been invited to bring a selection of our own slides for an evening workshop of comment and (positive) criticism.

'Try reflecting light into the flower by using silver tinfoil...'

'On a dull day, you can balance daylight with flash to add a little sparkle...'

'Remember the "rule of thirds" and avoid placing your subject dead centre in the frame.'

Malham House and Tarn

'A backlit shot can be very effective on a strong-sun day – but give a little extra exposure for detail on the shadow side...'

'A lens hood would have cut down that glare... '

'If you want to use daylight, not flash, shoot insects early in the day, before they've had time to warm up and become mobile. Look for comatose butterflies in long grass, or dragonflies on reed stems... '

On the last morning we were dodging showers again as we investigated the old stone walls around the house: biting stonecrop, ivy-leaved toadflax, and pretty mosses and lichens. Then the weather brightened and we walked up into the limestone hills. Rabbits hopped away and disappeared into holes. A wheatear flicked its white-patched tail and called '*Wheet*, chack-chack' from an old field wall: skylark song, meadow pipits flitting among the boulders, calling curlew.

On the sheep-grazed, rabbit-nibbled sward grew wild thyme, harebells, birdsfoot trefoil and tormentil.

Moving in close with our cameras, thinking in stops, considering depth of field, we 'got down' to it.

CHAPTER EIGHTEEN

Into the Heather Again

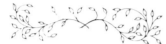

THE NATURAL HISTORY OF THE SOUTH-EASTERN HEATHS

John Sankey

•

Juniper Hall Field Centre,
Dorking, Surrey

THROUGH COPSE and spinney marched Bear; down open slopes of gorse and heather, over rocky beds of streams, up steep banks of sandstone into the heather again.

(A. A. Milne, *Winnie-the-Pooh*, Methuen, 1926)

It wasn't very long ago that Pooh Bear's heathery haven in Ashdown Forest was threatened with development. A. A. Milne fans rose up in protest and heaved a collective sigh of relief when the Sussex heath was given a last-minute reprieve. It was here, on a bridge, that Pooh Sticks was first played; that Tigger was taken to be Unbounced; that Pooh fell into a gorse bush. And it was here that Traps were dug for Heffalumps.

John Sankey, who lives with the heath on his doorstep, introduced me to my first Heffalump Trap; for however John may have explained it otherwise, 'I Knew Better'. John's Heffalump Trap was not on a Sussex heath, but in Surrey.

John retired in 1978 after two decades as warden of Juniper Hall. He still directs courses and we had joined him on an Expotition (as Pooh would have called it) to Thursley Common: home of the silver-studded blue butterfly, emperor moth, small red damselfly, raft spider and others of Rabbit's rarer friends-and-relations.

The heath in late summer is a glorious patchwork of misty pink and purple heathers. In a peace broken only by the chirrup of meadow pipits and the humming of insects on the wing, we followed the winding paths and began to look more closely at the three different kinds of heather.

Ling (common heather) dominates, with its spikes of tiny, pale pink flowers, each flower with four separate petals and four longer sepals, and tiny leaves in opposite pairs.

Bell heather and cross-leaved heath have sepals that are shorter than the petals, and joined to form a pendulous bell. Bell heather, with crimson-purple petals and hairless leaves bunched in whorls, is confined to the drier parts of the heath. Cross-leaved heath – rose-pink flowers and leaves in fours forming a cross at each node – grows in the wet.

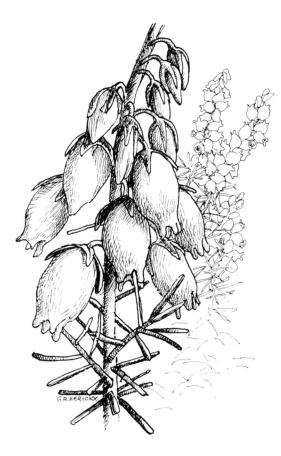

'Bell heather,' said John, 'is special to Britain, a rarity on most of the continent. If you want to give your European botanist friends a treat, introduce them to bell heather. It will send them into raptures.'

Heather is scratchy stuff to picnic in and it makes an uncomfortable bed for lovers. It offers no shelter in a sudden shower or shade on a blazing hot day. It is too prickly for sunbathing and not much good for playing French cricket on.

But people seek out a heath for the sense of solitude and space they crave, and for the beauty of its sea of purple petals in late summer. And heathland is home to certain animals that prefer it to any other habitat.

The Dartford warbler, woodlark, stone curlew and nightjar are birds of the heath. So, to a lesser extent, are hobby, grasshopper warbler, linnet, tree pipit, whitethroat and nightingale.

A shiny black beetle scurried across our track. Could it be Small? Short for Very Small Beetle? Last seen heading round a gorse bush? Rabbit, remember, Organized a Search. Pooh (a Bear of Very Little Brain) had asked him anxiously, 'Is Small the sort of friend – and – relation who settles on one's nose, or gets trodden on by mistake?' But Rabbit, as usual, was much too busy to reply.

Grasshoppers churred in the heather and leapt giddily high. Ants' nests were alive with frenzied worker ants scurrying to and fro, repairing elaborate stick-pile mounds. Spiders spun webs in a twiggy jungle. Honeybees buzzed, enjoying the sweet nectar and storing pollen away for Pooh's 14 (or was it 15?) pots of honey.

Gorse blossomed a cheerful yellow. Dwarf gorse was taking over from the common gorse, keeping, as they say, 'kissing in season'.

'A gorse bush,' said Pooh, 'is a sort of Surprise. Like an Ambush.' One had sprung out suddenly at him once when he fell from a tree and it had taken him six days to remove the prickles from his fur.

On sandy verges grew tormentil, heath bedstraw, sheep's sorrel, bristle bent, wavy hair grass and pixie-cup lichens. 'You have to be up early to see the pixies,' said John.

A beetle scuttled across the track

The warm, sandy verges are of importance to a number of heat-dependent insects. A solitary female digger wasp, striped yellow and black, hovered on fanning wings above the hole she had made in the sand. She zooms out across the heather to hunt down a small moth caterpillar, or perhaps a fly or other insect, paralysing it with her sting and dragging it back into the hole. Then she lays her egg on or near the still living, but paralysed prey. This is fresh food for the emerging wasp larva to feast upon and so the life-cycle continues.

We were walking through bracken now towards a windbreak of pines. Scots pines, with their distinctive orange-tinged trunks, were probably introduced to Thursley Common in the nineteenth century. Conifers make good shelter belts, but are very invasive. Beyond the pines, on sandy ground in another stretch of bracken, was the Heffalump Trap.

John said that the Very Deep Pit was a 'foxhole' left over from the Second World War – and John has Brain.

'You can read the history of the heathland by the different coloured layers in the soil profile,' he said.

And we all got down on our knees to examine the exposed walls of the pit.

Each layer (horizon) of soil is different in its chemical make-up from the others. The topsoil on the surface was a peaty brown.

'Rotting vegetation,' said John. 'Pine needles can take a long time to break down into spongy humus.'

The second layer was drained and impoverished where the rain had percolated through, leaching away all the minerals. So impoverished was the soil that sand grains had bleached to a pale ash-grey. This was the 'podsol' horizon: typical of a heathland soil profile. ('*Pod*' is the Russian for ash; '*sol*' = under.)

The hard black layer directly beneath was composed of compacted deposits of humus washed down from the surface. Then came a red-stained, impervious 'pan' layer rich in iron salts, followed by a layer of orange-brown soil. And below that was the basic, little altered, sandstone rock.

The story of heathlands can be read in the pollen grains preserved in peat bogs.

Much of Britain was covered with forest up to 8,000 years ago. Bog pollen tells us when the first farmers began to arrive to cultivate the land; pollen of arable weeds began to replace the pollen of elm and hazel, the dominant trees.

Farmers would clear a space for their animals and crops by burning. They felled the trees with flint axes. These early agriculturists probably sought out the lightest, sandiest soils, easiest to work with their primitive stone scratch-ploughs. But once the trees had been felled, the fertility of such poor acidic soils was quickly exhausted, for the deep roots of trees bring nutrients to the surface after rain and falling leaves rot down into a rich humus. Many of those early clearings were very soon abandoned. With no nutrients left in the sandy ground, the farmers had to move on in search of more fertile land.

And heather, probably confined to riverbanks, sand dunes and cliff edges, began to move in and colonize the bare, empty spaces.

'A mesolithic botanist would have done a dance,' said John, 'to see the spread of heather. At that time heather must have been a very rare plant.'

We were getting hungry. It was midday. The heat from the sun directly overhead was intense. It was time for a little Smackerel of something. Dragonflies darted to and fro across the bright green sphagnum moss of a small peaty pool: purple moor grass, bog cotton grass, bottle sedge, beaked sedge, round-leaved and long-leaved sundew, and bog asphodel with orange seedheads.

Thursley Common is now a National Nature Reserve. During the Second World War it was taken over by the army for manoeuvres and held for some years after. The heavy tanks wrought much destruction at the time and the vegetation suffered. But some of the rutted tracks left behind by the vehicles evolved into useful boggy ponds, attractive to dragonflies. With a little encouragement from local naturalists, army engineers have since dynamited more ponds and, to date, 26 dragonfly species have been recorded breeding.

We drove to Frensham Common, an SSSI. Small flocks of meadow pipits were on the move. A skylark chirruped and flew up in front of us. Yellowhammers wheezed from the tops of gorse bushes. Linnets twittered from the heather.

Clumps of Scots pines lined the path. In among the pine needles were larvae of pine sawflies, the favourite food of woodpeckers. The black-spotted larvae with yellow legs stood on end and waved their 'tails' in threat as we parted the needles. Pine bark riddled with holes showed where longhorn beetles had bored tunnels out of the wood.

(Was there a Spotted or Herbaceous Backson anywhere about? Pooh would have asked.)

Sharp taps with a stick on the branches of pine and birch sent thrips, spiders, bugs, beetles

Juniper Hall Field Centre

and a bush cricket tumbling down into an umbrella-like cloth 'beating tray'.

Meanwhile, John was sweeping his net from side to side across the tops of the heather: froghoppers, weevils and grasshoppers. Two ladybirds were identified as the eyed ladybird, *Anatis ocellata*, and the hieroglyphic ladybird, *Coccinella hieroglyphica*.

The eyed ladybird, a Scots pine specialist, has black spots ringed with cream on its russet-red wing-cases (elytra). Comma-shaped black markings on bronze is diagnostic of the hieroglyphic, a ladybird specific to heather.

Running parallel with John Sankey's 'Heathland' course was a 'Ladybird' course led by Dr Michael Majerus. So, back at Juniper Hall, we reported our ladybird findings.

Ladybirds are small beetles. Brightly coloured and patterned members of the Coccinellidae family. In two days, by visiting a variety of Surrey habitats, Michael and his group managed to record 20 out of the 24 ladybird species on the British list.

Michael became a 'ladybird man' quite by accident. As a research worker at the Department of Genetics, University of Cambridge, he became very interested in the 2-spot ladybird, *Adalia bi-punctata*, a difficult ladybird to rear. He fed it pea aphids cultured on broad beans and soon his 2-spots were laying lots of eggs.

'I realized that there was an awful lot I didn't know about ladybirds,' he told us. 'Where do they live? What do they do? Where do they all go in winter time? The reference library couldn't help me. There was surprisingly little ladybird literature, in spite of their attractiveness and place in nursery lore.'

Michael put out an appeal for information on the *Today* programme and on John Craven's *News Round*. Before the week was out, 600 letters had arrived on his desk. Such enthusiasm encouraged him to launch the Cambridge Ladybird Survey and he recruited a nationwide network of amateur recorders. The oldest was 97 years old, the youngest, just 3 years. Some of the students on his Juniper Hall weekend were participants in the Survey, now into its second decade.

With the help of the data collected by his surveyors, Michael Majerus, with Peter Kearns, wrote *Ladybirds*, published in 1989 by Richmond Publishing in their Naturalists' Handbook series.

John Sankey at The Very Deep Pit

Not all ladybirds are bright red with black spots, as so many people think. Ladybirds can be yellow, cream, orange and brown. The markings on the wings can be separate, fused, round, squarish, striped, even plain. Most ladybirds are carnivorous, the gardener's friend. Natural pest controllers, ladybirds in your garden feed on scale insects and aphids. But there are three species that feed by grazing on powdery mildews and one species – the 24-spot – is a true, leaf-eating vegetarian.

With John Sankey we visited more heathland. On the western edge of Headley Heath, limey chalk has pushed up through the acidic sand. It is curious, walking through heather, to suddenly come across flowers of the chalk: old man's beard, dogwood, wild basil, autumn gentian, squinancywort, salad burnet and rock rose.

We climbed Leith Hill, the highest point in south-east England, 294 m (965 ft) above sea level. British Trust for Conservation Volunteers were hard at work on the heathland below, trampling bracken, bulldozing birch and pulling up invasive pine seedlings.

Heaths are disappearing at an alarming rate. Ninety per cent of heathland in Britain has disappeared in the last eighty years. What remains is fragmented. It is the same story all over Europe. (No wonder Eeyore is Gloomy.)

Country people throughout most of history valued the heaths on their doorstep. Commoners plundered the heathland for bracken bedding, bilberries and besoms; raided it for honey, rabbit meat, roof-thatch and firewood; and grazed their sheep on it. Heaths were very much part of the rural economy and managed as such.

But in the eighteenth and nineteenth centuries the passing of the enclosure Acts heralded dramatic changes. A population explosion, and the invention of more efficient agricultural machinery, resulted in the ploughing up of large tracts of lowland heath. More than 800,000 ha (2,000,000 acres) of 'waste' were divided into fields and cultivated.

The twentieth century has seen a further acceleration in the destruction of heathland. Heaths are enriched with chemicals and converted to arable land; quarried for sand, drilled for oil; used by the military; turned into rubbish tips; planted with conifers; and bulldozed and built upon.

Hordes of visitors drive out from London at weekends to enjoy Surrey's remaining heaths. But the result of people pressure is erosion and huge areas have been scraped bare of vegetation.

'Thirty years ago,' said John, 'I stood beside Frensham Little Pond, and listened to the singing of reed and sedge warblers. A nightjar was churring. Natterjacks croaked. There was the buzzing of field crickets. All could be heard from the same spot – and all in one evening. It's unlikely I shall ever be able to repeat the experience.'

Astute and Helpful Action is called for. Fortunately, 80 per cent of remaining heaths have been designated SSSIs. The Ministry of Defence holds 60 per cent of Surrey heathlands. Other landowners are the National Trust, English Nature, Surrey County Council and the Surrey Wildlife Trust.

Heaths were largely created by humans in the first instance. Now their survival depends on humans taking deliberate steps to save them: by cutting, grazing and controlled burning; by creating new bridleways with barriers; by constructing firebreaks; by fencing off vulnerable areas and reseeding.

> 'When you wake up in the morning, Pooh,' said Piglet, 'what's the first thing you say to yourself?'
>
> 'What's for breakfast?' said Pooh. 'What do *you* say, Piglet?'
>
> 'I say, I wonder what's going to happen exciting *today*?' said Piglet.
>
> Pooh nodded thoughtfully.
>
> 'It's the same thing,' he said.
>
> (A. A. Milne, *Winnie-the-Pooh*, Methuen, 1926)

CHAPTER NINETEEN

Kingcombe Magic and Mushrooms

ILLUSTRATING FUNGI
Claire and Kery Dalby

•

The Kingcombe Centre,
Toller Porcorum, Dorset

'IT'S BEEN A POOR YEAR for the mycologist,' said Dr Kery Dalby as we set off with our baskets on an evening fungus foray.

The summer had been long and hot. Mushrooms and toadstools require moist conditions. Would there be any fungi for us to find?

We had little success at first as we walked across the pasture, until we came to a little spring that bubbles up where the greensand meets the clay. There we found milkcaps and Russulas growing in the bracken. And old logs – natural reservoirs of moisture – were sprouting fine crops of brackets and tufts. Back at the Kingcombe Centre, a gourmet dinner had been promised. However, we were not collecting fungi to eat, but to illustrate.

This was the Kingcombe Estate and we were staying in the renovated farm buildings on one small portion of it.

When the 240 ha (600 acres) of estate land went up for auction at Dorchester's Corn Exchange on 15 May 1987, the hall was packed with would-be buyers. Interest was immense, in spite of the ramshackle state of the properties and the remoteness of the site. Nigel Spring, a local biology teacher, was there with his wife Jill to join in the bidding.

'Lot 3, Fisherman's Cottage and adjacent Barns. An attractive collection of buildings in need of sensitive renovation, situated on an idyllic 4 acre [1.6 ha] site close to the River Hooke.'

Nigel put in a bid dangerously close to the ceiling he had set himself, the auctioneer banged the hammer and Lot 3 was his.

The Dorset Trust for Nature Conservation must have breathed a collective sigh of relief. Jill and Nigel Spring had bought the land as private individuals, but Nigel is a council member of the

Trust. Lot 3 was in safe hands. And, at very short notice, sufficient money was raised by Friends of the Trust to acquire a majority of the 15 lots on sale.

Set in a tangle of sunken lanes on the edge of chalk downland, the Kingcombe Estate had been farmed for decades in the old 'traditional' way, using no artificial fertilizers, no chemical pesticides and no mechanical flails or heavy agricultural machinery. Farmer Wallbridge, when offered grant aid to 'improve' his land, is said to have refused it. He died at the age of 94, and the land was parcelled and put up for sale for the first time in 400 years. Ninety-nine per cent of the 240 ha (600 acres) is a scheduled SSSI for the importance of its flora and fauna.

'The forgotten farm,' shouted the media, 'straight out of a Thomas Hardy novel.' 'Remnant of old England.' 'A piece of paradise.' 'Herb-rich meadows.' 'A butterfly bonanza.'

It's been a poor year for the mycologist

Jill was to write later in *The Kingcombe Kitchen*:

Here we have a unique place. There is a special atmosphere, a quality that is beyond description, which has captured the imaginations of so many. It is something which goes back further than the environmental aspect. The flowers, insects, birds and traditional agricultural setting are merely embroidery. It is an energy, founded in the land itself and nurtured by the people who have worked that land.

Their dream was to convert the derelict farm buildings into a residential field centre. But the problems were immense. The renovation would cost a great deal of money. The buildings were in a far worse condition than they had realized. Bales of hay served as stairs in the cottage. The ramshackle barns were full of rotting hay. The only recent occupants had been cattle and sheep, and the floors were hard-packed with mud and dung.

Fisherman's Cottage collapsed as soon as repairs began on a cracked wall. It was rebuilt as an exact replica and linked by passageway to the large barn. It proved a hard slog to get the property into good shape in time for the planned opening date, but the Springs managed it. A year on from the sale, the centre – converted with impeccable taste – was welcoming guests.

I was shown into a neat little bedroom in what had been the old cowshed. It looked out on to the smallholding with ducks, geese, hens, Jacob sheep, shorthorn cows and Tamworth pigs, which woke me in the mornings with their grunting.

The spacious barn serves as dining room, lecture hall, work room and studio. It is light and airy with white-washed walls, a quarry-tiled floor, Laura Ashley curtains, original watercolour paintings, baskets of fruit and pedestal vases of flowers.

The 'Illustrating Fungi' course was tutored by Kery and Claire Dalby, a husband-and-wife team.

Botanical illustration – they explain – requires an understanding best achieved by close collaboration between botanist and artist. Kery is a professional botanist and lecturer at Imperial College, London. Claire is a highly talented artist: an elected member of both the Royal Watercolour Society and the Royal Society of Painters and Printmakers.

Kery rose early the next morning. It had

Neat little bedrooms in the converted cowshed

rained in the night, fungi had 'mushroomed', and he was able to bring back more specimens from the meadow: puffballs, fairy clubs, ceps, a fly agaric toadstool – and a stinkhorn still at the bud stage. (Later it was to smell so vile that we had to banish it from the barn.)

After breakfast, we got to work.

'It is important to emphasize,' said Claire, 'that there is no "one way" to draw a toadstool: but many different ways.'

This weekend we'd concentrate on the true-to-life, naturalistic approach. First we'd need to know something of fungal structure and biology. And this was where Kery came in.

A fungus (Kery told us) for most of the year lives an underground life in the form of minute hair-like threads (hyphae). These develop into a cobweb-like net called the mycelium. Lacking chlorophyll, and so differing from other plants, the mycelium draws sustenance from decomposing plant and animal matter.

When conditions are right – humidity, temperature, light – the hyphal threads meet and knot together to form a tiny knob, often button-shaped, and sometimes wrapped in a membrane (veil) which stretches and tears as the button – with a sudden intake of water – pushes up through the earth to take on the form of a fungal fruiting body. The only purpose of these short-lived mushrooms, toadstools and their like is to shed spores, millions of spores.

'When identifying a toadstool, the position of the veil remnant, however tatty, is of key significance,' said Kery.

The veil can form a 'volva' at the base of the stalk (stipe), or a ring or 'collar' further up. Or it can fragment into flaky scales that stick to the cap.

The spacious barn served as a studio

Also important are the gills. Toadstools may have gills that are crowded – or gills that are well spaced. They can run down the stalk, join it at right angles, curve upwards or hang free. Or a toadstool may not have gills at all, but spongy pores instead.

It was time to start drawing.

'First choose your "victim",' said Claire and we selected the specimen of our choice from the wonderfully diverse collection on the table.

False chanterelle, *Hygrophoropsis aurantiaca*: gills decurrent (running down the stem) and an orange cap shaped like a shallow funnel.

Parasol mushroom, *Lepiota procera*: shaggy brown scales on the cap, felty-brown stem with a frilly ring.

Beefsteak fungus, *Fistulina hepatica*: a dark red bracket fungus that grows on trees and looks like a fillet of raw meat; when you cut it, the flesh 'bleeds' a red sap.

Cep or penny bun, *Boletus edulis*: spongy pores in place of gills, brown cap and a fat stem networked with fine veins.

But, as a novice illustrator, I selected the simplest shape I could find.

A field mushroom, *Agaricus campestris*: domed cap, veil-collar, stout stipe.

'Arrange your victim in a "meaningful" position,' suggested Claire.

With the help of a flower arranger's pinholder and Blu-tack, I tipped the mushroom slightly to reveal the pinkish-brown gills beneath the roughened cap. There! Was that 'meaningful' enough?

But, how to begin? And I looked helplessly at Claire.

She came to my rescue, adjusted the portable lamp to throw light and shadow where it was most useful, took up the pencil and – explaining as she went along – began to draw.

'Outline first: a few tentative lines available for renegotiation.... Sketch in the light and shade.... there's a subtle bit of shadow sneaking in here. Put in the highest highlight – and the lowest lowlight.'

Each tiny fine line and carefully placed dot had a purpose. She checked measurements with a pair of dividers, then picked up the pencil again.

'Emphasize this zigzag stretch-mark... shrunken – as if it hasn't got its teeth in. More shading on the stalk to make it look a solid thing. Darken where the "pelmet" throws a shadow. Delineate the sharp knife-like edge of the gills... beastly close together.... I shan't attempt to draw them individually but just check direction and overall pattern – and go right in.'

Claire paused to consider. She nodded and got to work again.

'We'll make use of this slug bite, a natural way of showing texture and colour of fungus flesh. But we'll "repair" the rain damage, doesn't do to be too literal.'

The secret, she said, is to keep a balance. There's no need to draw every blemish and imperfection, but too much 'repair work' results in a bland, less aesthetically pleasing drawing.

'If the cap is sticky, then show the bit of grass sticking to it to make the point,' she said. 'And

G.R.HERICKX

I'll indicate habitat by drawing in the beech leaf at the base of the stalk.'

An illustrator's task is to decide which aspects 'matter' and which don't, to try to capture the 'essence' of a species, to distinguish between characters that describe the species as a whole and the idiosyncrasies of the individual specimen in front of them. And Claire handed me back my pencil.

In the afternoon Nigel Spring suggested that we might like to accompany him on a walk around his Kingcombe domain. It was beginning to have an autumnal look. Leaves in the hedgerows were streaked orange and yellow. Scarlet hips and haws, ripening blackberries, blue-bloomed sloes and clusters of purple elderberries were all signs of a changing season.

'In midsummer there would be heath-spotted orchids growing in profusion on this slope,' said Nigel. 'And in that sheltered hollow, the small pearl-bordered fritillary scatters her eggs where violets grow. This little stream is the favourite haunt of our kingfisher. And here's a badger path leading to a sett.'

A pied wagtail landed, long tail quivering, then darted to snatch at a fly. A robin sang its wistful little song. Starlings were gathering at pre-roost sites in the tops of trees.

Kery pointed out a specimen of the false deathcap, *Amanita citrina*. This started a discussion on the edibility of fungi. False deathcaps smell of raw potatoes. They are not a lethal species, but nasty-tasting and best avoided. False deathcap can too easily be confused with the deadly poisonous deathcap,

Amanita phalloides.

'Illustrators of fungi bear a heavy responsibility,' said Kery.

Mycophagists – that is, eaters of fungi – rely on the accuracy of botanical drawings if they are to differentiate correctly between the edible and the lethal: 'that do suffocate and strangle the eater'.

We walked back past the renovated Sunnyside Cottage, and past Home Farm, where Farmer Wallbridge and his family had lived. The Dorset Trust owns the major part of the Kingcombe Estate. 'And it is lucky,' said Nigel, 'that the rest of the land has been acquired by landowners sympathetic to nature, determined to farm in the old, gentle, caring way.'

Back in the barn, some of us decided to continue with our pencil drawings. Others switched to painting specimens in monochrome, working with paintbrush and one colour only from the paintbox.

That evening, Kery introduced us to the work of professional artists who have tackled, at some time or other, the conventions of fungi illustration. An assortment of field guides was on display; colour plates varied in technique from the stylized to the decorative. Kery showed us slides from his collection, including examples of Claire's own work, to emphasize the problems and possible solutions.

Toadstools change form as they age, from 'tiny button' beginnings to the faded (often maggot-infested) final stage. Caps, weathered by rain and sun, may change colour. Gills darken or lighten as millions of microscopic spores ripen. Accurate illustrations are almost indispensable to anyone interested in fungi. Not many species have English names. Latin names change frequently as mycologists argue over nomenclature.

In their book *Biological Illustration* (FSC, 1985) the Dalbys write:

> For any drawing to be a success, the artist should always be influenced by the original inspiration or purpose for undertaking the work; the suppressing of one's own exuberance in dwelling on beautiful but perhaps irrelevant detail where this detracts from the aims of the drawing as a whole, but without losing one's enthusiasm for the subject. It is a delicate balance.

Claire is a convert of the 'dry-brush' method of painting: a style favoured by Francis Bauer (1758–1840). Francis and his brother Ferdinand (1756–1826) were born at Feldsburg, in Germany. Their father, Lucas Bauer, was court painter to the Prince of Liechtenstein and both his sons showed an early talent for flower painting.

Ferdinand was the adventurous brother who travelled around the world in search of botanical specimens to paint. Francis stayed at home. His life changed when he visited England around 1790 and met Sir Joseph Banks, the wealthy president of the Royal Society. Banks was, by appointment of King George III, director at Kew. Banks used his own money to subsidize promising botanists and artists. So impressed was he with Francis Bauer's work that he offered the artist a permanent post. Francis stayed on at Kew for 50 contented years. For a time, he tutored Queen Charlotte and her daughter Elizabeth.

The turn of the nineteenth century was an exciting age of botanical discovery. Many new plants were finding their way to England and to Kew. Francis Bauer's beautiful plant portraits can be seen in the Collections. His work is recognized as being scrupulously accurate *and* pleasing to the eye.

To demonstrate Bauer's technique, Claire chose a purple-capped *Russula*. First she mixed a dark undercoat: 'approximating to the colour of the toadstool in its shadows'. Then she drew, with tiny fine lines, using her paintbrush exactly as she had used her pencil and working a small section at a time.

'Keep the palette on your right-hand side,' she

advised, 'and each time you dip your brush in the paint, try out a few strokes first on a spare sheet of paper.'

While the undercoat dried, she mixed a wetter, paler topcoat for the final wash.

'Apply a wet wash. But not so wet that it goes into puddles and dilutes away the early strokes,' Claire warned. 'Make a note of the ingredients of the colours you've mixed in your palette. You may run out and need to mix more. It's an illogical-sounding thing to say, but choose your mistakes before you make them! Some mistakes can't be put right.'

She repeated the whole process – tiny fine lines and a wet wash for the stalk and the gills. The painting was allowed to dry before she added final touches of deeper colour where necessary. We had been advised in advance to bring with us sheets of hot-pressed Aquarelle Arches 185 g, sable brushes size 0, 1, 4 and 6, and colours for our paintbox: raw sienna, alizarin crimson, new gamboge, aureolin, cadmium red and french ultramarine.

Francis Bauer made much use of his microscope. Making careful dissections, he got to grips with detail. So Kery Dalby prepared slides of fungal tissue for us, slicing off vertical sections and mounting the slivers between glass. Hyphal threads, cobwebby veils, powdery spores, all were magnified hugely under the microscope.

The colour of spore prints is often diagnostic when identifying a difficult species, whether white, cream, yellow, purple, pink, brown or black.

To make spore prints, fresh caps of mature toadstools are placed, gill side down, on a sheet of white paper. Each cap is covered with a jamjar to stop it drying out and left for a few hours. The result is a clear spore print of each species.

Claire and Kery had one final challenge to throw at us. 'Make spore prints of your own and mix paint in your palettes to match the spore colour exactly.'

Kingcombe mushrooms – and magic.

CHAPTER TWENTY

Grey Seals of Pembrokeshire

SEAL-WATCHING
Malcolm Cullen

•

Broad Haven Youth Hostel,
Broad Haven, Haverford West, Dyfed

FIVE DAYS AFTER my 'seal-watching' weekend, I was still tweezering gorse prickles from the palms of my hands.

Grey seals come ashore to pup in the months of September and October. Malcolm Cullen, head ranger with the Pembrokeshire National Park Authority knows the local hideaways and where to go for the best views of breeding beaches.

It was mid-October, but on the species-rich cliffs, a few flowers blossomed still: sea campion, sheepsbit scabious, tormentil, wild thyme, toadflax and centaury.

Ivy clung to the ruins of an old stone wall; its flowers, sticky with nectar, had attracted two red admiral butterflies. A late bumblebee buzzed around a foxglove. Crane-flies with ungainly long legs sprawled about the grass.

Malcolm led the way through the bracken and along winding sheep tracks; past purple heather, yellow broom, yellow gorse and tussocks of thrift with a last few pink petals among the papery seedheads.

'Tell me if I'm walking too fast and galloping on ahead,' said our guide, pausing briefly after a steep uphill ascent.

'You're walking too fast and galloping on ahead,' I gasped, out of breath.

From the edge of the cliff above North Haven we looked out on to St Bride's Bay. The coastline stretches in a long U-shaped sweep around the bay and the scenery is dramatic: representing a huge geological time span, with old red sandstones to the south and ancient volcanic Cambrian rocks to the north.

It was a blustery day. The wind was blowing the waves into white crests. On Stack Rocks a cormorant, standing sentinel, took off and flapped low over the water.

Skomer Island was just in view, peeping behind the Marloes headland: a deer park (with no deer) now owned by the National Trust. Skokholm Island was out of sight. Ramsey Island, owned by the Royal Society for the Protection of Birds, lay to the north, off St David's Head.

Dale Fort Field Centre (FSC), a converted Victorian military fortification, has its own sea-going boat. Trips to the Pembrokeshire islands are a regular feature in summer. Thousands of exciting seabirds breed on the cliffs and plateaux: puffins, guillemots, razorbills, kittiwakes, fulmars, manx shearwaters and storm petrels. Grassholm is famed for its gannetry: 32,000 pairs of gannets breed on the remote, uninhabited island.

But by the month of October the majority of birds will have left: to roam the oceans all winter. Many seabirds are long lived and may return year after year to the same island or stretch of coast where they first bred.

If the weather permitted, our weekend itinerary would include a boat trip to Ramsey where nearly half of Pembrokeshire's grey seals are born, the most important seal colony in Wales. Approximately 200 females give birth to 200 pups each year on the rocky beaches and in the deep caves.

We continued along the Pembrokeshire coast path. Gulls fished offshore, dipping into the choppy sea. Grey-wigged jackdaws tumbled and acrobated at the cliff edge: 'Jack, jack, jack,' they called. We listened for the ringing 'chee-ow' of choughs, for they breed along this coast and stay around all year in family groups: glossy-black corvines with red bills and red legs, probing for soil invertebrates in the rough grass of traditional cliff-edge haunts. Marloes, Strumble Head, Bardsey and Ramsey Island are all strongholds for the attractive chough.

No sight or sound of choughs; but Malcolm had stopped at the top of a steep-sided gully. We had reached a grey seal breeding beach. Rocks broke the full force of incoming waves. And three seal pups lay on the shingle at the top of the beach. The smallest and youngest was so newly born that its woolly coat hung in loose folds; stained yellow still with the amniotic fluid from the mother's womb.

The two older pups, with coats of white fur, were as round as barrels. 'I should say, 2 weeks old,' said Malcolm. Seal milk is super-rich, thick and creamy, about 50 per cent fat, and pups put on weight very quickly. (A cow's milk is only 3.5 per cent fat.)

The baby was wailing pitifully, 'Waah, waah': a sound disconcertingly like that of a human baby. It was obviously hungry and began to hump its way down the beach. At the water's edge waves swept over it and we began to feel anxious for its safety. Seal pups can swim from birth, but many die in their first year, dashed against the rocks, drowned – or from malnutrition or disease.

But the pup's mother was paddling offshore and keeping an eye on it. She heard the wailing at the water's edge, sculled smoothly in and worked her way a few metres up the beach. The pup followed. She stroked her baby with a flipper, then rolled over and lay on her side. The pup suckled happily at the teats on her lower abdomen.

The seal cow's wet coat lightened as it dried in the sun. Dappled and blotched, the coat blended with the colours of the shingle: shades of grey, black, brown and silver. She was a hefty animal, 2 m (6.5 ft) long, with an elongated muzzle, stiff bristle-whiskers, bristly eyebrows and large liquid eyes, nostrils on the 'roman nose' almost parallel.

Every 5 to 6 hours the mother comes in to feed her pup and will continue to do so for 16 to 21 days. After that it will have to learn to fend for itself.

As we continued our walk along the top of the cliff we could hear the melancholy sound of seal 'singing' – 'mermaid music' – wafting from below us. It was low tide and, in the exposed oarweed, a cow and a bull seal were coupling: rolling over in the bronze fronds, surfacing and disappearing again beneath the water.

Cows become receptive at about 14 days after the birth of the pup. Before that the bull, patrolling offshore, keeping watch over his territory, is met with hostility: snarls and rude waves of the flipper. As the cow prepares to desert and to leave for the sea, an approach by the bull becomes acceptable.

Pups are normally born in the autumn; but spring pups do occasionally occur in Pembrokeshire.

'Birth takes only a few seconds,' said Malcolm. 'I've watched pups being born in the caves on Ramsey. Look away for a minute – and you miss it!'

The wind was blowing in great gusts towards us and we retreated to find a sheltered spot. A stonechat clicked – 'Chack-chack' – from the bracken. A tiny wren flicked through the brambles, scolding loudly, 'Tik, tik, tik'.

A solitary hiker, heavy rucksack on his back, gave us a nod as he passed by. The 168-mile long Pembrokeshire coast path, marked with an acorn sign, starts on the outskirts of St Dogmaels in the north and follows the coastline, with very few breaks, all the way to Amroth Bay. The wardened Pembrokeshire Coast National Park follows the coast traversing National Trust

Opposite: *We could hear the melancholy sound of seal singing*

property for much of its length. It sweeps inland to enclose the northern heather moors of the Mynydd Preseli and to encircle the estuary of Cleddau to the south.

We walked on and found another rocky cove – and, on the shingle below, a lone, very fat, rotund pup, with matted fur.

'Like a big fat ... *slug*,' said Malcolm.

The sluggish pup stirred, shuffled and began to rub itself against a rock, attempting to rid itself of the itchy baby coat. Patches of darker pelage, the short, coarse fur of the first adult coat, showed through; seals moult annually into a new coat: the females between late autumn and March, and the males between winter and May.

Soon the pup would be teaching itself to catch food: shrimps, crabs and fish. While learning the new skills, it would have to survive on the thick layer of blubber fat.

Malcolm took us to a less inaccessible beach where it would be possible to get a closer view of a seal. By slithering down a sandy slope and dropping the last 2 m (6.5 ft), we reached the beach and took cover behind a boulder. A grey seal pup was outside the cave entrance and we could smell the fishy smell of the breeding cave. But the pup sensed our presence and snarled in our direction. Not wishing to alarm it – or its anxious offshore mother – we retreated and scrambled up the sandy slope to the top.

We were staying at the Broad Haven Youth Hostel. The Youth Hostels Association, founded in 1930, aims to provide simple accommodation close to beautiful countryside for people, especially young people, of limited means. In recent years the YHA has opened several purpose-built field centres and, at some of their traditional hostels, has introduced 'activity' and 'special interest' holidays. Various courses, planned to appeal to all ages, are run by experts in the field.

The award-winning Broad Haven Youth Hostel was specifically designed with disabled people in mind; the wide corridors and doorways are suitable for wheelchairs. Designated a 'superior grade' hostel we expected – and found – better fare than the 'bangers and mash' some of us remember (with a smidgen of nostalgia?) from hostelling days in our youth.

A force 8 gale was blowing next morning, dashing our hopes of getting across to Ramsey. So we went next door to the Pembrokeshire Coast Visitors' Centre, and spent some time browsing among the books and displays, learning more about the grey seals.

Seals are beautifully adapted for life at sea. Fore limbs are paddle-shaped. Webbed hind limbs can be fanned out or fishtailed together to make an efficient sculling instrument. The body is smooth and streamlined for fast swimming and diving: 'stubby torpedo-shaped'.

The stiff hairs of whiskers and eyebrows are sensitive to vibrations. Before each dive, the nostrils close tightly. Oxygen is expelled, the heart rate slows down and blood circulates only to the most vital organs. Seals can stay under water for 30 minutes, although 6 minutes is the more usual duration. The clicking sounds emitted underwater are believed to be used as echolocation like bats.

Seals are long-lived animals, cows of 42 years being known. Age can be estimated in a dead animal by counting the annual growth rings

which are laid down in its canine teeth.

About half of the world population of grey seals breed in British waters: an estimated 92,000. Most colonies are concentrated in the Orkneys, Shetland and Farne Islands, the Isle of May, and the Outer and Inner Hebrides. The breeding colonies of Pembrokeshire hold 2,000 to 3,000 seals (NERC 1986).

Only one other seal species breeds off our shores: the common seal. Smaller size, more uniformly speckled, rounder head, snub nose, V-shaped nostrils almost meeting at the base – these features differentiate the common seal from the grey seal.

But common seals are only rarely seen on the Pembrokeshire coast. Characteristically, they breed on sandbanks and mudflats in the Wash and around the Western Isles of Scotland, particularly the Orkneys. Birth is often at low tide in June and July; common seal pups, only a few hours old, must slip into the sea with their mothers at the next high tide.

Later that day, the rain eased and we drove north: past the 3 km (1.8 miles) of sands at Newgale, through the pretty little harbour village of Solva, to St Davids, the 'smallest city'. A quick look around the cathedral, and we braced ourselves to walk the windswept peninsula with its Iron Age fort and lifeboat station. From the cliff top, the coastal views were spectacular. Across the sound, with its treacherous currents, and out of reach for us today, was Ramsey: Ynys Dewi – David's Island. Legend says that 20,000 saints are buried there.

A few late swallows struggled against the fury of the wind. Swirling flocks of linnets, twittering goldfinches, 'cronk'-ing ravens and the shrill piping of oystercatchers. And, offshore, grey seals were keeping watch over their pups, born on the wind- and sea-eroded secret beaches and caves of Pembrokeshire's lovely cliffs.

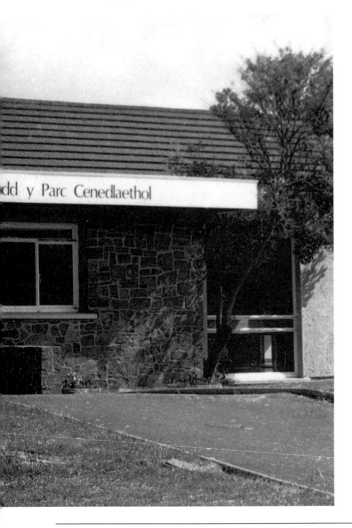

National Park Visitor Centre, Broad Haven

CHAPTER TWENTY–ONE

Catt's Countryside

BOTANIZING IN THE SOUTH HAMS

Martin Catt

•

Slapton Ley Field Centre,
Kingsbridge, Devon

WHEN MARTIN CATT was made redundant from his job as a research scientist at British Aerospace, he was offered a grant to retrain on the government's Business Enterprise Scheme. He had become very interested in natural history over the years and was much involved, in his spare time, with practical conservation work. He decided to do something that perhaps no one had ever done before on such a scheme: to retrain as a field naturalist/tutor.

With his wife and small son, he moved from London, where he had lived all his life, to the small village of East Prawle in South Devon. He made contact with local naturalists and the Field Studies Council gave him tremendous support. Devon County Council were soon making use of his conservation skills, and it wasn't many months before he was being asked to lecture and to lead field outings.

Slapton Ley Field Centre invited him to run week-long courses: 'Wildlife on the South Devon Coast', 'Natural History Afloat on Board the Egremont' and 'Dragonflies and Crickets'. I enquired, but the dates didn't suit. So, hoping for a wild flower rarity or two, I booked into a 'Catt's Countryside' weekend, which promised an emphasis on flowers, based at Martin's own home, Migrants' Rest. Guests stay with Martin and Ann or are found accommodation in the village.

South Devon is gloriously rich in wild flowers. East Prawle is within easy reach of rocky cliffs, estuaries, sand dunes, woodland and, a bit further afield, the acid bogs and granite tors of Dartmoor. Over 600 species of flowering plants have been identified in the South Hams alone. A total of 37 species of butterflies are listed locally and 270 species of birds.

On the first evening we botanized gently in the village lanes: ivy-leaved toadflax, wall pennywort, pineapple weed, crow garlic, wall speedwell, herb Robert, creeping buttercup, English stonecrop, nipplewort and swine cress.

Old stone walls were particularly rewarding: wall pennywort, rue-leaved saxifrage, pellitory-of-the-wall, wall speedwell, minuscule pearlworts (annual, sea, procumbent), tiny trefoils (hop trefoil, black and spotted medick), crucifers (scurvy-grass, swine cress, whitlow grass, hedge mustard), and ferns (rusty-back, wall rue, hart's-tongue, lanceolate spleenwort, maidenhair and southern polypody).

'Where the climate is mild and damp,' said Martin, 'old stone walls are adopted as suitable habitat by plants more normally associated with cliffs and rocky slopes.'

And it was on an old stone wall that we found the great green bush cricket.

The great green bush cricket, *Tettigonia viridissima*, is the largest and noisiest of Britain's ten species of bush cricket. The 'nymph' cricket hatches from the egg and undergoes several skin changes before its emergence as a mature adult. In late summer, the male 'fiddles' to attract the female, a loud harsh sound, like the long reeling of a sewing machine in action. To produce this 'courtship song', the cricket rubs a toothed 'file' on one wing against the 'scraper' on the other. The great green bush cricket is fierce: it will supplement a diet of leaves and fruit by overpowering and consuming insects smaller than itself. But in June the cricket is not yet fully grown. Its long, thread-like antennae were even longer than its green body, but there was no time for a closer look; it leapt skywards and vanished.

G.R.HERICKX

We continued botanizing, adding to our lists. Hedgerow lanes gave us dove's-foot cranesbill, alexander, rough chervil, red campion, stinking iris, dwarf mallow, wood sage, creeping cinquefoil, foxglove, wild madder, red campion, perforate St John's wort, lesser stitchwort, hedge bedstraw, meadow vetchling and common toadflax.

It was beginning to grow dark, time to turn back along Elm Lane, high above Gorah Rocks and the sea. A drinker moth caterpillar walked across the track: a furry caterpillar in a hurry.

'Drinkers always go walkabout before they pupate,' said Martin.

A greater horseshoe bat flickered by.

'Hawking after cockchafers.'

Below East Prawle, the South Devon Coast Path switchbacks from Start Point, via Prawle Point, Gammon Head and Mill Bay to the Salcombe estuary. Much of this wonderful cliff is National Trust land. Walkers on the coastal path enjoy some of the best scenic views in Britain. The rock is of ancient schist: sparkling grey mica and pale green hornblende. Wild flowers grow in profusion: thrift, sea campion, betony, sheep's-bit, birdsfoot trefoil, wild carrot,

Drinker moth caterpillars go walkabout

rock sea spurrey, rock samphire, dodder, sea plantain and bloody cranesbill... which, in his field guide, the Revd William Keble Martin preferred to call the 'blood-red geranium'.

The county of Devon, gloriously rich in wild flowers, was the happy hunting ground of Keble Martin: probably Britain's best-known botanist after Charles Darwin.

As a young man, he'd taken botany as his degree subject at Oxford. After his ordination, he worked for 18 years in the industrial north, served as chaplain to the forces in France in 1918 and, when the First World War ended, moved to Devon. A self-taught artist, he began drawing and painting wild flowers in his spare time. Illustrating flowers further afield involved midweek train journeys and walks on unknown territory. His famous field guide, *The Concise British Flora in Colour* took him 60 years to complete. It was finally published in 1965; he was 88 years old.

'The dedicated and painstaking skill which has gone into each plate in order to ensure complete accuracy in colour and detail will, I am sure, make this book invaluable to both amateur and professional botanists,' wrote the Duke of Edinburgh in the foreword.

Thirty years on, *The Concise British Flora in Colour* (Michael Joseph, 1965, 1991) is still as popular today: named 'the most preferred field guide' in a recent survey by the magazine *British Wildlife*.

Keble Martin wrote:

Botany is an interest that takes us out to the beautiful places of the earth. And if we really know the wild flowers around us at home, the plants almost speak to us of their struggles to grow. This interest stays with us to the end of our pilgrimage.

We decided to make a 'pilgrimage' ourselves next day and to search for one of Keble's rarities: heath lobelia, *Lobelia urens*, a pretty little bellflower with two-lipped blue flowers. It grows on the rough acidic grassland of a nature reserve owned by the Devon Wildlife Trust. In 1954 it was said to be 'too rare to have got itself an English name'. But in Keble's *Flora* he calls it 'blue lobelia'. Today, listed a *Red Data Book* species, it is more commonly known as 'heath lobelia', and survives at only a handful of sites in Britain: more at home on the damp heaths in western France, Spain and Portugal.

Heath lobelia... and heath spotted orchid, zigzag clover and perforate St John's wort. And yellow bartsia! Another *Red Data Book* species. *Parentucellia viscosa*: stickily hairy and semi-parasitic on the roots of other species.

The RSNC Wildlife Trusts Partnership lists 300 plus wild plants in its *Red Data Book* that are considered to be 'endangered' or 'threatened with extinction'.

Some flowers, Keble Martin pointed out, become endangered because of the misbehaviour of botanists. He did his best to persuade people not to pick flowers, but to preserve rare and interesting species on site for future generations.

'Gathering the flower prevents the casting of

seed,' he wrote. 'Real botanists understand this.'

We were leaving heath grassland now and approaching marsh. We found more flowers to 'tick off': early marsh orchid, southern marsh orchid, marsh bedstraw, marsh pennywort, marsh thistle, marsh woundwort, wild angelica and narrow leaved hempnettle.

A scarlet tiger moth, *Callimorpha dominula*, spun across the sunlit bracken. It settled on a frond and closed its cream-spotted, dark green fore-wings – concealing the gaudy scarlet hind-wings so conspicuous in flight and allowing the moth to merge into its sun-speckled background.

Now a golden-ringed dragonfly, *Cordulegaster boltonii*, zipped past and landed on a sorrel leaf. It had strong yellow ring markings on a black body, huge green eyes, and is Britain's largest insect: wingspan 100 mm (4 in), body length 84 mm (3.3 in).

Marsh changed to woodland: twayblade, broad-leaved helleborine, enchanter's nightshade, yellow pimpernel, square-stalked St John's wort and butterfly orchid.

A nuthatch was calling – 'Seet, seet, seet' – from the branches of a downy birch. Ringlet butterflies wavered over the grasses. And small puncture holes in alder buckthorn were signs that brimstone caterpillars were at home.

In a pond dug by young WATCH members, water crowfoot was in flower. Conservationists had felled trees to create a woodland glade: an attempt to bring back fritillary butterflies. If the violet seeds lying dormant at bracken edges could be encouraged to germinate again, the butterflies might return; violets are the food plant of most fritillary caterpillars.

On the way back to East Prawle, we stopped on the Kingsbridge estuary; not really an estuary at all, but a flooded valley (or ria) created when the ice melted on surrounding hills some 10,000 years ago.

It was low tide. Fish were jumping in the shallows. Wildfowl and waders fed in the narrow winding creeks. Shelduck paddled on the mudflats, swooshing their red bills to filter-feed for tiny *Hydrobia* snails. Four mute swans sailed by. A heron stalked, long neck jerking out and back, dagger-bill poised to strike.

As we watched, a fox came running along the foreshore opposite. It nosed about in the flotsam of the tideline, scratching through the seaweed and washed-up debris; then grabbed some edible morsel and ran off with it into the wood.

A large bird of prey had settled, half hidden, hunched up, on a stump. What could it be? Sparrowhawk, owl.... osprey, even? Three crows arrived to mob it and the mystery bird took to flight.... 'An abnormally pale buzzard,' decided Martin.

A flock of 30 black-headed gulls in full summer plumage, preening and drinking at a stream, proved another puzzle.

'Black-headed gulls don't breed in Devon,' said Martin, 'so what are they doing here? At this time of the year?'

He feared some disaster had struck at their breeding ground further north. Or perhaps they

had bred exceptionally early, raised their young and were already moving south.

But, it was time to get back to botanizing and two more *Red Data Book* plants: Italian cuckoo pint, *Arum italicum*, and balm-leaved figwort, *Scrophularia scorodonia*. Both grew in the undergrowth of a ditch beside the road at this point: a grotty roadside habitat for such very uncommon species, and known to Keble Martin.

We stopped at Slapton for flowers of the shingle: yellow horned poppy, sea spurge, sea campion, thrift, musk thistle, ribwort plantain, buckshorn plantain, sea beet, viper's bugloss and rest harrow.

The 3 km (1.8 mile) shingle ridge stretches from Torcross to Strete Gate, separating Slapton Ley and the sea. Where the pebbles meet the thin sandy, turf verge, small stabilizing annuals have moved in.

'Great for interesting clovers,' said Martin, getting down on to his knees.

Haresfoot clover, knotted clover, rough clover, clustered clover, dwarf clover: it was a botanist's paradise.

Birdwatchers were lining up with their telescopes, not to watch us (although no doubt we looked a little odd, on our knees, noses to the ground, looking for clovers), but to count scoters drifting across the bay. 'Rafts' of the black sea ducks bobbed up and down on the waves. Two hundred scoters? Three hundred?

We had time only for a cursory look at the Ley, the largest natural freshwater lake in south-west England. A nature trail open to the public leads past reedbeds, scrub and woodland. Certain vulnerable areas are closed, used by the Slapton Ley Field Centre for teaching purposes.

After dinner that night we went bat-watching.

Martin drove to a high-banked lane and parked beside a haystack. Ancient Devon lanes, over hundreds of years, gradually sink below the level of the surrounding fields. Sheltered and warm, they attract night-flying insects. Car headlights picked up moths, beetles and gnats. 'Bat grub,' said Martin.

With the windows open, he switched on the bat detector. Clicks, burps, buzzings and cracklings: noises like radio interference. Bats were on the wing, homing in on their prey.

Pipistrelles, in fluttery flight, twisted and swooped between the hedge banks. Silhouetted against the sky, a bat with long, narrow wings was flying high and fast; it spun into a dive and skimmed along the lane activating loud, clear sizzlings from Martin's bat detector.

'Fish-'n-chip shop sizzling. Probably a noctule.'

Noctules are often the earliest bats to appear, emerging from tree-hole roosts, chasing larger insects, scooping them up in the membranous tail and eating their catch on the wing. They are high-flying bats that hawk with the swifts on balmy summer evenings.

We saw more noctules, more pipistrelles and a 'possible' whiskered.

Next day, on an outcrop of the Torbay limestones at Orleigh Common, we listed lime-loving calcicoles: wild privet, spindle, wayfaring, traveller's joy, salad burnet, fairy flax, wild strawberry, marjoram, wild basil, thyme, rough chervil, burnet saxifrage, nodding thistle, hay rattle, common gromwell, hemp agrimony, dropwort and pyramidal orchid. And little-robin, *Geranium purpureum*: a *Red Data Book* species and another of the Revd W. Keble Martin's discoveries.

It is easy to overlook little-robin – teasingly similar to a very common geranium: herb Robert. Martin pointed out its smaller size and the bright yellow pollen – as distinct from orange – on the stamens. Little-robin grows at only a very few sites in Britain, usually close to the sea on fertile, calcium-rich soil.

We went on to another habitat: Avon Woods, north of Kingsbridge. This was the first wood to be owned by the Woodland Trust.

'Everyone should make an annual pilgrimage to Avon Woods,' said Martin, 'to do homage to Kenneth Watkins.'

When Avon Woods went up for sale in 1970, the Devon Wildlife Trust would have dearly liked to purchase the land but had insufficient funds. Kenneth Watkins, a local man, single-handedly sought donations from local people. He raised the money, bought the 40 ha (98 acres) and opened the wood up for everyone to enjoy.

Enthused by his success, Kenneth went on to found the Woodland Trust, one of the fastest growing conservation societies ever. Today the trust owns and manages more than 500 woods, many of them ancient woodlands. The policy of informal public access continues.

Avon Woods run alongside the banks of the River Avon for 3 km (1.8 miles). Some of the original coppice still survives. But during the First World War, most of the timber trees were felled. Neglected oak stumps sprouted again, and grew dense and tall. The Woodland Trust has the task of managing the wood in the way that is best for wildlife: the flora and the fauna.

Streams run down the hillside to the river below, where dippers and grey wagtails breed, and otters leave their spraint. The wettest sections of the path are bridged by boardwalks, constructed by British Trust for Conservation Volunteers in conjunction with the South Hams Environment Service.

Spring flowers were over. Midsummer flowers had taken their place: wood speedwell, honeysuckle, water mint, herb Bennet, greater stitchwort, wild valerian, opposite-leaved golden saxifrage, wood spurge, water figwort, tutsan, meadowsweet, crosswort and goldilocks buttercup.

Poised on a willow leaf was a dark green damselfly with metallic-bronze wings: the beautiful demoiselle, *Calopteryx virgo*. Honey bees droned over the hemlock water dropwort. The wasp beetle, *Clytus arietus*, scuttled about pretending it was a wasp; tapping with its antennae in a wasp-like way, the bold yellow stripes on its abdomen a waspy disguise.

We heard the yaffle call of a green woodpecker – and songs of woodland birds: willow warbler, chiffchaff, blackbird, robin, wren and redstart.

Interesting liverworts grew on a wet, slimy rock face. And sprouting from an old log was a fine cluster of oyster mushrooms, shell-shaped and fleshy pink.

'Oyster mushrooms are an expensive luxury at the local Tesco's,' said Martin. 'We'll take these home for supper.'

We were beginning to feel hungry. A cream tea was waiting for us at the converted Loddiswell Station, so we abandoned the wood and walked back along the old railway line: dog rose, common centaury, tufted vetch, knapweed, wild thyme and, another good 'tick', long-stalked cranesbill, *Geranium columbinum*.

The deserted station yard is now a weedy sunspot and extremely attractive to butterflies. Marbled whites – males – flew purposefully over the herbage on the look-out for females emerging from pupae below. Ringlets, small skippers, gatekeepers, common blues and wall browns flitted from flower to flower.

In a southward-facing patch of stinging nettles, caterpillars munched away inside the shelters they construct for themselves. Nettles are the favourite larval food plant of several butterflies: red admiral, small tortoiseshell and peacock. The red admiral lays its eggs singly, each on the upper surface of a different leaf. The caterpillar, when it hatches, makes a leaf tent, spinning the folded leaf edges together with silk. Inside its shelter, it feeds and grows, constructing new tents when necessary, leading a solitary life. Small tortoiseshells and peacocks lay eggs in large batches; emerging caterpillars spin a communal silk web and – a wriggling mass – stay together to feed.

Nibble-holes in the leaves of broad-leaved dock suggested the presence of the caterpillar of a small copper. What made those tears in the leaves of wild hop? Probably a comma caterpillar.

We had a delicious cream tea at the converted station and oyster mushrooms were on the menu for dinner. And we went on a badger watch at a sandy sett where Cetti's warblers flit in and out of willows, bursting intermittently into sudden loud and explosive song: '*Chu*-ti, *chu*-ti, *chu*-ti'.

Common blue butterfly

Martin Catt knows where the rare cirl bunting breeds on the South Hams coast. In spring and autumn, he leads birdwatchers on the 'twitch' for migratory birds to all the best local sites. A committee member of Butterfly Conservation, Martin can guide you to a woodland glade where a colony of the silver-washed fritillary – the largest and most magnificent of our fritillaries – feeds on bramble flowers.

On Monday morning we decided to take one last look at the village pond: marsh ragwort, water figwort, water crowfoot, brooklime, fool's parsley... and – an oddity! Out came the field guide again.

It was knotted hedge parsley, *Torilis nodosa*: a new record for East Prawle!

That would have pleased the Revd W. Keble Martin!

CHAPTER TWENTY–TWO

The Miracle of the Sea Pea

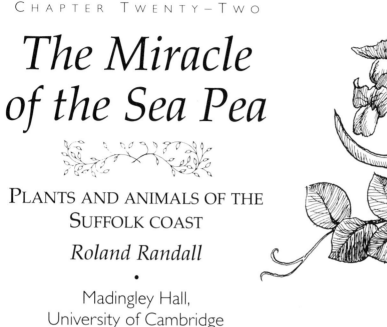

PLANTS AND ANIMALS OF THE SUFFOLK COAST

Roland Randall

•

Madingley Hall,
University of Cambridge

THE SEA PEA, *Lathyrus japonicus*, earned its reputation as a 'miracle plant' in 1555, the year of a disastrous famine. The seeds in their pea-like pods are said to have saved the lives of the hungry people of Suffolk.

An account of the episode appeared in William Camden's book, *Britannia*: 'a chorographical description of the most flourishing Kingdomes of England, Scotland, and Ireland' (published in Latin in 1586). Camden wrote: 'The starving people were very thankful to find a copious supply of edible sea peas at Aldeburgh and regarded the discovery as a miracle.'

The plant still grows on the Orford Shingles. Dr Roland Randall has recorded its presence there every year for the last 30 years.

Buffeted by east winds whipping in from Hollesley Bay, we followed Roland along the bleak shingle ridge.

'It's nearly always blustery at Shingle Street,'

he shouted above the sound of the waves and the wind.

But the sun was shining, and the sea and sky-scape of wide horizons, racing clouds, white crested waves and bobbing boats made Shingle Street an exhilarating place to be. Perhaps it is a miracle that *any* plant manages to survive in the extreme conditions of a bleak pebble beach, we thought as we battled on. Drenched by salt sea spray, dried by winds, bereft of soil and at the mercy of the glaring sun, shingle plants live in one of the most inhospitable habitats on earth – akin to mountain tops and arid deserts. But, somehow, seeds manage to germinate, put down roots and flourish.

Pioneer plants – colonizers of the driftline – make use of the flotsam and jetsam blown in on gales or washed up by waves: scraps of seaweed, fir cones, sea mat, driftwood, cork and dead animal remains. This is all organic detritus that rots down into humus, a useful, moisture-retaining mulch with nourishment enough to support the very specialized first-comers: sea campion, curled dock, yellow horned poppy – and sea pea.

The plants grow, shed their seeds, die and decay. And they, in their turn, are recycled themselves into nutrients for the next lot of colonizers: shrubby seablite, sticky groundsel, yellow vetch, sea beet and Babbington's orache.

Each is adapted in its own way to cope with the harsh conditions. Herb Robert appears in a maritime dwarf form, low and mat-like. Silverweed sends out runners over the shingle surface, its rootlets growing down from nodal points. Sea sandwort has the shape of a tiny Chinese pagoda and its opposite leaves trap

moisture in the spaces between. Maritime scarlet pimpernel produces petals and leaves that are fleshier than the same plant inland. Hoary mullein and yellow horned poppy survive the winter as low rosettes of leaves, then grow tall in late summer and shoot the seeds from popping pods.

Common features are waxy leaves for storing water, fleshy petals, succulent stems, salt-exuding glands, low rosettes, tough cuticles, miniature size and deep roots.

Rather surprisingly, plants with roots sufficiently long have some access to fresh water even on a shingle beach. Rain and dew collect in

Herb Robert in its maritime form

the spaces between the smaller pebbles and roots can reach down to tap this reservoir.

The alternating bands of coarse shingle and fine shingle on a beach help to determine the vegetation patterns. On coarse shingle, seeds often fall too deep for successful germination.

Sea pea was growing on its preferred habitat, a sparsely vegetated shingle ridge. An attractive plant, it blooms from May until August. It has lush, pink-purple petals fading to blue, large, fleshy leaves and woody rootstocks anchoring deep. In late summer, the pea-like seeds of the sea pea burst from their pods and are dispersed by the waves, remaining floating and viable for several years.

'I've seen feral pigeons fly across from Havergate to eat the peas,' said Michael Hall, a local ornithologist. He had come along at Roland's invitation to answer our 'bird' questions. Coincidentally, the entomologist in the group was also named Michael Hall.

Michael (the insect man) was watching the bumblebees that 'bumbled' from one flower to the next along the shore – sturdy, furry 'flying machines.'

'Yet, given the weight to wing-size ratio,' he said, 'any aeronautical engineer might well say that a bumblebee is poorly designed for flight.'

A bumblebee can only fly if its flight muscles are able to reach a certain temperature. The bee basks on sunny surfaces and can warm itself up by shivering its wing muscles. The furry body hair helps to retain heat. Once it has taken off, the act of flying itself generates heat. On each journey the bee must consume enough pollen and nectar to replace the energy it expends in its

foraging; it must also carry back to the underground nest, food for the hungry young.

Britain's 25 species of true bumblebee are all in the genus *Bombus*, meaning 'booming' – and the 'booming' of the bumblebee is a lovely, summery sound. Most species are rather patchily distributed; their range is restricted. Only six species are still widespread and fairly abundant. Fifty per cent of sand dune/saltmarsh/shingle plants are dependent on fertilization by bumblebees and other pollinating insects.

We watched as a bumblebee buzzed to and fro over the sea campion. Landing on a flowerhead, it probed with its tongue after nectar which it stores in its 'honey-stomach' to regurgitate later. Pollen from the anthers sticks to the bee's hairs and, later, it will comb this protein-rich yellow dust into the pollen bags on its legs.

'Sea pea... another clump, over here.'

Today the 'miracle plant' is rare and local. It has retreated from many of its former British haunts. But it is still to be found on certain stretches of shingle in Dorset. And it is present in Kent: in spite of the fact that, in 1937, a Kentish botanist wrote of the plant's 'disappearance' from the county. He claimed that its 'shyness in flowering, and therefore inability to reproduce itself' accounted for its demise. He blamed, too, 'the rapacity of collectors'.

That a healthy colony of sea pea remains on the Orford Shingles, in spite of the fact that the military have been active on the site for many years, is certainly something of a miracle.

A Martello Tower stands at Shingle Street, a relic of the Napoleonic Wars. Pillboxes are a reminder of the Second World War. Two world wars and the intervening period saw much of the shingle scraped bare of vegetation during manoeuvres. The sea pea survived practice bombing; barbed wire defences; the laying down of mines; bullets from the firing range; heavy vehicle movement; gravel excavation for coastal defences; road building; runways for

aircraft; and the construction of an early warning system. Five thousand unexploded bombs were dug up between 1967–86.

Dr Randall has been returning each year, and several times a season, to check that the sea pea is still present on its shingle habitat. In the 1970s he was able to report a slight increase in colony size.

'The sea pea is a perennial – as are most plants of the shingle,' said Roland.

Tiny plants known as 'winter annuals', such as toothed medick, early forgetmenot, sea mouse-ear, little mouse-ear, are an exception. They survive the harsh conditions by waiting for cool September days in which to germinate. As seedlings, they rest until early spring. Briefly they flower, set seed and then lie dormant once more, thus avoiding the hot summer sun and drying winds.

But the dominant plant on this shingle stretch is the perennial sea campion, *Silene maritima*. With its spreading mat-like growth and long roots, sea campion is an excellent stabilizer:

trapping wind-blown debris and preparing the ground for the plants that follow after. The white flowerheads are bell-like and pretty.

There is a pinkish variety of sea campion, peculiar to Shingle Street. After we'd admired it, Roland said, 'I'll take you to see another curiosity. Rock samphire. As far as I know, the only patch in Suffolk.'

Rock samphire is a plant more usually found growing on rocks and cliffs of the west coast of Britain. An umbellifer, with succulent tangy leaves, it was at one time popular as an ingredient for pickle. Roland discovered the plant when he first began monitoring the Shingle Street flora. His particular pride and joy, he keeps an eye on the clump with its blue-green leaves and yellow-green flowers. One summer he was distressed to find the rock samphire buried beneath charred wood and grey ash. The tenants of a caravan parked close by had made a bonfire of their rubbish on the site. But, somehow, the plant survived and the following year underground roots sent up shoots. It has continued to flourish ever since.

Two meadow pipits flew up suddenly from behind a cushion of sea campion: 'Ti-*zik*, ti-*zik*, ti-*zik*'. A raggedy line of lapwings, blown by the wind, gusted across the beach on round floppy wings and headed inland.

'Hornpies,' said Michael (the bird man). 'The local Suffolk name for lapwings.'

The squealing of little terns distracted us. Snowflake flocks were fishing in the channel off the point of Orfordness, a 15 km (9 mile) long spit stretching from Aldeburgh. Little terns nest on the shingle of the spit. We settled out of the wind, in the lee of a ridge, to eat our packed lunches. We could watch the dainty birds with their long tail streamers and grating 'Ki-ki-ki-ki' calls. Terns are agile, hovering with fast wingbeats, buoyantly swooping, dipping and diving, sending the spray flying.

Common terns, little terns and roseate terns all nest across the water on Havergate Island. The famous bird reserve is owned by the Royal Society for the Protection of Birds and can be reached by boat from Orford Quay. The island is also the site of Britain's largest nesting colony of avocets: around 100 pairs breed. Avocets are elegant wading birds with pristine black and white plumage, and uptilted bills. They sweep their long bills through the brackish water of lagoons to feed on tiny shrimps, ragworms and midge larvae.

Havergate Island/Orfordness/Shingle Street make up the complex known as the Orford Shingles, an internationally important SSSI.

A lesser black-backed gull flew low over the point. At once all the little terns on the shingle below rose up in a protesting cloud. They mobbed the gull, hassling the would-be predator with outraged squeals: 40 terns, shimmering white against a brilliant blue sky. What a sight and what a commotion!

The gull took evasive action, diving low over the shingle. The terns continue to mob the intruder and it flapped away defeated – chased by the little terns until it was out of sight. Peace returned once more as the terns resettled on the shingle of the point.

The eggs of little terns (said Mike) are particularly vulnerable – and not only to marauding gulls. Their shingle scrapes are exposed to high tides and strong winds. Many eggs are lost each year. Foxes can be a menace. Holidaymakers and their dogs may unwittingly disturb the birds. It has become RSPB policy to fence off little tern colonies during the crucial breeding season, appointing voluntary wardens to protect the birds and watch over them.

Human disturbance and trampling can also be a threat to the rare sea pea. The fleshy, brittle sea kale, another rarity, has already gone from Shingle Street. The wording of the polite sign in the Shingle Street car park reads:

Please help safeguard the shingle, plants and wildlife for which the beach is specially valued. Please respect the peaceful nature of the area, take your litter home, and do not drive vehicles on the beach. Thank you.

One-third of Europe's shingle beaches occur around Britain's coastline. Shingle is a rare habitat in global terms. Plants characteristic of mobile shingle – less than two dozen species – are rated as 'rarities' on a world scale.

A ringed plover was running along the edge of the waves. Seven oystercatchers, piping shrilly, flew low over the sea in a straight follow-my-leader line. And a skylark was striving to sing a few notes in the blustery air above.

The pebble stones scrunching beneath our feet are of flint, eroded from chalk and Suffolk's glacial cliffs, washed southwards along the coast by the longshore drift. Shingle is defined as: 'sediments larger in diameter than sand grains (2 mm [0.08 in]) but smaller than boulders (200 mm [8 in]).'

'Orfordness, a National Nature Reserve, is probably the finest example of a pure shingle spit to be found anywhere,' said Roland.

Like Topsy, it 'growed and growed', cutting off the Alde and Butley so that the two rivers have to follow a parallel course before being allowed to escape to the open sea at Orford Haven. But Orfordness itself is now threatened with a breach at its narrowest point, just south of Aldeburgh.

We were approaching the lagoon area. The dynamic shoreline of the Orford Shingles is one of constant change. Spits are breached and new spits evolve. Islands appear and disappear. Shingle is washed shorewards to pile up on the beach and high tides sweep it away again. Saltmarsh forms on the landward side. Lagoons of brackish water come and go.

Great storms, such as that of January 1953, sometimes have a constructive effect, throwing shingle to the top of the beach crest above the reach of ordinary waves. Or storms can destructively cut back the beach, as on one memorable day in August 1964 when 2 m (6.5 ft) of shingle was lost in 4 hours.

Dr Randall and his colleagues continue to map annually the shifting ridges and hollows, islands and lagoons, of this dynamic coastline. For 30 years he has been plotting the many changes that have taken place. Many features can be precisely dated, the vegetation giving an indication of age. Others are still a puzzle. Recent changes are recorded with accuracy by means of aerial photographs.

'Lagoon seven has gone since I was last here,' said Roland, studying his map.

Another lagoon had appeared close by, fringed with salt-tolerant plants that might have been more at home on a saltmarsh: glasswort, sea purslane, sea lettuce and sea lavender. Such brackish coastal lagoons are not a common feature of the British coastline. Salinity can vary and this is reflected by the flora.

We walked back to the car park along a path running parallel to the western ridge of sand dunes. Formed on a shingle skeleton behind the beach, these dunes have been stable since 1893 and an acid heath flora has developed, a rare and unusual habitat in Britain: false oat grass, sea couch grass, silver hair grass, sea storksbill, thrift, red fescue, common catsear, buckthorn plantain, lady's bedstraw, sheep sorrel, clovers, vetches, mosses and lichens.

And another curiosity: there are two species of stonecrop. The biting stonecrop, *Sedum acre*, is typical of the east coast of Britain, but English stonecrop, *Sedum anglicum*, is most often to be found on the west coast. At Shingle Street the two plants grow side by side.

Swishing sound of sea on shingle, wide skies, grating cries of fishing terns, vari-coloured pebbles, nodding white heads of sea campion... and the sea pea, 'miracle plant'.

But it was time to return to Madingley Hall and dinner by candlelight in the elegant dining hall of a Cambridge college: dating from the mid-sixteenth century and with gardens laid out by Capability Brown. Tomorrow we would be exploring more of the lovely Suffolk Heritage Coast.

As we walked back to the car park, Dr Roland Randall, author of a number of papers on the ecology and conservation of the Orford Shingles, told us that he'd first visited Shingle Street as a Suffolk schoolboy.

'My old schoolmaster was right. He used to say to us: "The Almighty just can't make up his mind. Shingle Street must be the last place on earth God created – and He still hasn't finished the job"!'

Madingley Hall, University of Cambridge

CHAPTER TWENTY–THREE

Fool's Gold and Devil's Darts

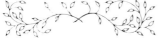

GEOLOGICAL GEMS OF THE NORTH YORK MOORS

John Whittle

•

Abbey House,
Countrywide Holidays,
Whitby, North Yorkshire

G.R.HERICK.

ABBEY HOUSE, perched high on the east cliff of Whitby, stands in the grounds of the ruined abbey of St Hilda. Visitors enjoy a fine view of the red roofs of the town, the boats in the harbour and the coastline beyond. Steps lead down from the abbey to the shore: 199 steps – we counted them on the first morning as we set off in search of geological gems.

'Here we come a-fossiling.' We were not interested today in the sandy beach packed with August holidaymakers, but in the rocky stretch beyond: flat shale rocks ripple-marked by the waves.

At each outgoing tide the smooth, black, wave-cut platform is exposed to view: a mecca for fossil seekers.

'Once you start fossiling you won't want to stop – so I'd better do my talking first,' said John Whittle.

In his introductory briefing, John told us that the sediment in the horizontal layers (strata) of rock clearly visible on the cliff face was deposited over millions of years. 'Young' (geologically speaking) strata are at the top, 'older' layers at the base: brown sandstones, rusty-orange ironstones, dark grey mudstones and black shales. In the Jurassic era some 140 to 195 million years ago, the continents were closer together. Europe was nearer the equator, and the climate was arid and hot. Shallow tropical seas cut the Britain we know today into two halves. Much of Yorkshire, the east Midlands, the Cotswolds, Welsh Border, Dorset and Devon was submerged under water.

Rivers flowed down from northern Britain, and deposited mud and silt, weathered from the land, on to the seabed where it settled and, under pressure, changed into sedimentary rock – mudstones and shales.

Preserved in these rocks are the fossilized remains of curious marine creatures that occurred in abundance in Jurassic seas. As soft parts decayed, so minerals replaced the body tissues, replicating the original animal. Gradually the minerals hardened and fossilized, and turned into stone. Our wave-cut platform was, in fact, an ancient graveyard of extinct species.

This explosion of life in the Jurassic was dominated by the dinosaur, which translates as 'terrible lizard'. Dinosaurs differed from the sprawling-gait lizards by having ball-and-socket joints which allowed an upright posture. The 'rule of the dinosaurs' lasted for 160 million years.

'But we are unlikely to uncover any dinosaur bones today,' said John, 'though there's a good chance of an ammonite or two.'

It was low tide. We had 3 hours in which to work our way across the mile-wide (1.6 km) Scaur – as the wave-cut platform is known locally – and round the headland into Saltwick Bay before risk of being cut off. There was no time to lose.

Andrea and Joanne, John's young daughters, donned their orange safety helmets and stood guard. If one of us wandered too close to the dangerously crumbling cliffs in our absorption, the girls would rebuke us gently with a polite tap on the shoulder.

It was not difficult to prise apart the compacted slivers of shale. The black stuff felt oily, full of decomposed and crushed microscopic organisms. By splitting and flaking off thin layers, I was able to extract my first fossil find, a 'devil's thunderbolt': the pointed internal guard shell of a belemnite.

A belemnite was a squid-like creature. Swimming about in the warm shallow seas, it used its long tentacles to ensnare smaller sea

Abbey House, Whitby

creatures. The outer shell covering was so delicate that it normally dissolved after death and the tough, bullet-shaped, internal guardshell is all that survives in fossil form. Cuttlefish are distant relatives of the extinct belemnite; and the white 'cuttlebones' we find washed up on the beach are the internal shells of the modern cuttlefish.

People once believed that fossils were endowed with magical or medicinal powers. Fossils acquired their own folklore. The Greeks thought that belemnites were 'darts from Heaven', flung down from the skies during thunderstorms, and *belemnon* is Greek for dart. That belemnites were somehow related to lightning was a widespread notion: perhaps due to the translucent yellowish to bluish (lightning?) colour of many specimens. Colloquially belemnites have been known as 'arrow heads', 'bat stones', 'gnomes' candles' and 'devils' fingers'. In Whitby, belemnites are still called 'scaur pencils' after the beach where many are to be found.

Devil's darts

'UFO over here,' called someone.

We hurried across to have a look at the 'unidentified fossilized object' embedded in a hard nodule of rock.

'Perfect specimens are most likely to turn up in a nodule such as this, as any professional collector will tell you,' said John. 'Who's got the big hammer?' he asked. 'This fossil's a whopper.'

Using a geological hammer and chisel of specially hardened steel, he worked round the nodule, levering gently. A portion of the surrounding rock broke clear. One sharp tap with the hammer split the lump in half to reveal the coiled shell of a fine ammonite.

John brushed off grains of debris and washed the ammonite in a handy pool, revealing the whorled pattern on the shell.

'*Hildoceras*,' he said, 'named after St Hilda, the Saxon abbess of Whitby (614–80). The story goes that the plot she chose for her convent was

G.R. HERICKX.

plagued by serpents. She prayed hard, and her prayers drove the serpents over the cliff and into the sea, where they lost their heads, curled up, and turned into stone.'

Whitby shopkeepers still make money by selling 'serpent stones', more often with 'heads' carefully carved into the stone by local craftspeople. *Hildoceras* features in Whitby's town crest; and tradesmen's tokens bearing a device of three coiled stones are known from as far back as 1667.

But Hilda shouldn't only be remembered for the silly serpent legend. She was the grandniece of King Edwin of Northumbria and rather a remarkable woman, according to the Anglo-Saxon historian, Bede. As Abbess of Whitby, she had complete charge of the monks and nuns who lived in two separate monasteries and came together for church worship. But her influence spread far beyond the monasteries. Bede wrote: 'Not only ordinary people, but even kings and princes sometimes asked and accepted her advice.' Whitby Abbey was chosen as the location for the great Synod of Whitby in 664: held to decide when the festival of Easter should be celebrated.

And an ammonite is not a 'stone serpent', of course, but the petrified remains of the shell of an extinct cephalopod, a soft-bodied creature distantly related to the squid, octopus and pearly nautilus.

Ammonites probably swam by jet-propulsion, shooting themselves forward by squirting out water. Each chamber in the shell was separated from the next by a thin wall. As the animal grew, so it would secrete a larger chamber to move into and, as the chambers filled up with gas, so the shell became buoyant.

The early Greeks named the spiral shell after Ammon, an Egyptian animal-headed deity whose horns were coiled like a ram's. So the fossils became known as the 'horns of Ammon', and eventually as 'ammonites'. In some parts of the western isles of Scotland ammonites were referred to as 'crampstones', because of the belief that a cow could be cured of cramp if the part affected was washed with water in which a crampstone has been steeped for some hours.

A *Hildoceras* ammonite is around 180 million years old, give or take a million years or so: an awe-inspiring thought. And here was I, carelessly wrapping it up in newspaper to put into my rucksack!

'Wonder what an ammonite tasted like,' said an irreverent companion, 'and what sort of sauce you'd serve with it?'

John was chiselling out a different species of ammonite. A rinsing in a rock pool revealed the distinctive pattern on the shell.

'*Dactylioceras*,' he decided.

Ammonites evolved rapidly in the Jurassic era. A complex and varied group, they exhibit an amazing succession of forms and ornamentations, although the flotable shell was a universal feature. Palaeontologists find ammonites invaluable as a means of correlating and dating the beds of the Jurassic which occur

worldwide. William Smith, a young engineer engaged in canal digging at the beginning of the nineteenth century, was the first to make this time-sequence connection and his book *Strata Identified by Organised Fossils* was published in 1816.

'What's this?' asked someone, holding up a hard coal-black object. 'Is it jet?'

Whitby is famous for its jet: a form of

Ammonite, petrified remains of the shell of an extinct cephalopod

fossilized wood from a swamp-growing tree, ancestor of our monkey-puzzle. Polished smooth and glossy by craftspeople, jet becomes a lustrous, midnight-black gemstone. Jet jewellery – bead necklaces, brooches and lockets – is on sale in most of Whitby's jewellery shops.

But the black fragment was identified by John as a piece of burnt-black twentieth-century wood.

Another curious find: the fossil of a bivalve mollusc that glittered and sparkled as if gilded with gold.

'Iron pyrite,' said John. 'Known as "fool's gold"!'

But by now the tide had turned. If we stayed fossil-hunting any longer, we would risk being cut off. It was time to hurry on round the headland to safety. The incoming waves would break up boulders and scour the flat surface of the rock platform, removing silt and exposing fresh fossils for others to find tomorrow.

We took the path up from the beach and joined the Cleveland Way, a long-distance path that follows the Yorkshire coast for some miles. Parallel to the clifftop edge, fulmars planed by: a short burst of flapping followed by a long glide on stiff wings. Below the lighthouse, on ledges in the soft rock of the cliff, were the nests of kittiwakes. They had built directly beneath the hard seams of doggerstone that jutted out from the cliff face, giving the sitting kittiwakes some needed shelter from the elements. We could hear the plaintive calls: 'Kitti-wa-a-ke, kitti-wa-a-ke'.

'Seabirds are good geologists,' said John.

Doggerstone was laid down as the sea retreated: at a time when dinosaurs wallowed in the creeks of the vast muddy river delta, leaving their footprints preserved in the sediment. Preserved too are the fossilized leaves and stems of swamp plants: cycads, gingkos, tree-ferns and horsetails.

Dogger is rich in iron. Mined at Rosedale in the nineteenth century, it formed the basis of the Tyneside iron and steel industry. Whitby Abbey is built from doggerstone.

From the Cleveland Way, we could see a tinged-pink headland. The pink is burnt shale, quarried extensively for its alum in the seventeenth, eighteenth and nineteenth centuries. Whitby alum was in demand by the textile and leather industries, used in the tanning and dyeing processes. Labourers, equipped only with picks, shovels and wheelbarrows, removed millions of tons of rock. Great mounds of shale were piled up on brushwood and set alight to extract the alum, and the burning would continue for up to a year at a time. To crystallize the mineral, ammonia was added in the form of urine brought in by boat from cities such as London and Hull. The industry finally collapsed when a cheap process of extracting alum from colliery waste was developed. Whitby's last alum works closed in 1871.

Patched with pink are the heather-covered cliffs around Sandsend, to the west of Whitby, where much of the burning went on. On another afternoon we were to visit the old Sandsend alum quarries which have been turned into a nature reserve. The trail leads through purple heather and past dragonfly-haunted pools. A pair of kestrels make their nest high on a quarry cliff. Frogs and newts breed in the marshy areas at the base of spoilheaps. Hemp agrimony has colonized the rough ground, attracting butterflies. Hartstongue fern grows on the walls of the old disused railway tunnel. Scrub provides cover for small migrant birds.

Back at Abbey House, our 'geological gems' were put on display. An informal social evening, traditional at Countrywide guesthouses, followed the evening meal. The activities, organized by John's wife Ann, were optional, but turned out to be an agreeable way of getting better acquainted.

Countrywide Holidays, first in the field of 'walking holidays', celebrated its centenary in 1991. A hundred years before, the Revd T. A. Leonard, minister of a Congregational church in the small Lancashire mill-town of Colne, felt that his flock deserved better than the traditional seaside holiday Wakes Week: 'A week of thoughtless spending, inane types of amusement and unhealthy over-crowding in lodgings', was how he described it in his journal.

He organized an alternative walking holiday, based at Ambleside. Thirty-two members of his

G.R.HERICKX

Young Men's Guild rambled through the mountains, climbed Wansfell and Helvellyn, listened to talks about wayside flowers and Wordsworth, and joined in a Sunday service held on a hillside against the roar of the waterfall at Dungeon Ghyll. The innovative walking holiday was an enormous success and proved to be the first of many.

'We made up our own trampers' lunches,' wrote Leonard in his autobiography. 'Dates, oatmeal biscuits, cheese – and butter, carried in pots, which melted in the rucksacks and greased our coats. It took years to attain the refinement of sandwiches, and when we added ginger biscuits to our dietary this was considered a luxury.'

Influential people began to talk of 'the birth of a pioneering movement of fellowship, idealism and equality'. In 1896, the comfortable Abbey House at Whitby was leased as the first of the Countrywide guesthouses.

Visitors' needs and expectations have changed with the times, and so has Countrywide Holidays. 'Special interest' weeks and 'wildlife breaks' are proving very popular. But walking holidays are still the mainstay and, next day, we were lacing up our boots and taking up our rucksacks in the long-established tradition.

'The North York Moors are full of history,' said John, 'and much of it can be read in the rocks. The best way to learn is through the soles of your feet. You can acquire more knowledge of geology in a week of walking than in a year in the classroom.'

A coach took us up on to the moors, John pointing out important features on the way: the flat-topped Tabular Hills, lifted high by great movements of the earth; the Bridestones, remnants of Jurassic grits, sculpted into bizarre shapes by wind erosion; the Cleveland Dyke, a ridge that stretches for 50 km (31 miles), formed when molten magma forced its way through the sedimentary rock; and the Hole of Horcum, a deep circular hollow, the work of Wade the local giant.

'Wade once got into a terrible rage,' John told us. 'His wife had displeased him in some way. He scooped up a handful of earth in his huge fist to throw at her – and there! You can see the great hollow in the ground that was left. Wade threw the earth but it missed his wife and landed ... right there,' John said, pointing to a small isolated hill, named on the map as Blakey Topping.

The coach stopped above the mighty waterfalls of Mallyon Spout and Thomason Foss. Steps led down to the plunge-pools below.

The force of the river had gradually eroded away the soft sandstone where it met hard doggerstone and spectacular waterfalls were the result.

From Grosmont station, we followed an old railway line to Goathland and boarded the famous steam train saved from demolition by the North Yorkshire Moors Historical Railway Trust, a group of railway enthusiasts.

The train chuffed its way along the scenic route to Pickering and through the spectacular Newton Dale Gorge. Some 10,000 years ago, at the end of the last Ice Age, glaciers in the hills had melted, releasing huge quantities of meltwater which poured down from the tops with tremendous force, gouging out a gorge some 90 m (300 ft) deep and 22.5 km (14 miles) long.

In the Pleistocene period of 'recent' geological time, the advance and retreat of ice sheets had shaped the North York Moors landscape all over again with snowfields and tundra vegetation, sticky brown boulder clay deposits and erratic boulders, frozen lakes and meltwater channels: geological gems of a *glacial* kind.

CHAPTER TWENTY–FOUR

Seabird Spectacular

BIRD-WATCHING
Peter Hawkey

•

Nether Grange Guest House
(HF Holidays), Alnmouth,
Northumberland

T RY AND VISIT the Farne Islands in May when the terns are due to return. And, if you can, take Peter Hawkey, former warden of the Farnes, along with you.

'Habitat is what it's all about,' said Peter at the beginning of his birdwatching week.

We went across to the estuary for curlew, shelduck and grey plover; inland to woods for pied flycatcher, willow warbler and redstart; to a scrubby marsh area for sedge warbler, reed bunting and linnet; up into the hills for ring ousel, wheatear and skylark; along the riverbank for dipper, grey wagtail and common sandpiper; and – the high spot of the week for most of us – across the sea to the Farnes for guillemots, puffins and terns.

At Seahouses we boarded Billy Shiel's boat, *Glad Tidings* II. It was 10 o'clock on a beautiful sunny morning.

'How long has Billy been running his boats to and fro to the Farnes?' I asked.

'Since St Cuthbert's time probably,' was Peter Hawkey's reply.

St Cuthbert was the hermit who lived on Inner Farne from 676 to 684 – and returned to die there in 687. He is remembered as the first bird protectionist for he framed rules to protect the eider. Eider ducks are still known locally as 'Cuddy's ducks'. When the Farnes were bought for the nation by public subscription in 1925, the National Trust took on St Cuthbert's traditional role, protecting Cuddy's ducks and all the other island birds.

Billy Shiel started up the engine. The sea was blue and amazingly calm. 'So calm that you could bounce a ball on it,' said Peter, 'and it isn't often you see it as calm as that.'

We left the harbour and headed for the Farnes. Inner Farne, with its prominent white lighthouse, is the nearest island: not much more than 1.6 km (1 mile) out from the mainland.

Past the Wideopens, past Big and Little Carr, and now we had hit the choppy cross-currents of Staple Sound. Spray blew back into our faces

as the boat rode the waves. Staple Island, Brownsman, and the North and South Wamses: reputed to be the island retreats of demons banished by St Cuthbert. Past Longstone with its red and white lighthouse, home of Grace Darling, the Victorian heroine.

And through the sea's tremendous trough,
The father and the girl rowed off...

wrote William Wordsworth in horrible verse.

On high cliffs, seabirds stood profiled against the sky: thousands of auks, gulls and shags. It was the beginning of a new breeding season: site prospecting, courtship rituals, nest building, egg laying, chick rearing.

Eider ducks are known locally as Cuddy's ducks

On rocks uncovered only at low tide, grey seals were basking: massive, dark-coated bulls and slimmer, paler cows. More seals bobbed in the water, regarding us curiously: whiskery heads, elongated muzzles, limpid brown eyes.

'As the tide creeps up', said Peter, 'so the seals on the rocks will be driven closer together until finally they are forced off into the sea.'

'Seals aren't really too keen on water,' he explained. 'Being air-breathing mammals, they probably prefer, like us, to be in the dry. Only when the state of the tide – or hunger – determines do seals voluntarily get wet.'

The boat turned and headed back towards

Staple Island. Gulls flew out to meet us. We saw small flotillas of puffins and whirring fly-pasts of guillemots. There was an unforgettable stench of seaweed and rotting fish, and kittiwake noise: 'Kitti-wa-a-ake, kitti-wa-a-ake'. The pretty white gulls, with softly rounded heads, lemon-yellow bills and gentle brown eyes, lined the ledges, the dark volcanic rock washed white with their guano.

Staple Island is wedge-shaped, like all the islands. It slopes down towards the north, the shape the glaciers left them. Surface rocks are rounded by glacial deposits of boulder clay and there are deep fissures between, striations carved by the ice still visible.

To the south are the spectacular Pinnacles. On tall pillars of black dolerite clustered hundreds of guillemots: shuffling, bobbing, bowing, preening. There were guillemots flying in from the sea to hover in mid-air before dropping into a space, guillemots squatting on ledges, facing inwards, backs to the wind, guillemots growling, 'Aarrrrrr, aarrrrrr' and guillemots already incubating eggs.

Guillemots (explained Peter) are birds that have evolved a way of working together as a unit. They arrive together, court together, nest together, lay eggs together, bring up chicks

Guillemots stood profiled against the sky

together, see off predators together and depart together.

An overcrowded narrow ledge is a dangerous place to bring up a chick. The parent bird carefully balances the single green egg on top of its webbed feet, tucking it under the loose skin of the belly. Male and female share the chores of rearing the young. Change-overs are precarious and sometimes an egg is lost. But being pear-shaped, weighted down at the rounded end by the embryo, the egg has a tendency to spin safely on the spot and not to roll over the edge.

Gulls are the auks' most dangerous predators. Herring, lesser black-backed and greater black-backed stay on the alert, waiting their chance to grab a lone egg or chick. Guillemot parents will even babysit for each other if one couple wants to go off and fish. As soon as the youngsters are strong enough – even before they can fly – the adults encourage them down from the vulnerability of the cliffs into the comparative safety of the water.

We scanned the Pinnacles for a 'bridled' guillemot and picked out two. Each had the diagnostic white spectacle markings around the eyes. An estimated 4 per cent of Farne Island guillemots are bridled.

Guillemots ... and a razorbill.

The black and white auk with the chunky white-lined bill was half-hidden by a boulder. Razorbills are not as gregarious as guillemots. Due to a shortage of suitable crevice-type sites on the Farnes, less than 100 razorbill pairs nest, compared to 14,000 pairs of guillemots and 26,000 pairs of puffins.

On the peaty soil of cliff edges, rotund little puffins stood in photogenic groups, loafing, yawning, sleeping and courting. They are super birds to watch, with their rolling gait, sociable habits and paintbox bright colours.

One puffin with a beakful of grass disappeared underground. Another took off for the sea. Others were flying in, stalling with orange feet spread, landing on the turf with gentle thuds. Later on in the season there will be fewer puffins visible on the slopes. Parents will

be taking it in turns to incubate their single egg in the burrow below ground; the 'off-duty' parent spending its time fishing out at sea.

By July and August the chicks will be feathered and fat. As the adults depart, so the young fledglings have to find their own precarious way, at night, to the cliff edge and the sea below.

Offshore, a fulmar petrel planed effortlessly, stubby-necked, stiff-winged. The birds are plankton feeders and they spit a revolting plankton oil at any intruder at the nest.

'The only thing to do with an anorak spattered with fulmar oil is to burn it, the smell is so disgusting,' said Peter.

But now we were approaching the main shag colony.

The common cormorant or shag
Lays eggs inside a paper bag.

goes the nonsense rhyme.

Not true. But, watching the birds on Staple Island, I learnt facts about the shag that are nearly as strange. Shags are most often seen as large black shapes flying rapidly across the bay and out of sight. Rather boring birds really. But not when you are standing only 1 m (3 ft) away and the shag's in its breeding finery. The black plumage is glossed an oily green/blue/purple. The long neck, and scaly wing feathers edged with velvet-black, give it a reptilian look. Eyes are a brilliant emerald green. The gape is bright yellow. Shaggy headcrest feathers curve forward jauntily. An adult shag in spring is a striking bird.

The sun was beating down and many of the shags were 'gular fluttering' to dissipate the heat: panting air in and out through the pouch of naked skin beneath the chin. The sitting females on their bulky nests were remarkably tolerant of our close presence.

'Courtship rituals strengthen the pair bond,' said Peter as we watched one pair displaying at a nest less than 2 m (6.5 ft) away from where we stood.

G.R.HERICKX.

Swaying her neck, quivering her feathers, the female was enticing the male to hand over his 'gift'. Bashfully he edged forward, trailing a long strand of dried seaweed, making curious little rasping noises. He dropped the weed; she began to tuck it into the nest structure with her bill; and an affectionate show of mutual preening followed.

'Older males get so exhausted by all this gifting,' said Peter, 'that they'll steal sticks from the nests of younger neighbours.'

But the ritual at the nest has the advantage of cementing the relationship. The chicks benefit. Shags are excellent parents.

'If a shag lays three eggs,' said Peter, 'then three chicks will be successfully reared.'

One parent broods the young continuously, shading them from the hot sun, keeping them warm on cooler days. The other parent sees to all the feeding: regurgitating partially-digested fish into wide open beaks.

And shags are so aggressive in defence of their territory that predator-gulls stay away. Other seabird species have learnt to take advantage. Guillemots and kittiwakes quite often build their nests close to a shag colony for a share of the protection.

'The common cormorant or shag', goes the rhyme. But the cormorant and the shag are two different species. The shag is almost exclusively marine, while you can find the cormorant on reservoirs and other inland waters. Shags normally fly low over the water with faster wingbeats than the higher-flying cormorant. And the shag lacks the white on cheek and chin, and also on the thigh, that identifies a flying cormorant in spring.

'Cormorants are shy, timid birds,' said Peter. 'If disturbed on the nest, they are slow to return. The gulls seize their chance, and swoop down to take unprotected eggs and chicks. That is why we keep visitors away from the cormorant colonies.'

Colonies of the more aggressive shags have expanded dramatically. At the beginning of the century there were only one or two pairs nesting on the Farnes. Now there are nearly 2,000 pairs, compared to only 200 pairs of cormorants.

It was time to leave Staple Island. We boarded the boat and headed back to Inner Farne. A lone gannet sailed past: yellow ochre head, dark-lined dagger-bill, long, snow-white wings tipped with black. It was probably from Bass Rock, the nearest gannet colony.

We landed in St Cuthbert's Cove on a small sandy beach. The National Trust warden greeted us and pointed out that there was a small landing fee (NT members exempt).

'Terns are back,' said the warden.

The sky above was filled with newly arrived Arctic terns. It was as if someone had shaken a giant pillow and, instead of feathers, thousands of snowy-white birds had flown out. Black-capped, scarlet-beaked, coral-legged Arctic terns hovering, side-slipping, buoyantly dancing on narrow translucent wings, steering with long delicate tail streamers.

Photographers reached for their cameras.

'Wait till the sun glints on the eye – *then* shoot,' advised Peter.

Without such a highlight, the black eye of a tern is easily 'lost' in the black feathers of the cap.

Courtship, clamour and copulation in the sea campion: the colony was seething with excitement; tern screeching was incessant. 'Kee-arr, kee-arr, kwek-kek-kek-kek...'

Within camera range a male was presenting a sand eel to its chosen mate. Held in the blood-red bill the gleaming fish drooped like a silver moustache. With mincing steps, the bird advanced. She responded coyly. He dropped the fish in front of her. She picked it up.

'Don't ever accept a fish if it is offered to you on the Farnes,' Peter warned, 'or you'll be there for another six weeks.'

Pair bonds are formed by this 'plighting of troth'. Birds will seek out the same partner year after year and Arctic terns are long-lived. Annually, for perhaps 20 to 30 years, they follow the sun and the food supply from the Arctic to Antarctica.

After the ritual gifting and coupling comes the scrape-making and egg-laying. Tail streamers sticking up out of the blanket of white sea campion betray where birds are already sitting on eggs.

But the terns resented our presence. We were soon under attack.

'If the terns worry you, stand next to someone taller than yourself!' was Peter's jocular advice.

Hurrying along the path to dodge hostile swoops, angry scoldings and sharp jabs from pointed bills, we reached the lighthouse. On the cliff below was the main kittiwake colony.

The cacophony of kittiwake sound reverberated in the steep gullies. Dainty gulls floated in the breezes, hanging in mid-air, struggling against the gusts to navigate their way back to the nest. Courting couples preened on ledges: nibbling, necking, billing, cooing.

In Churn Gut there were puffins. The thin soil had been denuded of its pink thrift vegetation by their seasonal burrowing. A cormorant stood with wings spread out to dry on Black Rock. Oystercatchers piped loudly from offshore boulders. A small flock of sandwich terns preened: 'pony tail' tufts of black feathers, black bill with yellow tip, harsher calls.

An eider duck, crouched at the base of a stone wall, was being mobbed by three Arctic terns. She raised her head in gentle protest as they squealed and swooped, her dowdy brown feathers insufficient camouflage.

Drake eiders are boldly patterned and handsome. In spring the head and breast are flushed with lime-green and creamy-pink, and the courtship crooning of the male resounds across the water: 'Ah-hOOO, Ah-hOOO, ah-hOOO...'

'He's the Andy Capp of the bird world,' said Peter. 'The drake takes charge until the eggs are laid – and then scarpers off to the mainland shoreline with the rest of the lads: to moult their feathers and obtain better feeding.'

The duck eider is left alone to incubate her large clutch of eight or nine eggs. It takes 4 weeks for the chicks to hatch. The devoted mother quits her down-lined nest for short periods only, to quench her thirst and, perhaps, to eat a little. After such a long incubation time, the young emerge well formed and able to swim. 'Aunties' (broodless ducks) help to round up the ducklings and to shepherd them across to the mainland where they learn to feed in the shallow water. These duckling crèches are a pretty sight on the rocky shoreline in late summer. Meanwhile, the mothers get a chance to recuperate and build up their strength.

'No man shall ever harm you,' said St Cuthbert to his beloved eiders, and the story is told that he even allowed his favourites to nest on the steps of his altar.

Female eiders on Inner Farne are so trusting that they will brood in the most curious places: on the boardwalk laid down for visitors; in the courtyard next to the gate; beneath wooden seats at cliff viewpoints; at the entrance to St Cuthbert's chapel.

The chapel was built in 1370 on the site of the

G.R.HERICKX.

hermit's cell. The remains of a second chapel have been converted into an attractive visitors' centre. A plaque reads: 'CARNEGIE INTERPRET BRITAIN AWARD. Presented to the National Trust for Inner Farne Interpretation.'

The nine seasonal wardens employed on the Farnes from March to December use the sixteenth-century tower as their living quarters. A well, believed to have been used by the saint, is today polluted and unsafe. Drinking water, and all the other necessities of life, have to be brought across by boat from the mainland.

Down on the rocks were oystercatchers, dunlin, ringed plover, rock pipits, turnstones.... But it was time to go.

The National Trust appointed Peter Hawkey as the first head warden of the Farne Islands in 1970. The name Farne is derived from the Celtic 'ferann', meaning 'land'. The chain of islands compose the most easterly portion of the Great Whin Sill, a shelf of hard volcanic dolerite rock that runs from High Forces on the Tees, through Durham and Northumberland, until it reaches the coast and is submerged by the sea. There are 15 to 28 islands in all, the number showing above water depending on the state of the tide.

'People ask: "What do wardens do all day?"' said Peter. '"Feed the birds?" I think they imagine we scrub the guano off mucky ledges at the season's end. Or that I'm there to serve cups of tea to visitors!'

Wardens census birds at key migration times; monitor the breeding species; engage in ecological research; write papers and reports; carry out policies which suit both birds and people. Birds must be protected. People want sensible access. Most importantly, wardens contribute ideas towards the management plan which is drawn up by the head warden and the National Trust Farne Island Local Committee. As circumstances change, so the plan is continuously updated.

In 1990, after 20 years as head warden, Peter retired. During his guardianship, numbers of breeding birds had more than doubled, increasing from 25,000 pairs to 55,000 pairs, in spite of the presence of 50,000 day visitors each season. For his services to conservation, he was awarded the MBE.

And, summer after summer, the kittiwakes, guillemots, puffins, shags and all the other seabirds return to the island, offering one of the most exciting seabird spectaculars in the western world.

Peter Hawkey, first head warden of the Farne Islands

Further Reading

Anderson, Sheila: *The Grey Seal*, Shire, 1990

Anderson, Sheila: *Seals*, Whittet, 1990

Andrews, E. & Crawford, A. K.: *The Otter Survey of Wales, 1984–85*, Vincent Wildlife Trust, 1986

Bang, Preben & Dahlstrom, Preben: *Collins Guide to Animal Tracks and Signs*, HarperCollins, 1990

Bassett, Michael: *Formed Stones, Folklore and Fossils*, National Museum of Wales, 1982

Beebee, Trevor: *Pond Life*, Whittet, 1992

Benton, Edward: *The Dragonflies of Essex*, Essex Field Club, 1988

Bertel Bruun (et al.): *The Hamlyn Guide to Birds of Britain and Europe*, 1970, 1986

Birks, Johnny: *Mink*, Mammal Society/Anthony Nelson, 1986

Boyle, C. B. (ed.): *RSPCA Book of British Mammals*, Collins, 1981

Bjarvall, A. & Ullstrom, S: *The Mammals of Britain and Europe*, Croom Helm, 1986

Bright, Paul & Morris, Pat: *A Practical Guide to Dormouse Conservation*, Mammal Society, 1989

Bright, Paul & Morris, Pat: *Dormice*, Mammal Society, 1992

Bright, Paul: *Where to Watch Mammals in Britain*, Mammal Society, 1991

Broom-Lynne, Catherine: *A Vision Established*, Field Studies Council, 1994

Brown, Valerie: *Grasshoppers*, Naturalists' Handbook, Cambridge University Press, 1983

Cameron, R. A. D.: *AIDGAP Key to the Slugs of the British Isles*, Field Studies Council, 1983

Cameron, R. A. D. & Pannett, D. J.: *Hedgerow Shrubs and Landscape History: Some Shropshire Examples*, Field Studies Council, 1980

Cameron, R. A. D. & Kerney, M. P.: *A Field Guide to the Land Snails of Britain and North-west Europe*, Collins, 1979 (out of print)

Cameron, R. A. D. & Kerney, M. P.: *Land Molluscs of Britain and Northern Europe*, HarperCollins, 1994

Catt, Martin: *Day-flying Moths*, Butterfly Conservation, 1994

Chanin, Paul: *Otters*, Mammal Society Series, Anthony Nelson, 1987

Chanin, Paul: *Otters*, Whittet, 1993

Chanin, Paul: *The Natural History of Otters*, Croom Helm, 1985

Chapman, Norma: *Deer*, Whittet Books, 1991

Chapman, V. J.: *Coastal Vegetation*, Pergamon Press, 1976

Chatfield, J. & Pfleger, P.: *A Guide to the Snails of Britain and Europe*, Hamlyn, 1983

Chinery, Michael: *A Field Guide to the Insects of Britain and Northern Europe*, Collins, 1972, 1986

Chinery, Michael: *Collins Guide to the Insects of Britain and Western Europe*, 1986

Churchfield, Sara: *The Natural History of Shrews*, Croom Helm, 1990

Churchfield, Sara: *Shrews*, Mammal Society Series, Anthony Nelson, 1988

Clark, Michael: *Badgers*, Whittet, 1988

Cloudesley-Thompson, J. L.: *How to Begin the Study of Spiders*, Richmond/BNA, 1987

Colebourne, Phil & Gibbons, Bob: *Britain's Countryside Heritage*, Blandford, 1990

Conray, J. (et al.): *A Guide to the Identification of Prey Remains in Otter Spraints*, Mammal Society, 1993

Corbet, G. B.: *Finding and Identifying Mammals in Britain*, British Museum (Natural History), 1989

Corbet, G.B. & Harris, S.: *The Handbook of British Mammals*, Blackwell, 1991

Crawford, Andrew & Andrews, Elizabeth: *Otter Survey of Wales. 1984–85*, Vincent Wildlife Trust, 1986

Cresswell, Penny, Harris, Stephen, & Jefferies, D.J.: *The History, Distribution, Status and Habitat Requirements of the Badger in Britain*, Nature Conservancy Council, 1990

Cresswell, Penny, Harris, Stephen, Jefferies Don & Cheeseman, Chris: *Problems with Badgers*, RSPCA, 1988

Cresswell, Penny, Harris, Stephen & Jefferies Don: *Surveying Badgers*, Mammal Society, 1989

Cresswell, Penny, Cresswell, Warren & Woods, Michael: *The Country Life Guide to Artificial Badger Setts*, 1993

Croft, P. S.: *AIDGAP Key to the Major Groups of Freshwater Invertebrates*, Field Studies Council, 1986

Dalby, Claire & Dalby, D. H.: *Biological Illustration*, Field Studies Council, 1985

de Bray, Lys: *The Art of Botanical Illustration*, Helm, 1989

Dunstone, Nigel: *The Mink*, T. & A. D. Poyser, 1993

Fairhurst, Alan & Soothill, Eric: *Trees of the Countryside*, Blandford, 1989

Fitter, R., Fitter, A. & Blamey, M.: *The Wild Flowers of Britain and Northern Europe*, Collins, 1974

Flowerdew, J. R.: *Mice and Voles*, Whittet, 1993

Flowerdew, J. R.: *Woodmice and Yellow Necked Mice*, Mammal Society, 1984.

Garard, Ian & Streeter, David: *Wild Flowers of the British Isles*, Macmillan, 1983

Gibbons, Bob: *Dragonflies and Damselflies of Britain and Northern Europe*, Hamlyn, 1986, 1994

Gilbert, Francis: *Hoverflies*, Naturalists' Handbooks, Richmond, 1986

Grigson, Geoffrey: *The Englishman's Flora*, Dent, 1955, 1987

Gubbay, Susan: *Coastal Directory for Marine Service Conservation*, Marine Conservation Society, 1988

Gurnell, J. & Flowerdew, J. R.: *Live Trapping Small Mammals*, Mammal Society, 1990

Hammond, Cyril: *The Dragonflies of Great Britain and Ireland*, Harley Books, 1983

Harding, Patrick & Lyon, Tony: *How to Identify Edible Mushrooms and Toadstools*, HarperCollins, 1994

Harding, P. T. & Sutton, S. L.: *Woodlice in Britain and Ireland: Distribution and Habitat*, Institution of Terrestrial Ecology, 1985

Harris, Stephen: *Foxes*, Mammal Society, 1984

Hawkey, Peter: *Birds of the Farnes*, Butler, 1990

Hopkins, Stephen: *AIDGAP Key to the Woodlice of Britain and Ireland*. Field Studies Council, 1991

Hurrell, Elaine: *The Common Dormouse*, Blandford, 1980 (out of print)

Hutson, Tony & Greenaway, Frank: *A Field Guide to British Bats*, Coleman, 1990

Jennings, Celia: *John Constable in Constable Country*, Radford, 1976

Jones-Walter, L. M.: *AIDGAP Key to the Families of British Spiders*, Field Studies Council, 1989

Keble Martin, W.: *The Concise British Flora in Colour*, Michael Joseph, 1965, 1991

King, Angela (et al.): *The Declining Otter*, Friends of the Earth, 1976

Kruuk, Hans: *The Social Badger*, Oxford University Press, 1989

Leach, Michael: *Mice of the British Isles*, Shire, 1990

Mabey, Richard: *Food for Free*, Fontana/Collins, 1975

Mabey, Richard: *The Complete New Herbal*, Elm Tree, 1988, 1991

Majerus, Michael: *The Natural History of Ladybirds*, New Naturalist, HarperCollins, 1994

Majerus, Michael & Kearns, Peter: *Ladybirds*, Naturalists' Handbook, Richmond, 1989

Marchant, John (et al.): *Population Trends in British Breeding Birds*, BTO, 1990

Marren, Peter: *Woodland Heritage*, David & Charles, 1990

Mason, Chris & Macdonald, Sheila: *Otters: Ecology and Conservation*, Cambridge University Press, 1986

Mattison, Chris: *Frogs and Toads of the World*, Blandford, 1987

Mattison, Chris: *Lizards of the World*, Blandford, 1989

Mattison, Chris: *Keeping and Breeding Amphibians*, Blandford, 1993

Mellanby, Helen: *Animal Life in Fresh Water*, Chapman & Hall, 1938, 1987

Miller, Peter: *Dragonflies*, Naturalists' Handbooks, Cambridge University Press, 1987

Moore, Norman (et al.): *Dragonflies*, Collins, 1960, 1985

Neal, Ernest: *The Badger*, Collins, 1948, 1975

Neal, Ernest: *Badgers*, Blandford, 1977

Neal, Ernest: *The Natural History of Badgers*, Croom Helm, 1986

Owen, Jennifer: *Garden Life*, Chatto & Windus, 1983

Philips, Roger & Foy, Nicky: *Herbs*, Pan, 1990

Pollard, E., Hooper, M. D. & Moore, N. W.: *Hedges*, Collins, 1974

Putman, Rory: *The Natural History of Deer*, Christopher Helm, 1988

Rackham, Oliver: *The History of the Countryside*, Dent, 1986

Ransome, Roger: *The Natural History of Hibernating Bats*, Christopher Helm, 1990

Richardson, Phil: *Bats*, Whittet, 1985

Robertson, James: *The Complete Bat*, Chatto & Windus, 1990

Shaw, John: *The Nature Photographer's Complete Guide to Professional Field Techniques*, Amphoto, 1984

Shaw, John: *Close-ups in Nature*, Amphoto, 1987

Skidmore, Peter: *AIDGAP Key to the Insects of the British Cow Dung Community*, Field Studies Council, 1991

Spring, Jill: *The Kingcombe Kitchen*, The Kingcombe Centre, 1990

Staniforth, Alan: *Geology of the North York Moors*, North York Moors National Park, 1990

Stebbings, R. E.: *Conservation of European Bats*, Christopher Helm, 1988

Stebbings, R. E.: *Bats*, Mammal Society, 1986

Stebbings, R. E.: *Which Bat is it?* Mammal Society, 1986

Stebbings, R. E. & S. T. Walsh: *Bat Boxes*, The Bat Conservation Trust, 1985

Strachan, Rob & Jefferies, Don,: *The Water Vole in Britain 1989–1990: Its Distribution and Changing Status*, Vincent Wildlife Trust/Joint Nature Conservation Committee, 1990

Sutton, S. L.: *Woodlice*, Ginn, 1972

Tate, Ann: *Birdwatcher's Year*, David & Charles, 1988

Thomas, Jeremy: *RSNC Guide to Butterflies of the British Isles*, Country Life, 1986

Thomas, Jeremy & Leington, Richard: *The Butterflies of Britain and Ireland*, Dorling Kindersley/National Trust, 1991

Thompson, Shirley: *Bats in the Garden*, School Garden Company, 1989

Thompson, Shirley & Richardson, Phil: *Bats Conservation Project Book*, Hodder & Stoughton, 1993

Tilling, S. M.: *AIDGAP Key to the Major Groups of British Terrestrial Invertebrates*, Field Studies Council, 1987

Waterhouse, Gordon: *Wildlife of the Salcombe and Kingsbridge Estuary*, Harbour Books, 1992

Wayre, Philip: *Operation Otter*, Chatto & Windus, 1987

Webb, Nigel: *Heathlands*, Collins, 1986

Yalden, Derek & Morris, P. A.: *The Analysis of Owl Pellets*, Mammal Society, 1990

Yalden, Derek: *The Scientific Names of British Mammals and Why They Change*, Mammal Society, 1979

Yoxon, Paul & Grace: *Wildlife of Skye and Ramsay*, Skye Environmental Centre, 1990

Yoxon, Paul & Grace: *Otter Survey of Skye*, Skye Environmental Centre, 1990

Useful Addresses

Badger Consultancy, The, 1 Tilling Walk, BRISTOL BS10 5AH

British Naturalists' Association (BNA), 48 Russell Way, HIGHAM FERRERS, Northants NN9 8EJ

British Trust for Conservation Volunteers (BTCV), 36 St Mary's Street, WALLINGFORD, Oxfordshire OX10 0EU

British Trust for Ornithology (BTO), The Nunnery, THETFORD, Norfolk IP24 2PU.

Butterfly Conservation, PO Box 222, Dedham, COLCHESTER, Essex CO7 6EY

Campaign for the Protection of Rural Wales, Ty Gwyn, 31 High Street, WELSHPOOL, Powys SY21 7JP

Common Ground, 45 Shelton Street, LONDON WC2H 9HJ

Council for Environmental Education, University of Reading, London Road, READING RG1 5AQ

Council for the Protection of Rural England, Warwick House, 25 Buckingham Palace Road, LONDON SW1W 0PP

Council for the Protection of Rural Wales, Ty Gwyn, 31 High Street, WELSHPOOL, Powys SY21 7JP

Countryside Commission, John Dower House, Crescent Place, CHELTENHAM, Gloucester GL50 3RA

Countryside Council for Wales, Plas Penrhos, Fford Penrhos, BANGOR, Gwynedd LL57 2LQ

Countrywide Holidays, Birch Heys, Cromwell Range, MANCHESTER M14 6HU

Derbyshire Wildlife Trust, Elvaston Castle, DERBY DE72 3EP

Devon Wildlife Trust, 188 Sidwell Street, EXETER, Devon EX4 6RD

Dorset Trust for Nature Conservation, 39 Christchurch Road, BOURNEMOUTH, Dorset BH1 3NS

Dyfed Wildlife Trust, 7 Market Street, HAVERFORDWEST, Dyfed SA61 1NF

English Nature, Northminster House, PETERBOROUGH PE1 1UA

Essex Wildlife Trust, Fingringhoe Wick Nature Reserve, Fingringhoe, COLCHESTER, Essex CO5 7DN

Fairfield Holidays, Proprietor John Whittle, 23 Fairfield Avenue, KIRKELLA, Hull HU10 7UG

Field Studies Council, Central Services, Preston Montford, Montford Bridge, SHREWSBURY, Shropshire SY4 1HW

Gilbert White Museum, The Wakes, Selborne, ALTON, Hampshire GU34 3JH

Gloucestershire Wildlife Trust, Dulverton Building, Robinswood Hill, Country Park, Reservoir Road, GLOUCESTER GL4 9SX

HF Holidays, Imperial House, Edgware Road, LONDON NW9 5AL

John Clare Society, The Stables, 1a West Street, Helpston, PETERBOROUGH PE6 7DU

Leicestershire and Rutland Trust for Nature Conservation (LRTNC), 1 West Street, LEICESTER LE1 6UU

Leicestershire Badger Group. Leicestershire Bat Group. Address as LRTNC

Leicester Literary and Philosophical Society, Natural History Section, Leicestershire Museum and Art Gallery, New Walk, LEICESTER LE2 0JJ

Mammal Society, Department of Zoology, University of Bristol, Woodland Road, BRISTOL BS8 1UG

Marine Conservation Society, 9 Gloucester Road, ROSS-ON-WYE, Herefordshire HR9 5BU.

National Federation of Badger Groups (NFBG), 16 Ashdown Gardens, Sanderstead, SOUTH CROYDON, Surrey CR2 9DR

National Institute of Adult Continuing Education, 19B De Montfort Street, LEICESTER LE1 7GE. (*Time to Learn* is an annual publication listing residential study breaks.)

National Rivers Authority, Sentinel House, Wellington Crescent, Fradley Park, LICHFIELD, Staffs WS13 8RR

National Trust, 36 Queen Anne's Gate, LONDON SW1H 9AS

Northumberland Wildlife Trust, The Garden House, St Nicholas Park, Jubilee Road, NEWCASTLE UPON TYNE NE3 3XT

North York Moors National Park, The Old Vicarage, Bondgate, HELMSLEY, North Yorkshire TO6 5BP

Peak District National Park, Aldern House, Baslow Road, BAKEWELL, Derbyshire DE4 1AE

Pembrokeshire Coast National Park, The County Office, St Thomas Green, HAVERFORDWEST, Dyfed SA61 1QZ

Ramblers Association, 1–5 Wandsworth Road, LONDON SW8 2XX

Robert Stebbings Consultancy, 74 Alexandra Road, PETERBOROUGH, Cambridgeshire PE1 3DG

Royal Society for Nature Conservation: The Wildlife Trusts, Witham Park, Waterside South, LINCOLN LN5 7JN

Royal Society for the Protection of Birds, The Lodge, SANDY, Bedfordshire SG19 2DL

Shropshire Wildlife Trust, 167 Frankwell, SHREWSBURY, Shropshire SY3 8LG

Somerset Trust for Nature Conservation, Fyne Court, Broomfield, BRIDGWATER, Somerset TA5 2EQ

Suffolk Wildlife Trust, Brooke House, The Green, Ashbocking, nr IPSWICH, Suffolk IP6 9JY

WATCH Trust for Environmental Education, RSNC, The Green, Witham Park, LINCOLN LN5 7JR

Wildfowl and Wetlands Trust, SLIMBRIDGE, Glos GL2 7BT

Wild Explorer Holidays, Skye Environmental Centre, Harapool, BROADFORD, Isle of Skye IV49 9AQ

Woodland Trust, Autumn Park, Dysart Road, GRANTHAM, Lincs NG31 6LL

World Wide Fund for Nature, Panda House, GODALMING, Surrey GU7 1XR

Yorkshire Dales National Park, Yorebridge House, Bainbridge, LEYBURN, North Yorkshire DL8 3BP

Yorkshire Wildlife Trust, 10 Toft Green, YORK YO1 1JT

Youth Hostels Association (YHA), Trevelyan House, 8 St Stephen's Hill, ST ALBANS, Hertfordshire AL1 2DY

Youth Hostels Association (Wales Area), 4th Floor, 1 Cathedral Road, CARDIFF, South Glamorgan CF1 9HA

Index